MISSION STRATEGIES THEN AND NOW

By the Same Author

This Holy Seed: *Faith, Hope and Love in the Early Churches of North Africa*

The Love of God, *book 1: The Quest for the Living God*

Biblical Missiology: *A University Course in Cross-cultural Mission*

Mission Strategies Then and Now

ROBIN DANIEL

Tamarisk Publications

The author welcomes comments, queries and corrections
addressed to him care of
Tamarisk Publications (tamariskbooks@yahoo.co.uk) or
Opal Trust (info@opaltrust.org).

Text and maps © Robin Daniel 2012
Cover illustration adapted with kind permission: Copyright 1973, 2005 David
C Cook. *The Picture Bible* published by David C Cook. Publisher permission
required to reproduce. All rights reserved.

First British Edition, 2012
ISBN: 978 0 9538565 6 5

Published by: Tamarisk Publications, Chester, United Kingdom
Email: tamariskbooks@yahoo.co.uk

Distributed by: Opal Trust
1 Glenannan Park, Lockerbie DG11 2FA, Scotland, United Kingdom
Phone / fax (UK): 01576 203670
Email: info@opaltrust.org
Web: www.opaltrust.org

Book design and production for Tamarisk Publications by
Bookprint Creative Services <www.bookprint.co.uk>
Printed in the United Kingdom.

CONTENTS

Acknowledgements   7

Dates   8

Introduction   9

1. **Jesus the Missionary**   13

2. **The Training of the Twelve**   17
    choosing, preparing and sending the disciples; the
    apostolic vision

3. **Culture and the Kingdom of God**   30
    the cultural sensitivity of Jesus. Was Jesus a cross-cultural
    missionary?

4. **The Mission of the Twelve Apostles**   37
    the greatest of all missionary events; the missionary
    experience of the apostles; the apostles' cross-cultural
    strategy

5. **Paul's Early Missions**   48
    Paul's first missionary journey (Acts 13:1 to 14:26): pioneer
    missions; new fellowships; Paul's ministry to the Church
    (Acts 14:27 to 15:39); Paul's second missionary journey
    (Acts 15:40 to 18:22): revisiting the churches; the mission
    to Europe; a strategic centre – Corinth; a new base and
    an old problem

6. **Paul the Missionary**   63
    Paul's synagogue ministry; his aim and achievement.
    Was Paul a cross-cultural missionary?

7. **Paul's Later Missions**   73
    Paul's third missionary journey (Acts 18:23 to 21:16):

a second strategic centre – Ephesus; news from Corinth;
a typical disciple – Epaphras; resolving tensions in
Corinth and Jerusalem

8. Paul's Missionary Methods   80
Paul's message; his guidance; his church planting
strategy: he proclaimed the gospel in public places, taught
his converts in private homes, created communities of
believers, encouraged spiritual growth, allowed local
leaders to emerge naturally, expected the gospel to
spread spontaneously.

9. Paul's Final Mission   100
Paul's mission to the Roman empire (Acts 21:17 to 28:30):
in Jerusalem; in Caesarea; in Rome; Paul's last years

10. Paul's Cultural Sensitivity   109
Social distinctions; dealing with cultural issues; minimizing
cultural resistance; cross-cultural evangelism; making full
use of cultural skills

11. Paul's Missionary Character   123
Paul's spiritual maturity, personal credibility, love for his
converts, servant spirit, constant prayer, devotion to Christ,
great vision

12. Paul's Missionary Team   132
apostles and evangelists; missionary recruits; the ministry
of women; missionary leadership; missionaries and churches;
financial support

13. The Value of Old and New
understanding Jewish scripture   151
technologies and strategies   155
global culture, gospel culture and local culture   161

14. Missionary Methods Then and Now
"tent-making"   165
strategic leadership   166
preparing for persecution   169
holistic ministries   174
miraculous healing   181

cross-cultural mission today 187

15. Our Glorious Hope and Expectation 197

Additional Notes

Understanding the Methods of Jesus
the gospel of the kingdom? 201
provisions for mission? 202
self-defence? 204

Understanding the Jerusalem Fellowship
all things in common? 206
lending and borrowing? 208

Understanding the Methods of Paul
the collection for the saints? 209
various kinds of languages? 211
itinerant evangelism? 214

Further Reading 216
By the Same Author 219

ACKNOWLEDGMENTS

I would like to thank Alan R Millard, David J Clark, Andy Warren-Rothlin, and A R (Bob) Turner for their helpful comments on preliminary versions of my manuscript. I am especially grateful to my dear wife Janet for sharing the life and experience that went into writing this book . . . and, as always, for correcting the final text.

Bible references are based on the *Greek New Testament* (4th edition, UBS 1993), usually following the *English Standard Version* or the *New International Version*.

DATES

Constructing an exact chronology for New Testament events (dated in years AD) is notoriously difficult, and my comments do not depend on any particular view of chronology. For convenience, the dates proposed by Schnabel for the ministry of the apostle Paul are noted as follows (*ECM*, pp.41-49). Paul's birth should probably be dated somewhere between AD 2 and AD 5.

AD 31 or 32	converted to Christ, preaches in synagogues of Damascus
32-33	active in Arabia, returns to Damascus, preaches in Jerusalem, finally settles in Tarsus
34-42	active in Cilicia and Syria
42-44	with Barnabas in church at Syrian Antioch
45-47	mission with Barnabas to Cyprus and southern Galatia (Pisidian Antioch, Iconium, Lystra, Derbe)
48	visits church in Syrian Antioch, then to conference in Jerusalem
49	mission with Silas heading towards Ephesus but redirected to Macedonia (Philippi, Thessalonica)
50-51	settles in Corinth
52-55	briefly to Jerusalem and Syrian Antioch, then settles in Ephesus
56	briefly visits Corinth
57-59	arrested in Jerusalem, then held in custody at Caesarea
60-62	under house arrest in Rome
63	? to Spain
64-65	with Titus to Crete
66-67	? imprisoned in Rome and finally executed by Emperor Nero

INTRODUCTION

"Go into all the world and proclaim the good news to the whole creation" (Mk 16:15). With these astonishing words, Jesus took leave of his disciples.

No one had ever before attempted or even suggested such a thing. Indeed, until this moment there had never been news so good that all the world must hear it.

But as they announced this good news, the followers of Jesus had another task to fulfill. They must prepare others to do exactly the same thing – in every country and every generation. So he told them, "Go therefore and make disciples of all nations . . . teaching them to do all that I have commanded you. And behold, I am with you always, to the end of the age" (Matt 28:19-20).

The mission that Jesus gave his disciples was the greatest and most wonderful assignment ever given to humankind. As they were responsible to fulfil it in their day, so are we in ours. But it is not easy. The need of the world has never been greater, and in some ways our task has never been more difficult.

In many countries our churches are under pressure from secular cultures and religious fanatics. Over wide areas Christian mission has become difficult or almost impossible. Doors are closing. Believers who speak of Christ are not welcome. Governments are resistant to foreign ideas and unwelcoming to foreign missionaries.

Elsewhere we may enter freely but then find that people will not listen to us. We may labour for many years, learning foreign languages, adapting to foreign cultures, but winning only a handful of converts who remain weak and unable to pass on their faith to others.

At the same time the world is changing rapidly. People are travelling more than ever before. No longer is each person restricted to his or her own culture and dialect. Many are studying foreign languages at school. Some are travelling to other countries for study, for business, for medical care, for tourism, and many are refugees. There is a steady flow towards the cities. Cheap technologies carry a form of universal culture almost everywhere. Old customs and beliefs are breaking down. By choice or necessity, men and women are learning new languages and new ways of thought. In the modern world many are becoming multi-cultural.

We may see the hand of God in these things, but the question is this: Are we adapting to our changing circumstances? Are we seizing the opportunities offered to us?

Many of our churches and societies have a vigorous mission programme. Some have excellent training schemes. Some have launched ambitious medical, educational and social projects. Some are sending missionaries into provinces and countries far away. New technologies are inspiring fresh forms of ministry. But much more could surely be done. And perhaps it could be done more effectively.

In our missions there are many issues of concern. It is not easy to start churches that quickly become self-supporting and able to plant other churches. We may face complex financial issues, desiring to move forward but lacking the money to do so. Tensions can arise when combining a holistic ministry with appeals for conversion to our faith. Conforming to a different culture, we may be anxious about compromising our character and stifling our message. There may be questions concerning ownership of property. Our leaders may feel more comfortable directing programmes for believers than going out with the gospel to unbelievers. Our converts may tend to remain weak and dependent, attending services but not becoming active in spiritual ministry. We need wisdom and guidance from above in dealing with all these issues.

Training the next generation is also our concern. Sending out young missionaries, we may wonder if they have been adequately prepared. Do our churches give them enough opportunity to develop their abilities through teaching, discipling, encouraging, visiting, answering hard questions and caring for people with serious difficulties? Have they had personal experience of explaining the gospel to outsiders and leading people of all conditions to faith in Christ? Do they possess sufficient strength of character to overcome the temptations and difficulties they will face among strangers in uncomfortable places far from home?

More important than any of these is the fundamental question: Have we really understood the gospel? Do we know what message we are called to proclaim in all the world? Do our churches teach the same gospel as Jesus and his apostles? Have we learned how to preach as they preached in New Testament times?

All this sends us back to the Bible with an urgent enquiry: How did Jesus and his apostles and the early churches approach the task of world mission?

The issues that concern us undoubtedly concerned them too. So how did they pioneer unreached areas, respond to new cultures and introduce the gospel to people with other beliefs? How did they overcome prejudice and persecution, helping new converts to become people of genuine Christian character? How did they recruit and train young missionaries and finance the work of church and mission? How did they keep a balance between teaching the word of God and launching holistic and caring ministries? How did they prepare and appoint effective indigenous leaders? How did they start churches that were self-supporting and able to plant other churches? We need to know.

What strategies did they use? How effective were they? And would their methods work today? Can the New Testament give us any guidance in our work of cross-cultural communication?

Nothing could be more helpful to anyone engaged in gospel mission than a careful and prayerful study of the life and ministry of Jesus himself, so that is where we will start.

1

Jesus the Missionary

Our Lord came to this earth on a mission. He left his home and his Father. He left a place where he was comfortable and at ease, a place where he had power and glory and honour, with angelic servants at his command. He came to live among difficult people, to bring them good news, to help them with their problems.

Scripture tells us he came as an *apostle*, a person sent from one place to another. He was sent by the Father. So he is called "Jesus, *the apostle* and high priest of our confession, who was faithful to the one who appointed him" (Heb 3:1-2).

He came as an *evangelist*, a person who brings good news. So he said, "The Spirit of the Lord is upon me, because he has anointed me *to proclaim good news*" (Lk 4:18).

For three short years Jesus preached the gospel of the kingdom and taught a small group of people how to continue his work after he had gone. He did this, of course, in a time and place far distant from our own, yet human nature and human needs do not change greatly from age to age, and the truth which sets us free does not change at all. We can learn much from his example.

Day by day our Lord encountered human frailty. He observed the fears, hopes, burdens, prejudices, ambitions and disappointments of men and women. He witnessed their selfish sins and frustrated ideals and the choices they made in wisdom or in folly. To the crowds, and especially to his disciples, he taught principles and facts of life and death that concern all mankind in every culture and every age.

In his life on earth Jesus had a clear objective which at any cost he must fulfil. "I must preach the good news" he said, "because I was sent for this purpose" (Lk 4:43). As an apostle and an evangelist, he had strong principles and he never wavered from them:

1. His desire was to do the Father's will. His greatest wish was not to please people, and never to please himself, but always to please the Father. He was not appointed by men or accountable to men, for he was sent by the Father and would do whatever his Father gave him to do. Even in Gethsemane he prayed, "Not my will, but yours, be done" (Lk 22:42).

He never compromised or lowered his standards. He never denied the truth. Opposition, danger, flattery, criticism, success or lack of success never caused him to waver or turn back. To do what the Father had called him to do was his greatest satisfaction. "My food," he said, "is to do the will of him who sent me and to accomplish his work" (Jn 4:34).

2. He went to where the people were. He spoke to men and women in the streets and markets, in the temple and the synagogue, at the lakeside and on the hill. He did not wait for them to come to him; nor did he erect a building and invite them to attend. He did not arrange religious ceremonies or rituals, or even regular meetings.

He travelled widely so that everyone might hear the truth, rarely staying for long in any place or with any group of people. He went to them where they were, in the towns and villages, at the roadside and the city gates. And he accepted invitations to their homes where he could see their true character and talk with them most freely about their personal circumstances.

3. He made friends with the people. He mixed with rich and poor, men and women, good and bad, young and old, and took a personal interest in each one. He talked with them about their needs, their heartaches and their anxieties (Matt 6:25-34). At leisure and at work, he shared their gladness and gave them joy (Lk 19:6).

He asked and answered questions about the real issues of life. Drawing parables and proverbs from the experiences they shared, he captured their attention and imagination, making them think carefully, and changing their attitudes and beliefs. Some of his hearers were wealthy, and for them he constructed parables about stewardship, inheritance, investment, servants, houses, banquets and the management of property and business. Others were poor, and for them he drew illustrations from the natural world of birds and flowers, trees, sheep and vines, light and darkness, grains of wheat and flowing water.

4. He taught the truth. Teaching the people was his first concern, for there were things they urgently needed to know. He taught them the love of God and the ideals of his kingdom. He told them how he must suffer and die as a ransom for many and then rise to eternal life. He spoke of judgment to come and how he would return in power and glory to raise the dead and bring peace on earth. He taught them as much as they could understand (Mk 4:33).

The miracles he did were "signs" proving that his word was true, that he was indeed their Messiah and that he alone could meet their deepest needs (Jn 2:11; 6:14; 7:31; 11:47; 20:30). But healing was never his priority. He did not ask them to come for healing, and he told them to say nothing when they were healed. Above all, he was a Good Teacher. "You will know the truth," he said, "and the truth will set you free" (Jn 8:32). We will speak more of this.

5. He lived by faith. He was constantly aware of his Father's presence (Jn 8:29). Everything that happened he received from his Father's hand (Jn 5:17). Always available, always approachable, he accepted every interruption as an opportunity rather than a hindrance. A group of lepers shouted to him, a rich man ran up to him, a woman touched his garment, another wet his feet with her tears, a paralysed man came through the roof, little children came for a blessing. Anyone sent to him by his Father must be a person in need of his ministry, and he had something of value for each of them (Jn 6:37).

Trusting his Father to supply all his need, he never asked anyone for money. He took no collections and received no wages. The rich young ruler should give to the poor, he said, not to himself or his disciples. He possessed very little and owed nothing but was welcome in many homes where friends who believed in him and his ministry were pleased offer hospitality (Lk 4:38; 5:29; 7:36; 10:38; 14:1 etc.). In due course we will speak more this too.

6. He spoke to individuals about personal salvation. He had a kind word for the Samaritan woman at Jacob's well, for the Pharisee who came to him by night, for the corrupt tax-collector who climbed a tree, for the religious young man with great wealth, for the penitent thief on the cross. There was something he would say to each that exactly met their need.

His concern was to develop individuals rather than society. He did not try to reform the established government or religion. Nor did he talk of political change or economic growth. He simply taught the people around him to put their trust in the Father and live a perfect life. The laws of the land he simply obeyed, without condemning Roman control or Jewish compromise (Matt 17:24-25; 22:21). The only fault he found with the religious leaders was their failure to follow their own teachings (Matt 23:3, 23).

In all this he never attempted to put a new patch on an old garment of religion or politics, but he totally transformed the individual men and women who believed in him (Matt 9:16; Jn 3:3).

7. He launched a movement with high ideals. He inspired his friends with his teaching about the love of God, the coming kingdom, and the new life that would never end. He restored the relationships of people with one another and especially with the Father. He proclaimed a vision and launched a movement that changed the character and destiny of his disciples.

In the accounts of his ministry we see how much Jesus was interested in people and how little in organisation. With no buildings to maintain and no employees to pay, his beliefs and ideals would spread naturally throughout the world as his followers simply passed on what they knew to those who had never heard (Acts 1:8).

For barely three years Jesus ministered to the people around him. His time was short, and he must prepare others to continue his mission after he had gone. Like him they would be apostles and evangelists, and he would train them with great care for the task entrusted to them. Now we must consider the method he chose for their missionary training.

2

The Training of the Twelve

The followers of Jesus often called him "Teacher" but they were not students in a seminary or theological college. For their lessons he took them into the street and marketplace, into the city and the open field, the rich man's villa and the meagre lodgings of the poor.

He was preparing them to go into the world and make disciples, and in the world he would show them how to do this. He would make them "fishers of people", and among people he would teach them to fish.

He did not merely give his disciples theories about mission; he showed them how to live and work as missionaries. And more than that, he showed them how to be men, as men should be.

Choosing the Disciples

For his closest friends Jesus did not seek out people of influence, culture, leisure, wealth or learning. His vision was not for a political revolution in the corridors of power but a transformation of character in the homes and workshops of common men and women. The kingdom of God must come to ordinary people, and with ordinary people it must start.

Although there were many who followed him and desired to be his disciples, Jesus chose only twelve for missionary training. He did not need a large number and he did not ask for volunteers.

A few had earlier been invited to join him as he taught in the villages of Galilee and Judea (Matt 4:18-22; 9:9; Jn 1:43). Others had been added to the company along the road. He observed each one and tested their worth. He knew the kind of men he wanted, men with a heart to learn, to serve others and to do the will of God. Finally he prayed all night for guidance, and then he called them to him.

The twelve he chose were drawn from families neither especially rich nor extremely poor. They were men accustomed to physical labour. Most had received very little schooling. The scribes and Pharisees would consider them "uneducated, common men" (Acts 4:13). Governors and priests would not suppose them capable of profound thought or high ideals. But each of the twelve had his own personality, his own perspective on life, his own family and his own experience of the world. Jesus could discern the potential in each of them, a potential hidden from those who did not know them or wish to know them.

He had special plans for their training. "He appointed twelve (whom he also named apostles) so that they might be with him and he might send them out to preach and have authority to cast out demons" (Mk 3:14-15).

First of all we see they must *be with him*. They must be prepared before they can be sent. They will be with him morning, noon and night, going where he goes, eating what he eats, sleeping where he sleeps, hearing what he says and watching what he does. They will pick up his habits, his character, his manner of conversation and his way of helping people. They will learn from his example how to pray, to seek the Father's will, to trust and to obey. They will learn to live as he lives. Only then will they be ready to go out to the towns and villages and do as he did.

We might wonder why Jesus did not choose any women for this missionary training. Firstly we should remember how physically demanding it would be. The disciples would walk long distances in the hot sun on dangerous roads through hills and valleys frequented by bandits, robbers and wild animals. They must manage large crowds, face angry opposition and handle fishing boats in all weathers. Every day they must get food and water and perhaps go far in search of it. Travelling two by two, they would seek shelter at night among strangers, and sometimes find no door open to them. Wives and children would be exhausted by such conditions, and single women quite vulnerable. On many occasions the disciples would all sleep together on the Mount of Olives, at Bethany, or by the roadside wherever they happened to be, and in these circumstances a mixed company of young men and women would always be at risk of vulgar comment, indecent gossip and dangerous accusations. Married women young enough to walk these distances would normally have little children to care for, even when not pregnant or breastfeeding, and while Jesus might ask a man to leave his nets or his tax accounts, he would not ask a mother to leave her baby.

Nevertheless on certain occasions there were women with them, and some of their names are known to us: Mary the mother of James and Joseph, Mary Magdalene, Susanna, Joanna the wife of Chuza, Mary the wife of Clopas and Salome the wife of Zebedee. Many writers have assumed that these women walked from place to place with the Twelve. It seems more likely that they, along with Martha and Mary of Bethany, were middle-aged or even elderly ladies who opened their homes and offered food and shelter to Jesus and his disciples in widely scattered towns and villages, and so "provided for them out of their means" (Lk 8:1-3).

We read that "many" of these women later went up to Jerusalem and witnessed his crucifixion (Matt 27:55). But most of those known to us were married and so would have a home and family to care for. They might physically "follow him" for short distances but could help him best by providing supper and a place to stay whenever he and his disciples came their way (Mk 15:41). The sisters in Bethany found him a most interesting guest and learned much from his teaching in their home (Lk 10:38-42).

Preparing the Disciples

Seventy-seven times the gospel writers speak of following Jesus. When he said, "Follow me" he called his disciples to become like him. In his company they would learn to think like him, to speak like him, to do as he did, to live as he lived, to trust his Father as he did, to care for others as he did. His disciples learned from his example. And so will we, as we consider it more closely.

1. His example in character

It was the character of Jesus that attracted men and women to follow him. As soon as he started his ministry it was clear to those who heard him that he spoke with authority (Lk 4:32). This was not the political or religious authority of a man appointed to office, but the assurance of one who thinks more quickly and deeply than other people, who knows things of which they are ignorant, who is able to deal wisely and effectively with situations far beyond their capacity.

He is a young man of quiet strength and awesome intelligence, feared by priests and governors yet loved by little children. He is severe towards any who oppress the elderly and the poor, yet gentle with those who weep for the wrong they have done. He is a man to respect and obey, but also a man to confide in and trust – a natural leader, bold, courageous and inspiring, yet a true friend, always full of kindness and warm sympathy. To become like Jesus is to become gentle and strong, and utterly dependable. He is a man you will follow to the ends of the earth, a man you will trust with your life.

Once the disciples had committed themselves to him, they learned much more of him. Day by day they found him faithful and true, always committed to his Father's will. They saw his patience, his meekness and his humility. They saw his purity of heart and mind. They saw him forsaking material security to live a life of faith, depending on his Father for his daily bread. They saw him, as the storm tossed the boat, trusting in his Father's care. They saw him troubled in Gethsemane, courageous and willing to lay down his life for the sake of them all. They saw him calm and brave through the pain of injustice, scourging and crucifixion. They saw him rise victorious over the powers of darkness. This strength of character they would need for themselves if they were to follow in his footsteps.

The character of a missionary is far more important than his knowledge or his skill. If his character is weak or worldly he will fail and bring shame on the name of Christ. If his character is strong and dependable he will be an influence for good wherever he may go.

Character is not formed in the classroom. Character is formed in the street and marketplace, in the workshop and especially in the home. Our character is shown by the way we face difficulties, opposition, popularity, success and failure. It grows through experience and becomes secure and reliable through perseverance. It brings assurance, confidence and high expectation: "Endurance produces character, and character produces hope" (Rom 5:4).

Maturity of character is not gained overnight. It is not picked up by chance. It is not acquired without effort. The mature are "those who have their powers of discernment trained by constant practice to distinguish good from evil" (Heb 5:14). Such spiritual growth takes time.

When Jesus ascended to the heavens, he did not leave his disciples inexperienced and immature. For three years he had been preparing them as men for their mission, helping them overcome personal weaknesses and besetting sins. He had watched over their spiritual progress, gently leading each one to the point where he would willingly deny himself, take up his cross and follow wherever his Lord might lead. The doubts of Thomas were transformed into a living faith. The hasty pride and fear of Peter became a rock-like commitment to the truth. James and John learned to place love above vengeance. Nathaniel overcame his prejudice against Nazareth. Philip, so slow to understand, became a faithful witness and apostle. Matthew, a collector of taxes, became a collector of prophecies and parables. The only exception was Judas, who never mastered his weakness for money.

Jesus had shown them how to have victory over worldly anxieties and selfish desires. He had accustomed them to habits of life that would remain to guide them long after he had gone. And these mature disciples were the men he left to continue his work. He knew they had the character to do it. All they needed now was a mighty baptism of the Holy Spirit to cement that character and make it firm. This they would receive on the Day of Pentecost.

2. His example in outreach

The disciples learned how to deal with people by observing how he did it. Every day he brought them face to face with young and old, men and women, rich and poor, good and bad, people of every sort. They sat with Pharisees and with thieves, with humble men and hypocrites, with seekers after truth and seekers after money, with the sick and the dying, with those who blessed and those who cursed, with those who mocked and those who flattered, with the ignorant and the learned, with officers and servants, rulers and slaves, rich and poor.

They learned how to discern the deepest needs of each, to warn those who were on the broad road to destruction, to encourage those who were truly seeking God, to reassure those who longed to be forgiven, and to offer a joyful message of eternal life to those who feared the dark and silent tomb.

He led his disciples into direct contact with the false religions and beliefs of the day. He showed them how to deal with the self-

21

righteousness of the Pharisees, the materialism of the Sadducees, the corruption of the Herodians. He let them see for themselves how the Law was being misused and misunderstood. They heard him talking with the ignorant, the wayward and the lost, and learned from him to have compassion on them all.

He introduced them to individuals such as Zacchaeus, Jairus, Bartimaeus, Nicodemus, the woman of Samaria, the godly centurion, Simon the leper and Mary Magdalene. They heard his reply to Mary and Martha, to the disciples of John, to the rich young ruler and to his own mother and brothers. The Twelve watched him dealing with all these people; they listened and remembered.

3. His example in teaching

When they were alone he discussed with his disciples the issues raised in these conversations so they would grasp the full significance of what they heard.

When a rich man went sadly away, he spoke to them of wealth, and also of salvation, sacrifice, the world to come, judgment and eternal life (Matt 19:22-30).

When the mother of James and John came seeking preferment for her sons, he drew lessons from this incident about suffering, about the Father's will, the coming kingdom, leadership, humility, service and his own imminent sacrifice as a ransom for many (Matt 20:20-28).

When John the Baptist sent asking for assurance, he taught them many things about John and about the kingdom of God (Matt 11:7-19).

When they saw how the Pharisees were offended with his parables, he taught them more about the parables and about the Pharisees (Matt 15:12-20).

When a poor woman put two coins in the temple treasury, he taught them the true value of the gift and of the temple (Mk 12:41-13:2).

To the crowds he spoke in parables, but to his disciples he explained the meaning of everything privately so they would understand (Mk 4:33-34).

In much of our teaching today, methods and theories are presented in the classroom and then perhaps applied and briefly tested in the real world. Jesus, in contrast, offered experience first, followed by discussion. For him and his disciples the purpose of learning was not to pass an exam or gain a diploma, but to acquire practical skills for effective mission. Teaching them how to work, he took them to where the work was done. He instructed them as a master craftsman initiates his apprentices into the secrets and skills of his trade – by practical demonstration and personal experience.

Jesus focused the attention of his disciples on what they really needed to know. They did not study the writings of false prophets, for they did not need to know much about error in order to teach the truth. They had only one textbook – the scriptures which they had heard from childhood in the synagogue.

But they studied the character of the people around them. From experience they learned to understand human nature and to know why men and women act as they do. They had no textbook on anthropology yet they learned the difference between good behaviour and bad behaviour. They had no textbook on philosophy but they could see how a bad philosophy will ruin a soul. They had no textbook on psychology yet they observed the consequences of wrong assumptions and foolish prejudices. They discovered how people can change their outlook and belief, and be transformed in their character and way of life.

We could say much more about how Jesus taught his disciples, how he drew vital questions from them, how he asked his own questions to make them think, how he left them a whole collection of parables and illustrations to clarify their message, how he identified key scriptures for them to quote, how he prepared them to stand alone when he would no longer be with them; but enough has been said to reveal the wisdom of his method.[1]

4. His example in perseverance

Jesus never expected his disciples to work harder than he worked, or to do what he would not do. They shared with him the fatigue of the road, the heat of the day, the storms on the lake, the clamour of the unruly crowds, the dangers, the hopes and disappointments, the mockings and the triumphs.

They saw how consistent and disciplined he was: "Every day he was teaching in the temple" (Lk 21:37). They learned from him how

---

1. For more on this subject, see *The Teaching Methods of Jesus*, by Douglas S Hubery, freely available on request from the publisher (email: tamariskbooks@yahoo.co.uk).

an honest and good heart will "bear fruit with patience" (Lk 8:15). He would explain the same fact in many ways: "Again I tell you . . ." and "Again I say to you . . ." (Matt 18:19; 19:24). He would repeat the same message many times: "I made known . . . and I will continue to make known . . ." (Jn 17:26). He would return to his Father only when his job was thoroughly complete, "having accomplished the work that you gave me to do" (Jn 17:4).

They learned from his example to work while it is yet day, always going on to the next village, always proclaiming the same truths, dealing kindly with every question and objection, waiting patiently for men and women to understand and respond in faith. They learned not to be discouraged by opposition or indifference but to sow the seed of the word everywhere, trusting that some would fall on good soil.

The disciples were with him as he walked the rocky paths, preaching and teaching until he was so weary he must rest at Jacob's well. Once he was so tired he was *taken* into the boat, and slept so deeply that even a storm would not wake him (Mk 4:36-38).

They learned from him to find a quiet place for rest and prayer when necessary, but never to be lazy and never to seek ease or luxury. They learned how to be servants, not seeking popularity or status in the eyes of the world. Bearing with every hardship and temptation, they became so familiar with this life that they would continue to live this way long after he had left them.

5. His example in prayer

The disciples often heard their Master pray. They saw how prayerfully he accomplished every task, seeking the guidance of his Father in every step he took. They saw him spend long hours and whole nights interceding for them and for the people around them (Lk 6:12). They saw him going to a hidden place for prayer (Matt 6:6; Lk 5:16). They heard him speak to his Father not with empty phrases and repetitions but earnestly from the heart (Matt 6:7).

From his example they learned how and when to pray. He always gave thanks before taking food (Matt 15:36; 26:27; Lk 22:19). He prayed for each of the little children brought to him (Matt 19:13). He prayed before raising Lazarus (Jn 11:41-42). He prayed when facing a great crisis (Jn 17:1; Matt 26:39). He prayed for Peter's faith, that it would not fail (Lk 22:32).

He taught them to pray as he prayed. As he said "Father, Lord of heaven and earth", they would say "Our Father in heaven" (Matt 11:25; 6:9). They learned from him to pray that the Lord of the harvest would send out labourers (Lk 10:2). They learned to pray, as he did, for the enemies who threatened and mistreated them (Lk 6:28). Through their failure, he taught them to pray against temptation (Lk 22:40). In their need, he taught them to pray for their daily bread (Matt 7:7-11). On their last night together he prayed earnestly for them and for all who would come to faith through their testimony (Jn 17).

By word and by example he taught them always to pray and not lose heart (Lk 18:1). They saw how his prayers were answered and his requests fulfilled (Jn 11:22, 42). After this rich experience of prayer, they would surely be prayerful people all their lives.

6. His example in love

Jesus loved his Father with intensity and joy, and from him the disciples learned to love the Lord their God with all their heart and mind and strength. And they learned to love each of their many neighbours as themselves.

They learned from him the true meaning of love. They saw his particular interest in all who suffer – the crippled, the blind, the deaf and the dumb, some made hideous by leprosy and others rendered bloody and violent by evil spirits. They saw his concern for a woman whose back was bent and a widow whose son had died. They saw his kindness to a corrupt tax-collector and a woman caught in adultery. They saw him stop for a blind beggar and hasten to a dead child. They saw how deeply the unhappy crowds affected him, "harassed and helpless, like sheep without a shepherd" (Matt 9:36).

It was his mission to care for such people. He loved the work his Father had given him to do. He loved the people around him with more kindness and compassion than the world had ever seen (Matt 14:14; 15:32; Lk 7:13). And he loved his disciples with a love that never wavered, no matter how slow or faithless they might be. He loved them to the end and to the uttermost (Jn 13:1). From him Peter learned that "love covers a multitude of sins" (1 Pet 4:8). Through him John discovered that "God is love" (1 Jn 4:16).

The disciples saw how love creates a deep and consistent longing to please the one we love (Jn 14:15, 23-24). It inspires a great desire to give. It moves us to do all the good we can. As missionaries these men would need the inspiration of this love – the love that believes all things, hopes all things, endures all things, the love that never ends (1 Cor 13:7-8).

7. His example in self-sacrifice

The disciples learned from Jesus how to devote their lives to a higher calling than earthly comfort or personal prosperity (Matt 16:24). They saw him ignoring his own interests and desires, giving up all he possessed for the benefit of others. They learned from him what it means for a person to deny himself and take up his cross. They saw how the Lord of glory had nowhere to lay his head, and how one born to eternal riches become poor for their sake (2 Cor 8:9). They saw in reality how it is more blessed to give than to receive (Acts 20:35). They observed how the Son of Man, the greatest of all men, came not to be served but to serve, and how as a servant he would wash their feet and suffer for their faults.

They saw how he accepted every interruption as an opportunity to help someone, every objection as an opportunity to teach something. A woman of Samaria came when he was tired and thirsty. An anxious father came as he climbed down a mountain. The Pharisees demanded signs, the Sadducees asked trick questions, the Herodians enquired about taxes. A ruler came to him at night, an ambitious mother by day, and finally a company of men armed with clubs and torches came to arrest him. He responded to each with compassion, dignity and grace, and in that hour taught them something they needed to know.

Jesus was a determined man. He did not flinch. "When the days drew near for him to be taken up, he set his face to go to Jerusalem" (Lk 9:51). Without complaint he endured reproach, hostility and finally the cross (Heb 13:13; 12:2-3). When Peter urged his Master to seek an easier path, the rebuke Peter received was the strongest ever given to a disciple (Matt 16:23).

There was in Jesus no trace of hypocrisy. He lived by what he taught. He described himself as a grain of wheat, willing to fall into the ground and die for an eternal harvest; and when the time came, that is exactly what happened (Jn 12:24). The disciples knew what kind of man he was and what kind of men they were called to be.

Sending the Disciples

When at last they were ready Jesus sent the Twelve out to the towns and villages of Galilee. He gave them authority to heal the sick, raise the dead, cleanse lepers, and cast out demons, and he told them to proclaim "The kingdom of heaven is at hand" (Matt 10:7). Later in the same way he sent out Seventy-two (Lk 10:1).

As his representatives bearing his name, they were entrusted with great responsibility. Indeed he staked his reputation on them. "Whoever receives you receives me," he said, "and whoever receives me receives him who sent me" (Matt 10:40). He would later go to the same places, meet the people they had spoken to and see the results of their labour (Lk 10:1).

On these short-term missions the character and maturity of the disciples would be thoroughly tested. None of them went alone, but always two by two. In this way they would learn to work together cheerfully and patiently, and to encourage and support and pray for one another as they went. They would remind one another of the many things they had learnt from their Master.

He sent them trusting their heavenly Father to provide for their needs, taking no money or change of clothing, and only the simplest of basic necessities. He did not pay them to serve God but said, "Freely you have received, freely give" (Matt 10:8). They would travel light, devoting all their attention to their mission and the people they would meet.

When they returned he took them away to a quiet place where they could talk together and pray about all they had seen and done. Nothing could be more valuable to these men than the personal experience he gave them and the opportunity to discuss it with him afterwards.

On his final evening with the Twelve they were gathered for the Passover meal. Then he did four things with them which they never forgot (John chapters 13 to 17).

1. **He taught them truths they must understand.** He spoke about servanthood, the Father, the Holy Spirit and his own deity. He taught them about death, life, prayer, fruitfulness and ultimate victory.

2. **He shared his heart with them in true fellowship.** He told them of love, betrayal, separation, glory, denial, persecution, sorrow and joy.

3. **He offered them a simple meal with a profound meaning.** He gave them bread as a symbol of his body broken for the sin of the world, and wine as a symbol of his blood poured out to secure a covenant of peace.

4. **He led them in prayer to his Father and theirs.** He prayed for them to have joy, protection, a true knowledge of God, holiness, unity, and a loving, joyful, glorious and effective witness to the world.

After this they sang a hymn and then went out.

We know that the disciples never forgot those last precious moments with their Lord. We know it because after Jesus had left them they continued to meet in Jerusalem for those four things: for teaching, fellowship, breaking of bread and prayer. Many times they enjoyed a simple meal together as they discussed what he had said and done, shared their personal concerns and prayed earnestly in his name. Whenever they broke open a loaf and poured out a cup, they remembered him.

As their numbers increased, when three thousand had been added to their company, the memory of that last supper continued to inspire them all. Whenever they met together they made sure of these four things: "They devoted themselves to the apostles' teaching and the fellowship, to the breaking of bread and the prayers" (Acts 2:42).

The Apostolic Vision

The Twelve had left their homes and occupations to become missionaries of the gospel. They were trained for pioneer outreach, for taking the word of God to strangers. Their work was to be like the work of their Master, proclaiming the good news far and wide. Such was the need of the world, and such was the task before them.

Jesus did not prepare them to be ministers or elders or pastors of churches. He did not build chapels for them in strategic places. He did not ask them to remain in one town or village, continually teaching the same group of believers and performing religious ceremonies. As leaders they must lead forward – to occupy new territories – and they would leave the ongoing care of local believers to local men with homes and families and secular occupations that tied them to that one place. His final word to them was both a command and a promise: "You will be my witnesses . . . to the end of the earth" (Acts 1:8).

These then were the methods chosen by Jesus for the training of his missionaries:

1. He chose his men carefully.
2. He trained them through practical experience.
3. He discussed everything with them privately.
4. He prepared them for pioneer outreach.
5. He taught them to live by faith.
6. He sent them on a short-term mission.
7. He then told them, "Go into all the world . . ."

When Jesus proclaimed the kingdom of God and taught the sermon on the mount he was introducing something new to the culture of his day. Every pioneer missionary is called to do this, and we may learn from the Master how to do it well.

3

Culture and the Kingdom of God

The culture of any group of people embraces the attitudes, traditions and beliefs they have in common. It will include language, behaviour, art, music, food, clothing, hair styles, habits and customs, indicators of status and honour, how they interact, things they consider important or unimportant, the way they build and furnish their houses, and the leisure activities they enjoy together. When everyone agrees on these things society is stable and people are comfortable with one another. But anyone who questions or opposes what is considered normal will cause a measure of tension, amusement or embarrassment to the men and women around him.

In the Bible we find many different cultures developed by people in many different places. In the time of Noah we read of music with flutes and harps, tools of bronze and iron, customs of marriage and family life, but also a great deal of violence and corruption. God was not impressed with this culture and swept it away in a great Flood. After this, a new culture arose with the construction of a towering temple at Babel, and God scattered the people who made it. The city of Sodom developed a notorious culture in the days of Lot, and God destroyed it. The culture of ancient Egypt, with its pyramids, statues, mummies and hieroglyphic writing, has astonished the world, but God sent plagues and led his people out of Egypt. Aaron adapted to local culture by making a golden calf, but God punished his people for it. Entering Canaan, the Israelites encountered a culture which burned little children to Moloch; God condemned it and removed it from the land. In all these cases the culture created by man was profoundly displeasing to God.

The Cultural Sensitivity of Jesus

As time passed, the Israelites developed a rich and complex culture of their own. It was derived from their common language and history, their tribal relationships, their worship, their scriptures, their food restrictions, purifications and other aspects of the Law. Many elements of their culture were given to them by God himself. Other elements they added as time went by.

Jesus grew up in this Jewish culture and accepted it as his own. He dressed and spoke as a young man of Galilee and attended the synagogue every Sabbath (Lk 4:16). He followed the Law of Moses in letter and in spirit (Matt 5:17-20). He paid the temple tax (Matt 17:27). He helped to make at least one traditional wedding a very happy occasion (Jn 2:10). Conforming to the culture of his day, Jesus would be accepted as a pleasant and agreeable young man. He could read well and speak well. People would like him and respect him, and be willing to hear what he said.

Sometimes, however, Jesus quietly ignored culture. People would find this surprising. He and his disciples did not fast when everyone else was fasting (Mk 2:18-19). He astonished his host by not participating in ritual washing (Lk 11:38). He touched a leper, took the hand of a dead girl, spoke to a Samaritan woman, all of which would make him ritually unclean. He was unimpressed with the great stones of Herod's temple (Mk 13:1-2). He would not become a legalist to please the Pharisees, or a ritualist to please the Sadducees, but made friends with irreligious outcasts (Matt 9:11). He expected his teaching to make and break relationships, and even divide families (Matt 10:35-37; 12:48-49). Why, in all these cases, did he ignore the accepted culture of his people? He ignored it because he had something better than the culture and was happy for everyone to see it.

On occasion, Jesus would go further than this. Sometimes he publicly defied culture. To ignore a culture is surprising but to defy a culture may be acutely offensive. He drove animals and tradesmen out of the temple (Mk 11:15). He allowed his disciples to pick grain on the Sabbath (Lk 6:1). He himself healed on the Sabbath, and perhaps healed more on the Sabbath than on other days (Lk 6:7). He refused to condemn an adulteress (Jn 8:11). He let a sinful woman anoint his feet (Lk 7:38). He called the Pharisees hypocrites (Matt

23:13). He spoke of judgment on Chorazin, Bethsaida and Jerusalem (Lk 10:13; 21:24). He opposed the conventions of divorce, swearing oaths, and legal accusation (Matt 5:31-32, 34, 40). Why, in all these cases, did he defy the culture? He did so because the culture had enslaved the people, and his desire was to set them free.

In the course of his life we see that Jesus usually followed the customs and expectations of the people around him. Sometimes, however, he would ignore their culture. Occasionally he would defy it. Yet the really important thing for him was none of these. His greatest desire was to introduce a new culture of his own.

It was the culture of the gospel, the culture of the kingdom of God, and it must supersede all human cultures. Jesus taught the principles of this new culture in his sermon on the mount, and he always lived according to those principles. He was concerned for inner purity more than outward show. He loved his enemies and the enemies of his people. He lived without selfish anger, greed, lust, dishonesty or desire for revenge. He was not interested in money or power, pleasure or status. He made up his own mind about right and wrong.

This is not normal behaviour. It made Jesus different from the men and women around him. When someone is willing to think for himself and decide on his own standards and ways of behaving, people will start to feel uncomfortable. His family were upset with him (Mk 3:21). Many of his disciples were embarrassed, and some of them left him (Jn 6:60-61). Others warned him, "Don't you know the Pharisees were offended?" (Matt 15:12). When he spoke to the inhabitants of Nazareth, "they were very angry" and tried to throw him off a cliff (Lk 4:28-29).

If we are following Jesus we will usually conform to culture. Sometimes however we may ignore it, and occasionally defy it. This may cause surprise and perhaps offence. When we live to please God more than men, and when we speak the truth in love, people may take a dislike to us. This is no cause for surprise. "If they have called the master of the house Beelzebul, how much more will they malign those of his household!" (Matt 10:25).

But our chief concern will be to introduce a new culture. We are commissioned to proclaim the gospel in all the world, and this is not normal behaviour in any culture made by man. We are introducing something different and unknown, something which may change the customs and beliefs of the people. This can be uncomfortable for them. It will arouse mixed feelings and sometimes resentment. We will never wish to cause offence but people may sometimes take offence. We can be equally sure that if our gospel offends some, it will powerfully attract others. We will speak more of this.

We have seen how Jesus introduced a new culture for his followers, that is a new way of life for all who believe in him. Because of this we can go anywhere in the world and find people like us. And the better we each know Jesus the more similar we will be. We are a worldwide cultural community. Jesus has called us "the light of the world". And he said, "Let your light shine" (Matt 5:14, 16).

Was Jesus a Cross-cultural Missionary?

We have seen how Jesus was a missionary, and an ideal missionary whose example the disciples would follow. We have considered how he related to his own culture – the customs and traditions in which he grew up. Now we must enquire how he approached other cultures. Was he interested in people who spoke foreign languages and followed different religions? Could we consider him a cross-cultural missionary?

It may seem strange that Jesus declared, "I was sent only to the lost sheep of the house of Israel" (Matt 15:24). With these words he indicated a precise cultural and racial limit to his mission. Born as a Jewish boy, he ministered in his own language to his own people, offering them the kingdom promised to their forefathers. He was their own Messiah, the son of David, the rightful king of Israel. He fulfilled their Law and their prophets. Scripture tells us that "he came to his own, and his own people did not receive him" (John 1:11). Although they did not receive him, he offered them all he had.

In his teaching and healing ministry Jesus never went outside the traditional borders of Israel. He never proclaimed the kingdom of God among the Gentiles (people of other races who were not Jews). He did not go to live among foreigners such as the Samaritans or Canaanites or Gerasenes. Although he sometimes passed through their territories, he never preached in their villages. He once went to the region of Tyre and Sidon but only to rest and instruct his Jewish disciples in a private house (Mk 7:24). He had no ministry to people of other cultures and religious beliefs.

The same is true of his twelve disciples when he sent them on their mission. He told them clearly, "Go nowhere among the Gentiles, and enter no town of the Samaritans, but go rather to the lost sheep of the house of Israel" (Matt 10:5-6).

When foreigners came looking for Jesus they found him reserved and unresponsive. A Canaanite woman begged for help but he did not answer her a word. Only as she insisted did he agree to heal her daughter (Matt 15:23). A man of the Gerasenes begged to go with him but was denied and sent away (Lk 8:39). A Roman centurion appeared extremely diffident about approaching him at all (Lk 7:1-8). Some Greeks asked to see him but his soul was troubled. Instead of answering their enquiry, his thoughts turned to a grain of wheat that must fall into the earth and die (Jn 12:20-27).

Why was he so strangely reluctant to receive these Gentiles? And why did he never go into all the world himself, healing and teaching among the nations and offering the gospel to every tribe and tongue?

A compassionate heart in these circumstances could only be checked by reason of a compelling hindrance. The reason is that the old covenant was still in operation. It was a specific covenant between God and Israel. A Gentile might enter it by presenting himself to a Jewish priest and receiving circumcision (in the case of a man) and by agreeing to obey the Law. But the old covenant did not resolve the deepest needs of mankind. It did not set the world free from human wickedness and the terrible consequences of that wickedness – disease, decay and death (Heb 10:4, 11). And it did not promise eternal life beyond the cold dark grave.

As yet Jesus had no gospel to offer these people. He had nothing new to give them. His death alone could secure what they so desperately needed. Only a new covenant in his blood would open the kingdom of God to the Gentiles. Only when the grain of wheat has died will it yield a harvest among the nations. Only when he is lifted up will he draw all people to himself (Jn 12:32). Only by his wounds can we be healed. Only by bearing our sins in his body on the tree can he free us from the guilt we bear (1 Pet 2:24). Only by dying and rising from the grave can he bring life and immortality to light through the gospel (2 Tim 1:10). Only when the price is paid, and the Spirit released, will all nations be able to seek and find peace with God and fellowship with his people.

So we see that Jesus learnt no new language; he adopted no new culture. He did not go into all the world proclaiming good news to all creation. He had no good news to offer the nations until he had died for the sin of the world. So Jesus himself was never a cross-cultural missionary.

Despite this we know he always had cross-cultural mission in mind. He was concerned for every tribe and tongue. He said, "I am the light of the world" (Jn 8:12). He said, "I did not come to judge the world but to save the world" (Jn 12:47). He said, "Go and make disciples of all nations . . . teaching them to observe all that I have commanded you" (Matt 28:19-20). And his final words to his disciples were, "You will be my witnesses in Jerusalem and in all Judea and Samaria, and to the end of the earth" (Acts 1:8).

We are so familiar with the idea of world mission that we may fail to appreciate how astonishing it was. Jesus was telling these men to go deliberately to other countries and try to change the beliefs and practices of people throughout the earth. Such a thing had never been attempted or even suggested by anyone else. It would seem highly unlikely to succeed.

But there is something more to note. Whenever Jesus himself met people from other cultures, he was glad for them to tell their own people what they had seen and heard. When the poor man among the tombs in Gadara was set free from a legion of demons, "Jesus sent him away, saying, 'Return to your home, and declare how much God has done for you'" (Lk 8:38-39). When he had spoken with the woman of Samaria, "many Samaritans from that town believed in him because of the woman's testimony" (Jn 4:39).

Although he had no covenant of salvation to offer these outsiders, Jesus was glad when they believed in him. Indeed, he marvelled at the faith of the Roman centurion and declared, "I have never found anyone in Israel with such a faith as this. I tell you, many will come from east and west and recline at table with Abraham, Isaac, and Jacob in the kingdom of heaven" (Matt 8:10-11). The conversion of many Gentiles was something Jesus looked forward to with keen anticipation, and his disciples observed all this.

He was preparing them to do greater works than he had done (Jn 14:12). He was preparing them for a great cross-cultural mission to be launched after he had left them and returned to his Father. They would proclaim to every tribe and tongue how the Saviour had died and risen to remove sin and all its consequences from the heart of man and in due course from the world itself.

This is confirmed by a curious fact. When Jesus selected his team of twelve, he did not choose a representative from each of the twelve tribes of Israel. He opted exclusively for men from Galilee (Acts 2:7). The Twelve were all Galileans apart from Judas Iscariot, whose origins probably lay in Kerioth to the south of Judea or perhaps in Moab.

There was a reason for this. Galilee was quite unlike the other regions of Israel. In "Galilee of the Gentiles" there lived a high proportion of immigrants – Egyptians, Arabs, Phoenicians, Greeks and others – who communicated with one another and with the Jewish populace in Greek (Matt 4:15).[1] The men whom Jesus chose for missionary training had grown up amongst people of other cultures. They already spoke two languages. In the days ahead this knowledge of both Aramaic and Greek would be extremely useful to them.

---

1. Schnabel, *ECM*, 249

4

The Mission of the Twelve Apostles

Jesus did not proclaim salvation to the nations and gather converts into churches. That could only be done once the new covenant in his blood had been secured. It could only be done when he had died and risen and ascended into heaven to intercede for all who would put their trust in him. It could only be done after he had poured out his Spirit on his people and granted them the spiritual gifts they would need for mission to the world and ministry in the church. Only then would his apostles have a message of salvation for the nations and the dynamic energy to proclaim it in the face of scorn and opposition.

Before this, there had never been news *so good* that all the world must hear it. But as he left them Jesus made sure they knew exactly what to say and where to say it. "Thus it is written," he reminded them, "that the Christ should suffer and on the third day rise from the dead, and that repentance and forgiveness of sins should be proclaimed in his name to all nations, beginning from Jerusalem" (Lk 24:46-47). With these words he identified both the gospel message and the sphere it must transform. Then he ascended to the Father.

The Greatest of all Missionary Events

After his ascension, ten days passed. Then came the great festival of Pentecost. To celebrate the occasion and enjoy the national holiday, many Jewish people who had settled in other parts of the world travelled back to their ancestral homeland. We are told they came "from every nation under heaven" (Acts 2:5).

Among these Jewish visitors were people of other races and cultures who had heard about the God of the Jews and committed themselves to the Jewish faith. They too had travelled hundreds of miles by ship and on foot in order to participate in the Jerusalem festivities. We are given a list of the places they came from (Acts 2:9-11).

Some of these Gentile converts to Judaism were known as *proselytes*, meaning "people who have come forward". Having believed in the God of Israel, they had committed themselves to the Law of Moses and in the case of men received circumcision. Others were identified as *God-fearers*, desiring to worship the God of the Jews without conforming to every point of the Law.

Attracted to a house where the apostles were assembled, these Jews and Gentile converts to Judaism heard a message that no one had ever heard before: "Jesus of Nazareth . . . God raised him up . . . and of that we all are witnesses . . . Repent and be baptized every one of you in the name of Jesus Christ for the forgiveness of your sins." But more remarkable still, to the astonishment of the crowd gathering there, "each one was hearing them speak in his own language" (Acts 2:5-41).

We can hardly fail to see that this was a divinely ordained and highly significant event. But rarely has its importance for mission strategy been fully appreciated.

Once the festival was over, many of these Jewish and Gentile visitors would return immediately to their distant homelands. They would tell their own people what they had seen and heard in Jerusalem. They would describe it all in their own local languages. They would carry the news through the Roman provinces to the west (to Cappadocia, Pontus, Asia, Phrygia and Pamphylia). They would take it deep into Persian territory to the east (to Parthia, Media, Elam and Mesopotamia). They would carry it along the coast of Africa (to Egypt and Cyrene in Libya). They would take it to Rome, Crete and Arabia (Acts 2:9-11). (See map: The Pentecost Mission.)

But some of these visitors would probably remain for a longer period in Jerusalem. They would ask the apostles to tell them more about the life and teaching of Jesus. When the time came for them to return home, these later travellers would have a deeper understanding of the gospel. They would be able to teach its biblical foundations and its practical applications, and to gather friends and family who accepted what they said in all the far-flung provinces and territories from which they had come. They would be able to form fellowships of believers in strategic centres throughout the known world.

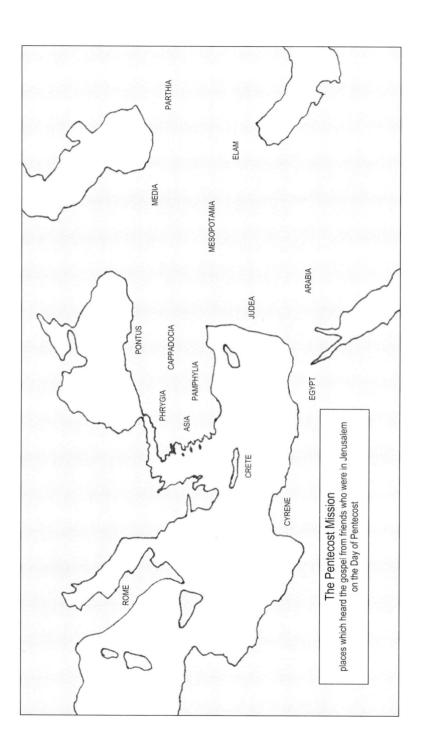

PARTHIA

ELAM

MEDIA

MESOPOTAMIA

ARABIA

PONTUS

CAPPADOCIA

JUDEA

PHRYGIA

ASIA

PAMPHYLIA

EGYPT

CRETE

CYRENE

ROME

The Pentecost Mission

places which heard the gospel from friends who were in Jerusalem
on the Day of Pentecost

Is it not remarkable that at the very start of the Christian Church, God showed its leaders the key to its mission? Immediately we are introduced to immigrants and visitors, people who had crossed from one culture to another *before* they heard the gospel, and were then able to carry it back to their own people in their own language.

It was a God-given strategy that minimized culture shock. It did this so well that the Pentecost event cannot be called cross-cultural mission at all. The Gentiles who heard the gospel on that day had already crossed culture before they heard it. And when they did hear it, they each heard it in their own language. They addressed Peter and the other apostles not as foreigners but as "brothers" (Acts 2:37).

This was both a miracle and a sign. It was a fulfilment of ancient prophecies which at first sight would seem entirely paradoxical. Isaiah had foretold that representatives of the nations would come to join the remnant of Israel (Is 45:20-22; 60:3), and also that the salvation of the Lord would reach the ends of the earth (Is 42:4-7; 49:6). In that momentous week of Pentecost the Gentiles came and joined the remnant of Israel and began to carry the salvation of the Lord to the ends of the earth.

The apostles themselves were not slow to appreciate this, and we will see the pattern of the Pentecost mission repeated many times throughout the book of Acts. But first we must enquire how the disciples began to apply the lessons they had learned from Jesus during their intensive missionary training.

The Missionary Experience of the Apostles

The example of their Master was one the apostles could never forget. He had proclaimed the good news far and wide, and so would they. He had travelled ceaselessly, tirelessly, fearlessly preaching and teaching. He did not wait for circumstances to be favourable. He had come to seek the lost, and so he went out to find them. He gave no thought to himself. As a true Shepherd of the sheep, he tramped through city and countryside, over mountain and desert, in cold of winter, in heat of summer, through regions infested with mosquitoes, flies, snakes and wild dogs, giving no thought to comfort or where he might sleep or what he might eat, devoting himself and his days and all his energy to seeking the harassed and helpless and leading them to safety.

MISSION STRATEGIES THEN AND NOW

The disciples had received his Spirit, and they would do as he did. They had been with him and knew what the missionary life was like. They would walk from dawn till dusk and teach the truth and seek the lost as their Teacher had done, until they had followed every highway and byway, and proclaimed his message throughout the whole land of Israel and to the ends of the earth.

But they could not start immediately. First of all they had been told to wait in Jerusalem until they received power from on high (Acts 1:4, 8). Then after the Spirit had come, they still could not leave because three thousand converts in the city needed teaching and establishing in the faith (Acts 2:41). Soon the number had risen to at least five thousand (Acts 4:4). And before they could travel elsewhere they must give their united testimony to the rulers of Israel – to the high priest, the council of elders and the royal court. For the empty tomb had proved beyond doubt that Jesus was indeed the Messiah, crucified by his people but raised by God and willing to accept all who would turn to him in repentance and in faith (Acts 2:36-38).

All this would keep them fully occupied for several weeks or months. While others carried the news throughout Israel that the Lord was risen, the Twelve remained in Jerusalem, with Matthias taking the place of Judas the traitor. "Every day, in the temple and from house to house, they did not cease teaching and preaching Jesus as the Messiah" (Acts 5:42).

But from their base in Jerusalem they were more than willing to walk out to neighbouring towns and villages. So "when the apostles at Jerusalem heard that Samaria had received the word of God, they sent Peter and John to them" (Acts 8:14). This took the two men forty miles to the north of Jerusalem. On their way back they did something they had never done before. They proclaimed the good news in many villages of the Samaritans (Acts 8:25).

Further journeys followed. "As Peter went here and there among them all, he came down also to the saints who lived at Lydda," a town about twenty-five miles north-west of Jerusalem (Acts 9:32). Then we see him thirty-five miles away with the believers in the port of Joppa. Next we find him further north along the coast at Caesarea, sixty-five miles from Jerusalem. Here too he was breaking fresh ground as he explained the gospel to the Gentile household of Cornelius (Acts 9:38; 10:23-24).

The other apostles no doubt did the same, visiting groups of believers wherever they were found, and taking every opportunity to speak with strangers along the road. From time to time they would return to Jerusalem where they could discuss their experiences and pray together, just as they had done when their Master was with them.

The early Christians became well known throughout the region and their message widely heard. They spoke freely about Jesus in public places – in the streets of Jerusalem (Acts 2:14), in the temple courts (3:11-12), in the synagogue (6:9-10), before the council of Jewish leaders (4:5-8; 5:27-32; 6:12-7:57), outside the city walls (7:58-60), throughout Judea and Samaria (8:1, 4-8), in many villages (8:25), on a desert road (8:26-38), in all the towns (8:40), and in the crowded house of a wealthy Roman (10:34-43). Their enemies alleged, "you have filled Jerusalem with your teaching" (Acts 5:28). Indeed they had.

But every day they also met privately in their own homes for the apostles' teaching, fellowship, breaking of bread and prayer (Acts 1:13ff; 2:1ff; 4:23ff; 12:12). The idea of reading scripture and praying together in an ordinary house was not new to them. The majority of synagogues had no special building at this time but met wherever they could find space in a Jewish home.[1] The word *synagogue* simply means a gathering of people.

Throughout this period, Peter and the other apostles would stay in the homes of believers wherever they went. News of their arrival would quickly spread, and a wider circle of family, friends and neighbours would be made welcome to benefit from their ministry (Acts 9:32-35).

The book of Acts shows us the crucial importance of hospitality for the early church and its mission. As an example let us take Simon the tanner and his house beside the sea at Joppa (Acts 9:43). Peter had already stayed with him "for many days", and while a meal was being prepared he saw his vision. Then Simon opened his door to a company of strangers sent by Cornelius. They too stayed overnight. Next day Cornelius welcomed Peter and other believers from Joppa into his own home, where he and his friends and family were gathered. After proclaiming his message, Peter remained with them "for some days", during which he would teach them many things (Acts 10:1-

---

1. Schnabel, *ECM*, 205

48). Such a ministry depended entirely on a culture of cheerful and generous hospitality.

It is clear that the believers enjoyed the company of one another and of strangers who showed an interest in their faith. This was not just once a week but every day. Day by day they went to testify in the temple courts, and day by day they came home together for a simple meal, breaking bread from house to house with gladness and sincerity of heart. And day by day the Lord added to their number those who were being saved (Acts 2:46-47). We might do well to learn from their example.

When the Jewish authorities finally resolved to reject the testimony of the apostles, severe persecution came upon them. But although many of the believers left Jerusalem, the Twelve still had no liberty to go. Indeed, we read that "they were all scattered throughout the regions of Judea and Samaria, except the apostles" (Acts 8:1).

At risk of their lives the Twelve remained in the city, refusing to seek safety in some quiet Galilean village. We may assume that many enquirers were still coming to consult them about matters of fact and of uncertainty. Indeed they were all present when a most serious controversy arose. It concerned the Gentiles, and whether the Gentiles must obey the Law of Moses. So "the apostles and the elders were gathered together to consider this matter" (Acts 15:6).

When agreement was reached, the Twelve were finally free to go into all the world and proclaim the gospel to all creation. The evidence available to us confirms that they did so.

We know that Peter travelled to Antioch in the province of Syria (Gal 2:11). From there he probably journeyed on to Babylon where a significant Jewish population would give him a warm welcome. This would be an ideal centre for outreach to the east (1 Pet 5:13).[1]

---

1. Many writers have assumed that when Peter says Babylon he means Rome. This seems unlikely. Babylon with its large Jewish community would be far more accessible to him than the imperial capital in Italy. The journey eastward from Syrian Antioch to Babylon along the famous Silk Road and down the Euphrates would be about 550 miles (880 km), whereas the distance to Rome was almost three times as far. In Babylon he could speak Aramaic, his first language, whereas in Rome he would be expected to use Greek or Latin. With news of Paul's progress in the west, Peter might very naturally turn east. Visitors from Babylon (Mesopotamia) had heard his Pentecost proclamation in Jerusalem and would no doubt offer him a warm welcome. A famous collection of Jewish writings, known as the Babylonian *talmud*, testifies to the strength of the Jewish community there at a slightly later period.

From this base in the east Peter addressed a letter to the west, to the "exiles of the dispersion in Pontus, Galatia, Cappadocia, Asia, and Bithynia" (1 Pet 1:1). As far away as Corinth it was common knowledge that Peter and his wife travelled together on apostolic mission (1 Cor 9:5). Peter was deeply concerned for the progress of the gospel throughout the world.

Before long his old friend John is also found far from home, on the island of Patmos in the Aegean Sea. Here he was a missionary, and perhaps a prisoner, "on account of the word of God and the testimony of Jesus" (Rev 1:9). From Patmos John sent messages to seven congregations, probably familiar to him, on the mainland of western Turkey. Both Peter and John took the trouble to write in Greek so their readers far away would easily understand what they said.

Later writers report many traditions of the Twelve travelling widely and proclaiming the word of God in the furthest reaches of the known world. Thomas, for example, is said to have established thriving Christian communities among the Jewish settlers in India, and those churches survive to this day.

It is sometimes suggested that the Twelve were reluctant to leave Jerusalem and fulfil the great commission, and that in this they were disobedient. There are not two witnesses able to prove such an allegation (1 Tim 5:19).

The missionaries so carefully trained by Jesus did not disappoint him. They justified his confidence in them, and his confidence in the Holy Spirit working through them. They followed the exact sequence he had given them: "You will be my witnesses in Jerusalem and in all Judea and Samaria, and to the end of the earth" (Acts 1:8).

The Apostles' Cross-cultural Strategy

We have seen how Gentile converts to Judaism came at Pentecost from many parts of the world and heard Peter's testimony in Jerusalem. These proselytes and worshippers of God had already adopted many aspects of Jewish culture. Attending a local synagogue in their homelands, they would be on friendly terms with many Jewish families. Whatever their language of birth, they could now speak Greek, and some might be learning the rudiments of Hebrew.

The book that informed and guided the Jewish communities

outside Israel was the *Septuagint*, a Greek translation of the Hebrew scriptures. Hand-written portions of the Septuagint were probably available in every synagogue. In its pages, evangelists such as Stephen and Philip would find many prophecies concerning Christ which they would later use to great effect in proclaiming the way of salvation.

Six of the seven men appointed to care for the practical affairs of the Jerusalem fellowship were probably Jews. But the seventh is identified as "Nicolaus, a proselyte of Antioch" (Acts 6:5). He was a Gentile, and one of many who had entered the Jewish culture and travelled far from home before hearing anything of the gospel. In the persecution when the Jerusalem believers were scattered, it would be natural for Nicolaus to return, at least for a while, to his home in Syria. Here he would share his experiences with his family and friends, explaining everything to them in their local dialect. The gospel would come to them as something discovered by one of their own people and therefore as something for them. Perhaps this was the beginning of the church in Antioch which later sent Saul and Barnabas on their pioneer mission to the Gentiles of the west.

Certain synagogues were especially popular with foreigners who had settled in Jerusalem. One of these was the "synagogue of the Freedmen" where Africans and Asians were accustomed to meet. Here Stephen told the assembled company about Jesus. Some of the men argued vehemently with him but then we are told, "they could not withstand the wisdom and the Spirit with which he was speaking" (Acts 6:10). A number became angry and eventually stoned him to death. But we may assume that others were convinced by what he said. Believing in Jesus, they would be able to carry their new faith back to their homelands: to Cyrene in Libya, to Alexandria in Egypt, to Cilicia in the south-east of modern Turkey (where Saul of Tarsus was born) and to Asia Minor (where Saul would later work). They too had crossed culture before they heard the gospel and were then able to take it back to their own people in their own tongue.

Shortly after this we read of an Ethiopian on his way home from a pilgrimage to Jerusalem. He too is a Gentile convert to Judaism, and he has with him a precious scroll of Isaiah, probably acquired on his visit to the city. This man has willingly crossed culture to embrace the faith of the Jews and to study their scriptures in a foreign language, almost certainly Greek. He is so eager to read that he cannot wait till he reaches the comfort of his home. When Philip tells him about Jesus, the Ethiopian believes and is baptized, and then goes on his way rejoicing. As a court official of the queen and in charge of all her treasure, we may assume he was a man of intelligence and influence, and well able to explain his new-found faith to his own people in their own language (Acts 8:26-39). He probably came from the kingdom of Meroë on the banks of the Nile in what is now Sudan.

Around this time Peter was invited to the home of Cornelius, a Roman soldier and centurion of the Italian Cohort (Acts 10:1). Cornelius too was a Gentile who had embraced the religious culture of the Jews. He was "a devout man who feared God with all his household, gave alms generously to the people, and prayed continually to God" (Acts 10:2). Hearing what Peter said, he immediately accepted the gospel. We do not know where Cornelius was posted after his assignment in Caesarea or what happened to the "many persons" with him who heard Peter's message, but we may assume that some went back to their military headquarters in Italy. Others, from different parts of the Roman Empire, may have returned there. The message which they heard from Peter in Greek, or perhaps in Aramaic, went with them, to be explained to their own friends and family in Latin or in their own local dialect (Acts 10:1-47).

In all this we see that a study of the races and places in the early chapters of Acts can shed a great deal of light on the mission methods of the early churches in Judea. It reveals the key role played by people who had already crossed from one culture to another before they heard the gospel, and who could then carry it back to their own people in their own language. This is the simple and obvious way for news to spread. This is the way that God providentially arranged for it to spread, and the way that the Holy Spirit led the apostles and the early evangelists to spread it.

But was it a strategy that would work beyond the borders of Israel? That is what we will now consider.

CHAPTER

5

Paul's Early Missions

Paul's First Missionary Journey (Acts 13:1 to 14:26)

Pioneer missions

Saul of Tarsus had travelled a long way from his home town in the province of Cilicia when he met the risen Christ on the Damascus road. Joseph Barnabas had travelled a long way from his home on the island of Cyprus when he heard the gospel in Jerusalem. It is significant that these two great missionaries were both converted far from home.

At Antioch in Syria, where they now lived, the church was led by five men whose origins were equally diverse. Indeed they were probably born in five different countries. Lucius was from Cyrene in Libya. Manaen had grown up with Herod Antipas in Judea. Simeon Niger, whose name means "black", may have been African. Barnabas was from Cyprus, and Saul himself came from Cilicia in what is now south-eastern Turkey. It is likely that these men all heard and believed the gospel while visiting or living in what was, to them, a foreign land.

As one of the leaders in the Antioch fellowship, Saul was already an experienced missionary. For ten years or more he had been refining his methods. After his conversion, he had not been led immediately to the ends of the earth but had simply started where he was, proclaiming the gospel in the synagogues of Damascus and "proving that Jesus was the Christ" (Acts 9:20-22).

From his base in Damascus he then headed into the region of Nabatea in northern Arabia. This was a fertile irrigated land with important trading activities, where the people spoke Aramaic and some Greek. There were Jews living in the larger towns but Saul may have tried to communicate directly with the pagan populace. He tells us he did not consult anyone, but having received his commission from Christ went immediately to "preach him among the Gentiles" (Gal 1:16). At this time there were political tensions between the Jews and Nabateans, and Saul's activity created such a stir that eventually the governor determined to arrest him. Returning to Damascus he was obliged to leave the city secretly (Gal 1:17; 2 Cor 11:32-33).

At this point Barnabas introduced him to the apostles in Jerusalem, and for a while "he stayed with them and moved about freely in Jerusalem, preaching boldly in the name of the Lord" (Acts 9:28). Eventually he was forced to leave the city when Jewish agitators threatened his life.

Settling once more in Tarsus, Saul became well known in the synagogues of Cilicia and Syria (Acts 11:25; 9:30; Gal 1:21). In these two provinces there were twenty or thirty large towns and he probably helped establish Christian fellowships in each of them, for we hear that about six years later "he went through Syria and Cilicia, strengthening the churches" (Acts 15:41). How he supported himself during this period is not clear. As an artisan skilled at making tents, he may have found ways to exercise his craft.

Meanwhile in Antioch, a large number of Gentiles had responded to "the good news about the Lord Jesus" (Acts 11:20). These new converts were greatly in need of teaching. Although Barnabas himself had a gift for encouraging believers, he appreciated Saul's outstanding ability to explain the gospel effectively to both Jews and Gentiles. Barnabas went to find him in Tarsus and invited him to join the work in this strategic regional capital. For a year the two men continued preaching and teaching in Antioch until the fellowship with its local leaders was well established (Acts 11:26).

It was then that their thoughts turned to nearby provinces which had not yet heard the gospel. They were sent on their mission by the church and by the Holy Spirit, and they took with them a young relation of Barnabas who had known the earliest disciples. His name was John Mark (Col 4:10).

Their first destination was Cyprus, the homeland of Barnabas himself. He probably had friends and family there and would know of Cypriot believers who had returned home to escape persecution in Jerusalem (Acts 11:19-20). Walking from town to town, Barnabas and

Saul visited the synagogues throughout the island. In each synagogue there would be opportunity to address the assembled company.

In the town of Paphos they came upon a Jewish sorcerer who vigorously opposed them. He was attached to the court of the Roman governor, Sergius Paulus, an intelligent man who sent for the apostles "because he wanted to hear the word of God" (Acts 13:7). Attempting to intervene, the aggressive sorcerer was for a time struck blind. The governor was astonished by what he saw and heard, and became a believer in Jesus (Acts 13:12).

Sergius Paulus had been appointed to Cyprus in the service of Rome but his family origins were probably in the region around Pisidian Antioch (central Turkey). Like other early converts in the book of Acts, he responded to the gospel far from home. As governor of Cyprus he was an influential man, and his testimony would be heard with interest by his extensive social circle. Barnabas and Saul must have been greatly encouraged by his conversion, knowing that other believers on the island would now have a friend in very high places if they needed protection or help in any way.

From this point onward Saul is known not by his Hebrew name but by the Latin name Paulus (Paul). It seems likely that he adopted the name of his first influential Gentile convert as a token of their unity in Christ and their fellowship in the work of the gospel.

After these positive experiences in Cyprus, the missionaries took ship to Attalia on the Turkish coast, not far from Tarsus where Paul had grown up. Heading inland, they came to the city of Pisidian Antioch. "On the Sabbath day they went into the synagogue and sat down." They did not have long to wait. "After the reading from the Law and the Prophets, the rulers of the synagogue sent a message to them, saying, 'Brothers, if you have any word of encouragement for the people, say it'" (Acts 13:15).

By now Paul had learned exactly how to speak in a synagogue, and a summary of his sermon is given to us in the book of Acts. His message awakened great interest, and he was invited to speak again. In the face of growing Jewish opposition, a number of Jews and Gentiles believed. Before long "the word of the Lord was spreading throughout the whole region" (Acts 13:49). With teaching and encouragement, "the disciples were filled with joy and with the Holy Spirit" (Acts 13:52).

Persecution eventually forced Paul and Barnabas to leave Pisidian

Antioch for the neighbouring city of Iconium, where once again "they entered together into the Jewish synagogue". Here too "a great number of both Jews and Greeks believed" (Acts 14:1). They remained teaching and encouraging their converts "for a long time" until opposition again compelled them to move on to Lystra and then to Derbe.

New fellowships

The exact location of provincial boundaries at this period is difficult to define, especially as the boundaries themselves were frequently changing. The area which Paul calls Galatia probably included Pisidian Antioch, and possibly Iconium, Lystra and Derbe too, so when he later wrote his letter to the Galatians, it would be to here that he sent it. He reminded them, "You know it was because of a bodily ailment that I preached the gospel to you at first." The healthier climate of the higher ground may have attracted him to these places if he was suffering from malaria or an uncomfortable eye condition, and despite the trouble his illness caused them, he recalled how the people received him "as an angel of God, as Christ Jesus" (Gal 4:13-14).

In every synagogue the apostle would explain that Jesus was the long-awaited Messiah, foretold in the scriptures, rejected and crucified by wicked men, then raised by God as Lord and Saviour for all who would turn to him in repentance and faith. They proclaimed their message clearly and boldly. It was highly controversial and would quickly become a talking point among the Jewish community and the Gentiles who worshipped God. And it would not remain within the walls of the synagogue. Gentiles who did not attend the meetings would learn about it from their friends and family who did.

Many questions would arise in the minds of those who heard this synagogue preaching, and it would be natural for them to invite Paul and Barnabas home for further discussion. Those who accepted the message and sincerely believed in Jesus were then baptized in his name and met as often as they could for further teaching, for fellowship, and for breaking of bread and prayer.

The mission of Barnabas and Paul was not a hasty flight from place to place scattering seed and leaving it to sprout or perish on its own. Their objective was to establish a permanent fellowship of believers in each place, and they would stay as long as necessary to accomplish this.

Their converts had much to learn. Assurance of salvation, the guidance of the Holy Spirit, the meaning of prophetic scripture, the varied gifts for ministry, the fellowship of the church, financial stewardship, prayer and intercession, the responsibilities of believers to one another and to those outside, the wonderful ministry and teaching of Jesus himself – all this would be thoroughly discussed. And every new believer had opportunity to ask questions, seek counsel, and receive personal guidance and prayer for his or her spiritual growth and usefulness. Each must gain sufficient understanding and confidence to share the gospel effectively with friends, family, customers and workmates, and to share it too with strangers throughout the locality.

After the missionaries had left them, the believers would be dependent on the Holy Spirit and on the insights and abilities granted by the Spirit to the members of their own company. Each day they would make fresh discoveries in the scriptures, find new answers to old questions, and overcome the bad habits of their past lives. They would see friends and family changing and growing, gaining confidence and wisdom as their Lord filled them with the good fruits of patience and loving kindness.

After some months, having completed their mission in Derbe, the apostles decided it was time to revisit the congregations they had left in Lystra, Iconium and Pisidian Antioch. On this return journey, they would look to see how leaders had emerged in each fellowship. In every place they found some who had already shown ability to teach, to comfort and encourage, and to set an example of Christlike character. After prayer and fasting, they recognised these men as elders. It was only a year or two after their conversion.

These elders were not paid to bear responsibility. They earned their own living and in general needed no financial support. There was no minister or pastor brought from elsewhere to direct any of these groups. Each was led by its own senior men, and when the believers met together in their homes, freedom was allowed for all to participate. We will speak more of this in due course.

In total, this first mission trip of Barnabas and Paul probably took about three years. Throughout that time they were never more than 200 miles (320 km) from where they had grown up. In every place, they had looked for a Jewish synagogue, where they would find an immediate welcome. The two men were quite comfortable in this environment, speaking languages they had always known and ministering to people like themselves. We could not yet describe their work as cross-cultural mission.

At one point during this trip, however, we have a genuine cross-cultural incident. In the city of Lystra, Paul healed a crippled man, but the pagan populace could not understand what Paul was saying. He did not know their language and they did not know his. They started shouting in their Lycaonian tongue, "The gods have come down to us in the likeness of men!" (Acts 14:11). The priest of Zeus brought oxen and garlands to the gates, desiring to worship the missionaries with ritual sacrifices and ceremonies. Then some Jews came and stirred up the crowd. There was an uproar and they stoned Paul and left him for dead. In this cross-cultural context we see that he was much less effective than in the synagogues.

Paul's Ministry to the Church (Acts 14:27 to 15:39)

Making their way back to Syrian Antioch, Barnabas and Paul then no doubt received a warm welcome from the congregation which had sent them out. For a period of about two years they would remain there, sharing in the ministry of the church. This was not an interlude in their missionary service but a continuation of it, for the Antioch congregation had urgent need of them.

As we have seen, the fellowship included many Gentiles. Some of these had previously been proselytes and circumcised according to the Law of Moses. But others had accepted Christ without circumcision or any commitment to the Law. They had been assured of acceptance with God and his people simply through faith in the Saviour. While Paul and Barnabas were away, teachers had come from Jerusalem, saying that faith in Christ was not enough. Circumcision and obedience to the Law were also necessary for salvation.

Paul and Barnabas could not accept this emphasis on Law. In truth, "Christ has brought the Law to completion, so that by faith a person can be right with God" (Rom 10:4). "We are released from the Law," they said, "so that we serve in the new way of the Spirit and not in the old way of the written code" (Rom 7:6).

By this time there were many Gentile Christians in Cyprus and on the mainland who had accepted the gospel without the Law. If these were all rejected by the Jewish believers in Jerusalem and Antioch, they would be compelled to form separate churches. The body of Christ would then be divided on racial grounds derived from the old covenant rather than the new.

The Antioch congregation decided that a delegation must go to enquire whether the apostles and elders in Jerusalem supported what these visiting teachers said. They sent Barnabas and Paul and several others.

After some discussion, the leaders in Jerusalem reassured the Antioch representatives of their commitment to the simple gospel of salvation through faith in Christ alone. They affirmed that the teachers who insisted on the Law had not been sent by them or with their approval. To ease the tensions, the assembled company also agreed that Gentile believers should avoid causing unnecessary offence to Jews through indulgence in things abhorrent to them. This agreement, with its emphasis on unity, was put in writing so that all the churches could see that no division existed and take care that none occurred.

Once this controversy had been resolved, Paul's greatest concern was for the believers that he and Barnabas had left in the neighbouring provinces. "Let us return," he said, "and visit the brothers in every city where we proclaimed the word of the Lord, and see how they are" (Acts 15:36).

Barnabas suggested again taking John Mark with them, but Paul had lost confidence in the young man, for Mark had quickly abandoned them on their previous mission. Unable to agree, they decided to separate. Barnabas and Mark went back to Cyprus. Paul invited Silas to accompany him overland through Syria and Cilicia and then to regions beyond.

Paul's Second Missionary Journey (Acts 15:40 to 18:22)

Revisiting the churches

Paul's second mission probably lasted about four years. Passing through his native Cilicia, he travelled west with Silas to revisit the congregations in Derbe, Lystra, Iconium and perhaps Pisidian Antioch. All these had been continuing under their own leadership for two years or more. As Paul's concern was especially for the believers meeting together in their homes, we do not read that he preached again in the synagogues or in other public places. The task of outreach in these localities was now the responsibility of the Christians who lived there.

As the fellowships were doing well, Paul turned his thoughts to the provinces further west which had never heard the gospel of Christ. Entering these territories he would be moving out of the Aramaic environment familiar to him and into a context where the superstitious philosophies and occult paganism of Greek culture were more deeply rooted.

In Lystra there was a young man named Timothy. He was "the son of a Jewish woman who was a believer, but his father was a Greek," and the church spoke highly of him (Acts 16:1). Despite their Jewish ancestry his mother and grandmother both had Greek names, and Greek would be the language of the family home.

A person such as Timothy would be particularly useful for mission to the west, for he was multi-cultural – more so indeed than Paul himself. As Timothy was half Greek, Paul knew he would be well accepted by Gentiles in the provinces they were about to enter. But he was also half Jewish, and Paul advised him to be circumcised so he could enter Jewish homes, speak in their synagogues and be fully accepted among the Jews. It was a significant moment, for in himself Timothy personified the unity and diversity of the Church where Jew and Greek were united in a single body. He became one of Paul's most trusted and useful companions.

Heading west, the missionary team passed rapidly through the central regions of Asia Minor (Turkey), forbidden by the Holy Spirit to proclaim the gospel in those parts. The flourishing congregation at Pisidian Antioch was not far away and might perhaps take the message to them within a year or two.

After this, the road led Paul and his companions through wild and dangerous country. They were forced to negotiate mountain passes, cross angry torrents and traverse arid regions infested with robbers and malarial mosquitoes. The New Testament writers rarely mention the physical hardships they endured on their journeys. Only when compelled to defend his ministry would Paul reluctantly catalogue some of them (2 Cor 11:23-27). But the suffering of the evangelist is as necessary as the suffering of Christ if the world is to receive the gospel (Col 1:24).

The mission to Europe

There are signs that the further Paul travels away from his homeland, the more sensitive he becomes to cultural differences. When his road through Asia Minor finally reaches its terminus at the coast, we find him quite uncertain about crossing the sea to Europe.

On that continent he would encounter an alien cultural environment. There would be fewer Jewish people and far fewer synagogues. He may have wondered whether his usual methods would work at all. Would he be able to communicate? Would the Greeks give a hearing to someone so obviously a Jew? He needed reassurance.

His mission, indeed, was facing frustrations and even appeared somewhat uncertain of its guidance: "When they had come up to Mysia, they attempted to go into Bithynia, but the Spirit of Jesus did not allow them. So, passing by Mysia, they went down to Troas" (Acts 16:7-8).

The port of Troas was as far as a traveller could go on the mainland of Asia. Ahead of them was water, the Aegean Sea, and beyond that the continent of Europe. It was then that "a vision appeared to Paul in the night: a man of Macedonia was standing there, urging him and saying, 'Come over to Macedonia and help us'" (Acts 16:9).

The whole team was involved in the decision to go. Their number had been strengthened by the addition of Luke, an educated man and a physician, and now a believer in Christ. We cannot be sure whether Luke was a Jew or a Gentile proselyte. In either case, his Latin name might have been given to him by a former master or benefactor. But most significantly, he could write excellent Greek and would be at ease in a Greek environment.[1]

The missionary team landed in the province of Macedonia and made their way to Philippi, the leading city. Here, if anywhere, there would be a synagogue. On enquiry it seems they could not find one,

---

1. The usual reason for supposing that Luke was a Gentile is that Paul calls him a "fellow-worker" in Philemon 24 whilst distinguishing him from his fellow workers "of the circumcision" in Colossians 4:11 and 14. There could be other explanations for this. If his mother or grandmother were Jewish, for example, he might have remained uncircumcised. Luke's writing contains many Jewish idiomatic expressions and demonstrates a detailed knowledge of the temple in Jerusalem. His presence with Paul never caused the same embarrassment as that of Trophimus who was a Gentile from Ephesus (Acts 21:29).

so on the Sabbath they went down to the river, looking for a Jewish place of prayer. They met some women there, spoke with them about Christ and won their first convert in Europe, a lady of great character and probably some wealth, by the name of Lydia. She was a Gentile worshipper of God.

Like others we have seen, Lydia was a long way from home when she heard and believed the gospel, for she was originally from Thyatira in Asia Minor. The church in Thyatira was later commended for its "love and faith and service and patient endurance" (Rev 2:19). It may be that Thyatira first heard the gospel from Lydia or from members of her household who heard Paul speak that day. Luke gives special mention to Lydia's generous hospitality in Philippi, so we may assume that she and her home continued to be of importance to the believers there and to Paul himself.

In Philippi, however, there was no wider Jewish community that might give a hearing to the message. It was a pagan city settled largely by Romans, and soon afterwards Paul had another difficult cross-cultural experience. He cast out an evil spirit from a slave girl, so destroying her ability to tell fortunes and depriving her owners of a substantial income. This immediately caused a riot. He and Silas were arrested, severely beaten and imprisoned. They had undoubtedly offended against the local culture. As their accusers alleged, "These men are Jews, and they are disturbing our city. They advocate customs that are not lawful for us as Romans to accept or practice" (Acts 16:20-21).

The inner cell of such a prison would be overcrowded, smelly, noisy, extremely dirty and totally dark at night. Despite the danger and discomfort he was in, Paul did not immediately claim protection as a Roman citizen. He would never demand privileges unavailable to his converts or to fellow-missionaries such as Silas. To prove his citizenship might also be a costly and time-consuming process if witnesses and documents would need to be brought.

At midnight, with their feet secured by heavy wooden bars, the missionaries were praying and singing hymns to God, while the other prisoners listened to them. A hymn may be more valuable, indeed, as a comfort in time of trouble, and a means of outreach to the suffering, than as a form of worship in days of ease. The only time we know that Jesus sang a hymn was when he went out to die (Matt 26:30).

Luke was pleased to record that this imprisonment led to the conversion of the jailer and his family, and that somewhere a small company of believers began to meet, perhaps in Lydia's home. But the missionaries were required by the Roman authorities to leave the city immediately. In comparison with the fruitfulness of their synagogue ministry, this attempt at cross-cultural mission in a pagan city was not notably successful.

Travelling on, "they came to Thessalonica, where there was a synagogue of the Jews. And Paul went in, as was his custom, and on three Sabbath days he reasoned with them from the Scriptures" (Acts 17:1-2). In this context he was far more effective. A large number of Jews and God-fearing Greeks believed, before Jewish opposition again forced him and Silas to leave.

Moving on to Berea they were again glad to find a synagogue, and especially pleased to see how keenly the Bereans studied the scriptures. Many of the Jews there accepted the gospel message, and also "a number of prominent Greek women and many Greek men" (Acts 17:12). When Jewish agitators stirred up the crowds Paul was forced to leave, while Timothy and Silas remained to teach and encourage the believers. Paul and Luke went on to wait for them in Athens.

This famous city was one of the three great intellectual centres of the Roman Empire, along with Tarsus and Alexandria, and superior to the others in reputation. The inhabitants of Athens spoke a cultured form of Greek and were trained to view all religions with calm academic detachment.

Paul found a Jewish synagogue here but its members seemed less responsive than in other places. So he went outside to talk with any Greeks who happened to pass in the public square, engaging them in religious discussion. Again, in this cross-cultural context, he was not very successful. Some sneered, "What does this babbler wish to say?" Others replied, "He seems to be a preacher of foreign divinities." Having preached a sermon well-adapted to their pagan worldview, he found the response from their leading intellectuals decidedly lukewarm. Some mocked, some wanted to hear more, and a small number accepted what he said. With that he had to be content. This experience did not increase his respect for Greek wisdom and philosophy, as we see when he mentions it shortly afterwards (1 Cor 1:18-25; 2:1-2).

Paul and his team did not stay long in Athens but moved on to

Corinth, a city they must have hoped would prove more responsive to their message.

A strategic centre: Corinth

Corinth lay in the Greek province of Achaia. Unlike Athens, it was a place where energetic activity was valued more highly than philosophical theory. It was also a major seaport with a constant flow of people from every part of the Mediterranean Sea. In fact the city had two harbours, one facing east and one facing west. If a church could be established in Corinth, its converts might readily carry the gospel throughout the known world.

While Timothy returned to Thessalonica to help the believers there, Paul and Luke settled in Corinth. Their aim was to establish a strong Christian community at this strategic location.

As this would take some time, they must find some means of support. The apostle looked for work and a place to stay, and he found it with a Jewish couple, Priscilla and Aquila. In his earlier days Paul had learned the specialized craft of making tents. These may have been heavy black tents sewn from woven goat hair, or perhaps lighter tents and awnings made of leather. It was a remarkable provision for him that he came upon this couple working at the same craft in Corinth.

Aquila and Priscilla were originally from the province of Pontus, on the northern coast of Turkey. But they had recently come from Rome, where the emperor ordered the expulsion of all Jewish residents. Their household probably included children, servants, friends, relatives and perhaps a number of tent-making assistants, suppliers, customers and employees.

When Paul explained his faith and his mission to Priscilla and Aquila they were convinced by what he said. Like many others, when they first heard the gospel they were far from home. We may assume that in due course they would share it with their own people whenever visitors came from Pontus or if they returned there to see friends and family.

Making tents during the week, Paul attended the synagogue every Sabbath, discussing the scriptures with the Jews and Gentiles who gathered there and seeking to persuade them of the truth. When Silas and Timothy brought a financial gift from Philippi, he could put aside his needle and thread for a while and devote all his time to this outreach. Stephanas and his household were the first converts from among the local people, and Paul himself baptized them (1 Cor 1:16; 16:15).

Before long however, Paul began to face opposition and abuse from some of the Jews in the synagogue. Tensions grew when "Crispus, the ruler of the synagogue, believed in the Lord, together with his entire household" (Acts 18:8). No longer welcome in the synagogue itself, Paul moved next door, to the house of a Gentile worshipper of God named Titius Justus.

In fact this would be an ideal location for continued contact with the synagogue community and also with the wider Gentile populace known to Titius Justus. Indeed, at this time, "many of the Corinthians, hearing Paul, believed and were baptized" (Acts 18:8).

The apostle saw this as a remarkable work of God rather than something attributable to his own abilities. As a foreigner he could not speak with the style and panache of the popular Greek speech-makers. He later recalled that he came to Corinth "in weakness and in fear and much trembling". He admitted, "My speech and my message were not in plausible words of wisdom, but in demonstration of the Spirit and of power, so that your faith might not rest in the wisdom of men but in the power of God" (1 Cor 2:3-5).

It is likely that the first believers met initially in the home or workshop of Aquila and Priscilla, or perhaps with the family of Stephanas. The house of Titius Justus would now be an additional meeting place, perhaps larger and more convenient than the others. Paul's disciples were already gathering regularly for teaching, fellowship, breaking of bread and prayer.

When he later wrote to this fellowship in Corinth he recalled how they would all "come together to eat" (1 Cor 11:33). Their common meal probably consisted of the simplest food and drink, readily available in every household – bread and water, or perhaps wine, which would be more healthy than most water in those days (1 Tim 5:23). This was probably provided by the host, although some of the guests might bring their own. After work in the evening friends and neighbours would arrive at the house in ones and twos or larger groups. It might take a while for everyone to assemble, and some were tempted to start eating without waiting for the others (1 Cor 11:21).

For Christians there was a special significance in sharing a simple meal, which Paul had explained to them in Corinth as elsewhere. Later he reminded them, "I received from the Lord what I also delivered to you." And this is what he taught them: "The Lord Jesus on the night when he was betrayed took bread, and when he had given thanks, he broke it, and said, 'This is my body which is for you. Do this in remembrance of me.' In the same way also he took the cup, after supper, saying, 'This cup is the new covenant in my blood. Do this, as often as you drink it, in remembrance of me.'" And then Paul concluded, "For as often as you eat this bread and drink the cup, you proclaim the Lord's death until he comes" (1 Cor 11:23-26). Whenever they ate together, they remembered what their Lord had done for them.

Paul remained in Corinth for about two years (Acts 18:11, 18). This was long enough to win a large number to the faith, to establish a warm and supportive Christian fellowship, and to teach his converts all they must know in order to continue on their own. In fact they were already taking the good news to the towns and villages throughout the region, so that before long he could write to "all the saints who are in the whole of Achaia" (2 Cor 1:1).

But he had not yet established a comparable centre in Asia Minor, and to his mind the ideal place would be Ephesus.

A new base and an old problem

Like Corinth, Ephesus was a great seaport, sending and receiving traffic from throughout the eastern and central Mediterranean, and from Africa to the south. It boasted many fine buildings, including the magnificent temple of Diana, one of the Seven Wonders of the World. And in Ephesus there was a large synagogue community whose spiritual potential had not yet been tapped. It was time for Paul to leave southern Europe and cross back to Asia Minor.

He expected to remain in Ephesus at least two years and during this time would again need some means of financial support. Aquila and Priscilla agreed to accompany him and establish a workshop in the city. They travelled together, and after an encouraging visit to the synagogue, he left them to make a start in Ephesus while he went to find a ship heading east.

It is very surprising that at this key moment Paul decided to leave his friends and return to Jerusalem and Syrian Antioch. We can only assume he had received word of serious problems there. It seemed likely that he would need to rally the Jewish factions to his cause once more with news of good progress among the Gentiles, and also to reassure himself that the agreed unity of teaching and fellowship had been preserved in his absence.

It was probably on this trip that he found Peter in Syrian Antioch. His old friend Barnabas was also there. To Paul's obvious dismay the two men and a number of others had been persuaded by teachers from Jerusalem to separate themselves from Gentile Christians who did not follow the Law of Moses. Now they were refusing to eat with uncircumcised believers. The old problem had resurfaced (Gal 2:11-21).

To Paul's mind this segregation denied the truth that believers are all one in Christ Jesus, saved and sanctified not by Law but by faith. The culture of the Jews was destroying the church. Indeed he saw a danger of permanent division on racial grounds, leading inevitably to separate Jewish and Gentile congregations.

He must have been discouraged to find men of such standing and experience as Peter and Barnabas so unclear about the basic principles of the faith or so incapable of upholding them. But others in Antioch agreed with Paul. His protest was accepted and unity restored. Paul remained with the fellowship there for several weeks, and his presence ensured a measure of stability "so that the truth of the gospel might be preserved" (Gal 2:5).

It sometimes happens that a missionary, coming from outside, can identify and help resolve problems like this in a local fellowship. But if men such as Peter and Barnabas could be so seriously mistaken about basic doctrine and practice, we should not be surprised at errors and delusions so seriously corrupting the churches of a later age in Europe and elsewhere.

Twenty years had now passed since Paul's conversion and the start of his missionary career. From long experience he had refined a strategy that worked extremely well. We must now examine more carefully the methods that he used.

6

Paul the Missionary

Paul's Synagogue Ministry

Like the twelve disciples, Paul had met the risen Christ. It was Jesus who appointed him as an apostle, and especially as an apostle to the Gentiles (Acts 9:15; Rom 11:13). His call to the Gentiles was confirmed by the leaders in Jerusalem, as he himself tells us, "that we should go to the Gentiles and they to the circumcised" (Gal 2:9). But in his mission to the Gentiles, Paul adopted a surprising strategy.

Whenever he came to a city he looked immediately for a Jewish synagogue, and if there was no synagogue he sought out a Jewish place of prayer. At first sight, this seems a very curious thing to do. If he was an apostle to the Gentiles, why would he look for a synagogue of the Jews?

The synagogue, in fact, was the best place to meet Gentiles. Not all Gentiles, of course, but those among the Gentiles who would give him a hearing when he spoke of Christ. We must look more closely at these synagogues.

At this period five or six million Israelites, known as the Jewish *diaspora*, were living outside the land of Israel. That is five or even ten times the number of Israelites dwelling in their ancestral homeland.[1] They had established communities in many parts of the Roman Empire and in the Persian territories to the east. In the major cities around the Mediterranean Sea, these Jewish families formed ten to fifteen per cent of the urban population. (See map: Jewish Settlement in the Mediterranean Basin.)

---

1. Schnabel, *ECM*, 559

Jewish communities were entitled to establish a synagogue wherever ten responsible men could be found. Here they would read and expound the scriptures, pray to God, and teach their children the customs of their people. After many years of exile, Hebrew was no longer spoken among them. Greek was the language used in their meetings, and the Greek Septuagint was their Bible. This was of great significance for the mission of the early church.

We have seen that the synagogue communities included proselytes and worshippers of God from various different races. These Gentiles had adopted many aspects of Jewish culture and belief. They had long been attracted to the God of the Jews. They believed in him. But they were seriously hindered in their worship and in their spiritual duties by the racial distinctions of the old covenant and by its ritual requirements.

Gentiles who attended the synagogue remained always to some degree outsiders. A proselyte, despite being circumcised (in the case of a man) and committing himself to obey the Law, could never belong to one of the twelve tribes; nor could he speak of Israel's history as his own. The larger number who were merely worshippers of God, without circumcision and observance of the Law, could only be third-class members of the synagogue community. They would never be accepted as leaders or as teachers on terms of equality with the Jews. If this applied to the men, it applied even more to the women. If it was true for the wealthy and influential, it was doubly true for the servants and slaves. A Gentile convert remained always a Gentile.

Additional problems would be raised for them by the customs and requirements of the Jewish covenant. To a sophisticated Greek, the strict food laws of the Israelites might seem singularly pointless and in practice highly inconvenient. Sabbath observance would curtail many normal and necessary activities. Circumcision must seem like a bloody mutilation akin to the grotesque practices of the pagan cults. And if reference were made to the Hebrew scriptures they were at a disadvantage, for the meaning was unknown to them.

When Paul came among them he offered not just full acceptance with God; he offered full acceptance with God's chosen people. This made the gospel immensely attractive. Under the new covenant these Gentiles would no longer be second- and third-class believers. Indeed, Paul insisted that "there is neither Jew nor Greek, slave

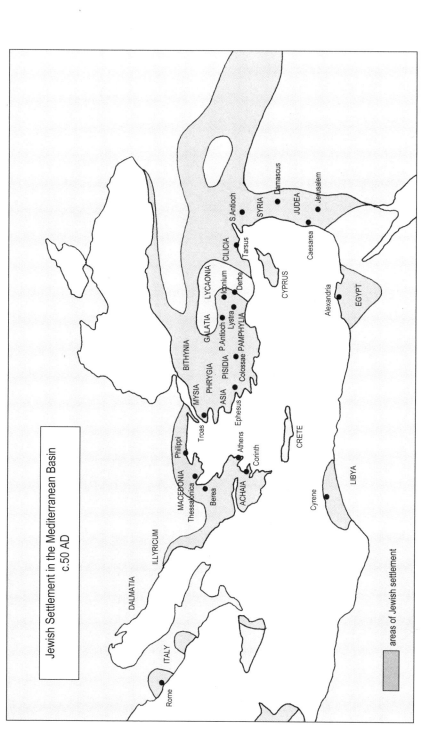

Jewish Settlement in the Mediterranean Basin
c.50 AD

ITALY
Rome

DALMATIA

ILLYRICUM

MACEDONIA
Thessalonica
Berea
Philippi

Troas
MYSIA

ACHAIA
Athens
Corinth
Ephesus
ASIA
PHRYGIA
BITHYNIA

CRETE

Colossae
PISIDIA
P.Antioch
Lystra
PAMPHYLIA
GALATIA
Iconium
Derbe
LYCAONIA

CILICIA
Tarsus
S.Antioch
SYRIA
Damascus
JUDEA
Jerusalem

Caesarea

CYPRUS

Alexandria
EGYPT

LIBYA

Cyrene

areas of Jewish settlement

nor free, male nor female, for you are all one in Christ Jesus" (Gal 3:28). He offered baptism instead of circumcision as a dignified and painless initiation into a life of high ideals, without any of the food restrictions and other ritual obligations of the Law. He spoke Greek, a language familiar to them, and he taught from the Greek Bible, the Septuagint, which they understood and accepted as the word of God.

In the synagogues many Gentiles proved willing to receive his message, and with it the obvious call to tell others. Speaking local dialects in addition to the Greek of their education, they would explain what they heard to their family, workmates, servants, tutors, employers, customers, friends and strangers. Many of their social circle had no particular interest in Judaism but adhered to a wide variety of local religions, philosophies, cults and idols. These were now hearing the facts of the gospel and its practical implications, not from a foreign missionary such as Paul, but from one of their own people whom they already knew and respected.

The Gentiles of the synagogue communities were of varied social classes. The God-fearers tended to be property owners, administrators, army officers and people whose social position and contact with the ritual defilements of the world made it impossible for them to adopt Judaism in its entirety. A man of wealth and status in a Gentile city would have to work on the Sabbath, for example, and attend public functions where idolatrous practices were observed.

The proselytes, on the other hand, were more often from a humble background, and many had previously been slaves. Finding work in a Jewish household or business they could more easily keep the Law.

Both these classes would attend the synagogue, and by introducing his message there, Paul could expect it to reach every level of pagan society. By going to the synagogues and persuading proselytes and God-fearers to believe in Jesus, he was effectively training a corps of Gentile missionaries for outreach to wider communities that spoke their language, shared their culture and mixed with them daily at work and leisure in the most natural way.

Although the good news about Jesus had initially come "to the Jew first and also to the Greek", Paul was now offering it in every synagogue to both at the same time (Rom 1:16). It is sometimes said that, in principle, he presented the gospel first to the Jews in every city and only turned to the Gentiles after the Jews in each place had rejected him. A careful study of scripture shows this to be quite false. In every synagogue he would speak to a mixed company of Jews and Gentiles, and from the very beginning both were present among his converts. In Athens, for example, "he reasoned in the synagogue with the Jews and the Gentile worshippers" (Acts 17:17) In Corinth "he reasoned in the synagogue every Sabbath, and tried to persuade Jews and Greeks" (Acts 18:4).

This synagogue strategy was highly effective. At Iconium "they entered together into the Jewish synagogue and spoke in such a way that a great number of both Jews and Greeks believed" (Acts 14:1). In Thessalonica "there was a synagogue of the Jews . . . and some of them were persuaded and joined Paul and Silas, as did a great many of the devout Greeks" (Acts 17:1, 4). In Pisidian Antioch "after the meeting of the synagogue broke up, many Jews and devout converts to Judaism followed Paul and Barnabas" (Acts 13:43).

Paul's Aim and Achievement

We often think of the apostle Paul as a great theologian and a great writer, and so he was. But he had a very simple aim in life. "I make it my ambition," he said, "to proclaim the gospel where the name of Christ is not known" (Rom 15:20).

Paul was a pioneer missionary, and a highly successful one. At one point in his life he could state as a simple fact, "From Jerusalem and all the way around to Illyricum I have fulfilled the ministry of the gospel of Christ . . . I no longer have any room for work in these regions" (Rom 15:19, 23).

We know that Illyricum (Albania) is a long way from Jerusalem. The distance between them is about 1560 miles (2500 km). In a period of probably less than twenty years Paul had introduced the gospel so effectively to these twelve or thirteen provinces that he believed there was no more work there for him to do.

Now what exactly does he mean by this? Has he preached in every town and village, on every farm and hillside? Has he spoken to every man, woman and child throughout these vast territories? Such a thing would be impossible for one missionary to do in many lifetimes.

What then has Paul accomplished? His aim was "to proclaim the gospel where the name of Christ is not known," and this is what he has done. But where has he done it? In the synagogues. The name of Christ is now known and accepted by Jews and Gentiles of the synagogue communities from Jerusalem to Illyricum, and Paul is confident that through their testimony everyone else will hear. But how could he be so sure of them?

He knew his converts were soundly converted and well taught. They were thoroughly committed to Christ, growing in Christian character and active in Christian ministry.

In their meetings Paul knew they were all accustomed to contribute. "When you come together," he said, "each one has a hymn, a lesson, a revelation, a tongue, or an interpretation" (1 Cor 14:26).

They knew what they believed and why. "Brothers," he observed, "you excel in everything – in faith, in speech, in knowledge, in all earnestness" (2 Cor 8:1, 7).

They shared the gospel freely with other people. In the earliest days of persecution, "those who were scattered went about preaching the word" (Acts 8:4). And now he recalled, "Not only has the word of the Lord sounded forth from you in Macedonia and Achaia, but your faith in God has become known everywhere, so that we need not say anything" (1 Thess 1:8).

The New Testament shows us believers filled with the Holy Spirit, participating freely in the fellowship and outreach of the Christian community. They knew how to proclaim the gospel with gladness and full conviction. They knew how to plant churches that would grow and in turn plant other churches throughout their province and the wider territories beyond. This is why Paul had such confidence in them.

But why did Paul stop at Illyricum? Why did he regard this as the limit of his work? It seems surprising that he would come to a halt when the Illyricans were still ignorant of Christ and the further provinces of central Europe remained unreached.

In fact the Illyrican border marked a cultural and linguistic boundary between the eastern half of the Roman empire and the west, a point where Paul must move out of a Greek context into a Latin context. It meant he would have to speak a language much less familiar to him. But of greater importance was the fact that in Illyricum he would find far fewer Jewish synagogues – perhaps none at all – in which to launch his mission. There is no evidence that he ever worked in the province of Illyricum. He never suggested he was about to enter Illyricum or continue his outreach in the provinces beyond. He was not the best person for that territory.

This raises an obvious question: Who will take the gospel to Illyricum? How will the good news reach a place where there are no synagogues to welcome a Jewish rabbi such as Paul? What can his expectation be?

Illyricum will surely hear the gospel from Illyricans who happen to live in Corinth, Thessalonica or some other city, and who hear about Christ there. They will return to their native land and share their discovery with their own people in their own language.

They must find a way to do this that suits the culture of their day – perhaps in schools or social clubs, perhaps in guild halls or market places or at the public baths, perhaps through preaching and testimony in the open air or even from door to door. And once they have won converts from among their own people, they may invite Christian friends of other races and cultures to come and help them in the planting of Illyrican churches.

Illyricum was barely 250 miles (400 km) from Corinth. It was an easy place to reach and Paul expected his converts to carry the gospel far further than this – westward along the Mediterranean coast of Europe, as far as Spain and beyond, and then across the sea to Africa. Several of the Corinthian believers mentioned in his letters have Latin names (1 Cor 1:14; 16:17). They were probably immigrants from those western provinces of the Empire where Latin was spoken, and they would be ideally equipped to take the gospel to their place of origin and birth. Of the seventeen individuals or groups known to us from Corinth at this time, nine are engaged in travel.[1] In due course, Paul himself hoped to head west from his base in Corinth and help them with this outreach (2 Cor 10:15-16).

By the time he took stock of his work from Jerusalem to Illyricum, the gospel had probably reached all the Jewish synagogues in the known world. The exception would be a small number in Italy and Spain, which he himself hoped to visit soon, and perhaps some scattered beyond the borders of the Roman Empire. In the synagogues of the east (Mesopotamia, Babylonia and Persia) the gospel message had probably taken root through friends present in Jerusalem on the day of Pentecost, and then through Peter and perhaps some other apostles. It will have reached the Jewish communities of northern Africa in the

---

1. The travellers are Priscilla and Aquila, Phoebe, Erastus, Stephanas, Achaicus, Fortunatus, Chloe's people and Sosthenes.

same way, and through the Cyrenians and Alexandrians who heard Stephen.

So a clear pattern emerges. The conversion to Christ of both Jews and Gentiles occurred first of all in the scattered outposts of substantial Jewish settlement. From these synagogue communities Paul expected the movement to spread throughout the world. The olive tree, as he said, grew from Jewish roots (Rom 11:17-18).

Once his converts had been well taught, he would leave them to carry the message into the surrounding towns, villages and countryside. It would be obvious to him, and to them, that they could do this much more effectively than he could himself. They would have personal contacts throughout the region – friends, relations, clients and suppliers. They would know the local customs and dialects, the beliefs, superstitions, fears and aspirations of the people. They could communicate naturally and effectively with the populace as a whole and establish a complete network of Christian fellowships where their own converts would be taught, encouraged and equipped for outreach.

Paul's vision was never limited to one town or one city. He thought and spoke in terms of provinces: Asia, Galatia, Macedonia, Achaia, Spain and Italy. But his vision was for the world. His concern was for "all the nations (Rom 1:5). "Your faith," he said, "is proclaimed in all the world" (Rom 1:8). This was his strategy and he confidently expected it to succeed.

Was Paul a Cross-cultural Missionary?

We have enquired whether Jesus might be considered a cross-cultural missionary, and whether the early evangelists in the book of Acts engaged in cross-cultural outreach. We found that they worked essentially within their own culture. Now what shall we say of Paul? Did he attempt to enter new cultures? Did he learn a foreign language? There is no evidence that he did. On the contrary, he moved in cultures already familiar to him and he used languages he already knew.

From childhood Paul was at home in at least four cultures (Jewish, Syrian, Greek and Roman). Among his boyhood friends in the synagogue community at Tarsus there would be many from Gentile families, both proselytes and God-fearers. He spoke three and possibly four languages (Hebrew, Aramaic, Greek and Latin). A Jew would not regard him as foreigner. Nor would a Syrian or a Greek, nor perhaps even a Roman – especially as many of the Roman elite had learned Greek. They would have no difficulty understanding his speech. Paul was like thousands of educated people who had migrated from various parts of the Empire to settle in its major cities. He was at home in the multi-faceted culture of the Mediterranean Basin. As a Roman citizen he would be treated with respect wherever he went (Acts 22:27-29).

For most of his life Paul was working in cultural environments where he was comfortable. Although he endured constant conflict from Jewish authorities and fanatics, this conflict took place within his own Jewish culture. Although he faced religious hatred from the worshippers of pagan deities, he was familiar with their Greek language and worldview, quoting effectively from their own poets and philosophers. When he went to Arabia and then back to Damascus, he could speak with the people in their own native Aramaic.

Does this justify us in saying that Paul was *not* a cross-cultural missionary? Surely he was called by Christ as a missionary to the Gentiles, whose culture was quite different from his own as a Jew. But Paul was already comfortable with these Gentiles – and especially with the proselytes and God-fearers among them – far more comfortable than James or Peter or John would be. And these Gentiles were comfortable with him. He could talk with them in Greek or Aramaic or possibly even Latin, and some of them may have learnt Hebrew. In the synagogues they would accept him as a learned rabbi and a man of God. They had already entered his culture before he proclaimed the gospel to them.

So we could argue that Paul was not a cross-cultural missionary. He did not have to learn a foreign language or adapt to a foreign culture as most missionaries do today. From childhood he was multi-cultural and this made him extremely adaptable. A multi-cultural person is ideally equipped for mission.

At the same time, we should note that Paul was highly sensitive to culture, and there is evidence that he became increasingly so as his experience of mission increased. With this in mind we will return to the unfolding narrative of his missionary career.

7

Paul's Later Missions

Paul's Third Missionary Journey (Acts 18:23 to 21:16)

A second strategic centre: Ephesus

When Paul set out once more from Syrian Antioch, he had two things especially on his mind. He was keen to establish a strong Christian community in the strategic port of Ephesus. And he wanted to see what progress was being made in Corinth.

The next five years of ministry are often called Paul's third missionary journey. But it was much more than a journey. At times he was indeed moving fairly rapidly from city to city, but other times he was settled for a period of months or even years at a base from where he and his fellow-workers travelled out to surrounding areas. During this period he wrote a number of letters to the churches, and sent his colleagues to resolve problems arising in various places.

From his starting point in Antioch, Paul headed west as usual. On his previous trip he had passed rapidly through the nearer provinces (Acts 16:6), but this time he "went from one place to the next through the region of Galatia and Phrygia, strengthening all the disciples" (Acts 18:23).

It would take many hours for Paul to walk from city to city. Only the very rich would think of riding a horse or hiring a mule carriage. The apostle must have carried a thick woollen cloak for cold or rainy weather, a purse tied round his waist, a leather or pottery water bottle, and a bundle containing a change of clothes, a lamp and a small jar of oil, a wash cloth and some soft soap, cooking utensils, a knife and plate, perhaps a few books and writing implements. At night he would sleep in his cloak. This was minimal equipment for a traveller but would still weigh heavily on the back of a middle-aged man labouring up hills on roughly paved roads. No doubt Paul appreciated the company of younger companions who might willingly help him when he grew tired, but for the time being it seems he was alone.

This would be Paul's third attempt at launching a mission in Ephesus. On his first trip he had been directed further north, "having been forbidden by the Holy Spirit to speak the word in Asia" (Acts 16:6). More recently he had made a start but could not continue (Acts 18:19-20). Arriving now in the busy metropolis, we may assume he went immediately to see Aquila and Priscilla.

They told him about a Jewish visitor named Apollos who had spoken fervently about Jesus in the synagogue while he was away. Inviting this man home, Aquila and Priscilla had explained some matters he had not fully understood, before he travelled on to Corinth with their encouragement. Like Paul, he had identified the synagogue as a strategic place for gospel outreach.

At this point Paul settled down to make tents during the week whilst teaching boldly in the synagogue every Sabbath.

After three months' synagogue preaching, his message had become a talking point throughout the Jewish community in Ephesus and was beginning to arouse serious opposition. With an increasing number of disciples he decided to move away from the synagogue, this time to a building identified with the name of Tyrannus. The property is described as a *scholē*, often translated "school" or "lecture hall" but probably in actual fact a guild hall – a social club where local craftsmen and tradesmen would spend their leisure hours. Here Paul continued to explain the gospel to many Jewish and Gentile enquirers. While this outreach was going on, those who had believed were meeting together for further teaching and fellowship, for breaking of bread and prayer, probably in the home of Aquila and Priscilla, or perhaps with the household of Onesiphorus (2 Tim 4:19).

By now a large number of Gentiles from the synagogue community – proselytes and God-fearers – had accepted the gospel. But it did not remain within the confines of the synagogue community. They were sharing their knowledge and belief confidently with other friends and relations, customers and employees, and before long many pagans and idolaters had also put their trust in Christ. Indeed the name of Jesus was heard in conversation everywhere. So we read, "This continued for two years, so that all the residents of Asia heard the word of the Lord, both Jews and Greeks" (Acts 19:10). The gospel had crossed culture rapidly and with great effect.

But Ephesus was a city haunted by terrifying occult powers. There were countless sorcerers and magicians who exploited every superstitious fear to make money and gain power over the people. In this intimidating context we read that "God was doing extraordinary miracles by the hands of Paul, so that even handkerchiefs or aprons that had touched his skin were carried away to the sick, and their diseases left them and the evil spirits came out of them" (Acts 19:11-12).

Conversion to Christ in such circumstances would totally transform a life. The old culture must imperatively yield to the new. We read that "many of those who were now believers came, confessing and divulging their practices. And a number of those who had practiced magic arts brought their books together and burned them in the sight of all" (Acts 19:18-19).

But some of the populace were decidedly unhappy about this. The craftsmen making pagan idols began to complain at their loss of trade. As they alleged, "Not only in Ephesus but in almost all of Asia this Paul has persuaded and turned away a great many people, saying that gods made with hands are not gods" (Acts 19:26).

Despite the antagonism and personal danger he faced, Paul was thankful that by the providence of God "a wide door for effective work" remained open for him in Ephesus (1 Cor 16:9).

In these large cosmopolitan Gentile cities the Roman authorities and pagan inhabitants were generally far more tolerant of Paul's ministry than were the leaders of the Jews. Only when commercial interests were threatened would pagan opponents be roused to violence and soldiers summoned (2 Tim 4:14). He was able to complete his preaching and his teaching in Ephesus, so that a substantial body of believers were thoroughly established in the faith. And he could see how effectively the Gentiles among them were passing on the message to their own people.

He later spoke of the methods he used: "You yourselves know how I lived among you the whole time from the first day that I set foot in Asia, serving the Lord with all humility and with tears and with trials that happened to me through the plots of the Jews; how I did not shrink from declaring to you anything that was profitable, and teaching you in public and from house to house, testifying both to Jews and to Greeks of repentance toward God and of faith in our Lord Jesus Christ" (Acts 20:18-21).

Finally after three years of intensive ministry, Paul believed there was nothing more he could do for the fellowship in Ephesus or indeed for the city itself: "Therefore I testify to you this day that I am innocent of the blood of all of you, for I did not shrink from declaring to you the whole counsel of God" (Acts 20:26-27).

The responsibility now lay with the local believers to continue the work he had begun and to follow the example he had set: "For three years I did not cease night or day to admonish everyone with tears . . . I coveted no one's silver or gold or clothing. You yourselves know that these hands have supplied my own needs and the needs of my companions. In all things I have shown you that by working hard in this way we must help the weak, remembering the words of the Lord Jesus, how he said, 'It is more blessed to give than to receive'" (Acts 20:31, 33-35).

In terms of strategy and character there could be no better example for any missionary to follow than the example of Paul in Ephesus.

News from Corinth

Although he was fully occupied in Ephesus during these months, Paul was equally concerned about the fellowship in Corinth. News from there was mixed. It seems that no elders had been appointed and a measure of anarchy and rivalry was dividing the believers. Some were critical of Paul himself, and a number of "super-apostles" were teaching a different gospel. In comparison with their brilliant Greek eloquence, Paul as a foreigner seemed "unskilled in speaking" (2 Cor 11:5-6).

As the believers met in family homes, which would normally be the domain of the women, it seems that some of these women were inclined to dominate proceedings, to claim authority and to lay down the law. This was causing disorder. Paul was happy for the women to pray aloud and to share their understanding of God's word, but he believed that the teaching and the authority must be the responsibility of the men in the church as in the synagogue (1 Cor 11:5; 14:34-35; 1 Tim 2:11-12).

He had written three times to the Corinthians but the time had come to visit them personally and see if he could help establish the fellowship on a more secure footing. With the prospect of this trip to Europe, where Greek culture and pagan morals predominated, he again refined his strategy. He sent ahead of him his Gentile converts Timothy and Erastus. They might prove more acceptable to the Corinthians than he was himself, and so prepare the way for his intervention (Acts 19:21-22).[1]

A typical disciple: Epaphras

Meanwhile in Ephesus around this time, or perhaps slightly earlier, a man named Epaphras was converted to Christ. He was probably a Gentile from the synagogue community, but he came originally from the city of Colossae about 120 miles (190 km) inland. After a period of missionary experience with Paul, he felt ready to take the good news to his own people in Colossae and to the neighbouring cities of Hierapolis and Laodicea (Col 4:12-13).

In each of these places, some responded to the testimony of Epaphras and began to meet together in their homes. Paul later wrote to these groups, telling them that although he had never met them he was delighted to hear about their faith and was praying earnestly for them. He took pains to summarize and clarify the main points of his teaching, "just as you learned it from Epaphras our beloved fellow servant" (Col 1:7). At a later date Epaphras rejoined Paul and shared his imprisonment in Rome (Philem 23).

In many ways Epaphras was typical of Paul's fellow-workers. At the time when he met the apostle and heard about Jesus, he was away from home in a large cosmopolitan city. He watched Paul at work there and learned through experience how to lead people to faith and maturity in Christ. In time he was led back to his own people to explain the gospel and help them form fellowships of their own.

There were no doubt many others discipled by Paul in the same way – immigrants converted in Ephesus who then returned to their own people in Smyrna, Pergamum, Sardis, Philadelphia and the other cities of the region. This discipling strategy was so effective that within two years, as we have seen, "all the residents of Asia heard the word of the Lord" (Acts 19:10).

---

1. Although Timothy and Erastus were sent to Macedonia, we may assume they would travel on from there to Corinth in Achaia as Paul had this itinerary in mind for his own trip (Acts 19:21-22).

Resolving tensions in Corinth and Jerusalem

Eventually the pagan agitation in Ephesus grew so intense that Paul believed the time had come to make his long-anticipated trip to Europe. He took the road up the coast of Asia Minor to a convenient crossing point. Landing in Macedonia he then made his way inland to Philippi and finally south to Corinth.

Three months he stayed in Greece, where Corinth was located, but we are not told how he was received or what he said to the church (Acts 20:2-3). From the content of his earlier letters we may surmise that there were ongoing tensions, intensified no doubt by the fact that he was a Jewish rabbi among Greeks who possessed a dynamic culture and worldview of their own. Having visited Corinth three times, written at least three letters, and sent a number of colleagues to confer with the leaders there, Paul was now hopeful that the fellowship would continue in the truth of the gospel and become the effective base for outreach to the west that he had envisaged.

This trip was productive in at least one respect. Paul had gained the company of several Gentile Christians who now travelled back with him visiting groups of believers along the road. Their names are carefully listed. "Sopater from Berea . . . and of the Thessalonians, Aristarchus and Secundus; and Gaius of Derbe [or Douberus], and Timothy; and the Asians, Tychicus and Trophimus" (Acts 20:4).

The cultural background of these men meant they would be welcome in the churches of Achaia and Macedonia, where Paul would undoubtedly look and feel like a foreigner. But their chief significance for him lay in the fact that they were *Gentile* Christians carrying contributions for famine relief to the *Jewish* believers of Judea. These men were accustomed to mix freely with Christians of all races, as was normal in the fellowships they belonged to, and they would set an excellent example to anyone with racist inclinations in Jerusalem.

The gospel mission had lost much of its Jewishness as it extended into Gentile territory. Moving beyond Judea and Syria, there is no further reference in the New Testament to the practice of tithing, and only once to fasting (Acts 14:23). No longer do we read of obligations relating to sacred times or places, or food restrictions. Like circumcision, these Jewish customs were appropriate for the old covenant but were never part of the new. Gentile converts were unfamiliar with such things and were never taught to observe them (Col 2:16-17).

This is not surprising. Jesus himself had condemned people who laid great emphasis on tithing (Lk 11:42; 18:12), and after his forty days in the wilderness we do not read that he ever fasted. Indeed, he was criticized because he did not teach his disciples to fast. He replied that he came to bring gladness, not mourning; fullness, not emptiness. "As long as they have the bridegroom with them," he said, "they cannot fast." Grieved by his death, they might abstain from food for some days, but their sorrow would turn to joy as he rose to be with them for ever (Mk 2:19-20; Jn 16:20). It was this resurrection message that Paul and his companions preached, a joyful proclamation of freedom and of victory. It was the gospel of the new covenant.

8

Paul's Missionary Methods

Paul's Message

In every generation there have been preachers who "distort the gospel of Christ" (Gal 1:7). They proclaim "another Jesus" and "a different gospel" (2 Cor 11:4). Their position is dangerous for they can lead many astray and will indeed "be judged with greater strictness" (Ja 3:1). It is vitally important for us to know the content of the true gospel message as we find it in the word of God.

Although he could expound the scriptures at great length when appropriate, Paul could also summarize his gospel in a few short words. He had identified a clear and simple message to pass on wherever he might go. So he says, "I would remind you, brothers, of the gospel I proclaimed to you." He then gives them five clear points:

1. "by which you are being *saved* . . .
2. that Christ *died* for our sins . . .
3. that he was *raised* on the third day . . .
4. In Christ shall all be made alive . . . at his *coming.*
5. Then the end will come, when he delivers the *kingdom* to God the Father" (1 Cor 15:1-4, 22-24).

In every place Paul taught these five basic truths: the urgent need for rescue, the atoning death of Christ, the resurrection of Christ, the return of Christ to raise the dead, and his coming kingdom for all who will put their trust in him.

He summarized his message in similar terms for the pagan

Thessalonians: "You turned to God from idols to serve the living and true God, and to wait for his Son from heaven, whom he raised from the dead, Jesus who delivers us from the wrath to come" (1 Thess 1:9-10). Here again he emphasized the need for salvation, the death and resurrection of Christ, and the future return of Christ to save those who believe in him.

In his letter to Rome he likewise shows the need for rescue (chapters 1-3), the death of Christ atoning for sin (chapter 5), the resurrection of Christ giving new life (8:1-11), and finally the return of the Saviour to raise the dead and establish the new creation (8:18-25).

But we see from the book of Acts that the apostle was creative and flexible in how he introduced his basic message. In each place he would start with one particular point, perhaps in response to a question raised, or a scripture read, or a strong belief held in that place. In Pisidian Antioch, for example, he explained how Jesus, risen from the dead, has fulfilled the hope of Israel (Acts 13:32-33). In Thessalonica he showed that "it was necessary for the Christ to suffer and to rise from the dead" (Acts 17:3). In Athens he preached "Jesus and the resurrection" (Acts 17:18). In Corinth he focused on "Jesus Christ and him crucified" (1 Cor 2:2). In Ephesus he spoke about the kingdom of God (Acts 19:8). To the Jewish council in Jerusalem he proclaimed the resurrection of the dead (Acts 23:6). With the elders of the Jews in Rome he again discussed the kingdom of God (Acts 28:23).

We may be sure that having opened with one particular facet of the gospel message, he would then teach the remaining truths so that his hearers might know enough to be saved for time and eternity. They must hear about the need for rescue, about Christ's atoning death, his resurrection, his return to raise the dead, and his coming kingdom. And in closing, Paul would call for a personal response of faith.

On at least two occasions, when required by the authorities to give an account of himself, he shared his own testimony, emphasizing the same truths – that Jesus died and rose from death, saved him from his own folly and wickedness, and then sent him to lead others to repentance and faith so they too might receive forgiveness and eternal life (Acts 22:6-21; 26:12-23).

He was not afraid to make a personal appeal. So he asked, "King

Agrippa, do you believe the prophets? I know that you believe." To which Agrippa replied, "In a short time would you persuade me to be a Christian?" Then the apostle affirmed, "Whether short or long, I would to God that not only you but also all who hear me this day might become such as I am – except for these chains" (Acts 26:27-29).

Paul did not preach theological theories, or impose religious rules, or attempt to awaken a sense of sin. He did not make unrealistic promises of health or wealth. He gave a positive message of good news, focusing on Jesus as Saviour and as victor over death. If one element of his basic message needed to be emphasized, other elements might be left for proper explanation the next time he spoke. In Pisidian Antioch, for example, his long account of Israel's history left no time for a discussion of the Saviour's second coming. That must be the subject of another sermon on another day.

The gospel that Paul proclaimed was not his own invention. He preached the same message that Jesus had entrusted to his disciples immediately before leaving them (Lk 24:45-48). It was the message Peter declared repeatedly in Jerusalem and in the house of Cornelius (Acts 2:23-24, 38; 3:12-15; 10:39, 43).

The gospel, for Jesus and for Peter, meant the death and resurrection of the Saviour, the new possibility of restoration to God (forgiveness of sin) and the need for a personal change of heart and mind (repentance). If Paul added anything to this, it was the certainty of Christ's future return to complete his work of salvation and to usher in the kingdom. But Peter too had emphasized this point when he spoke in Jerusalem about the "times of refreshing" to be enjoyed by God's people at the return of Christ, "whom heaven must receive until the time for restoring all things" (Acts 3:19-21).

Whenever he spoke, the apostle Paul aimed for clarity of fact and practical application. He knew the moral and intellectual difficulties of the people around him. He identified exactly what they needed to know in order to believe. And he expected them to turn away from anything that would hinder such belief. We have seen how the Thessalonians abandoned their idols. The Corinthians must also give up their temple prostitutes and drunken orgies, and the Ephesians renounce their magic charms and incantations.

Paul picked up popular "buzzwords" and adapted them to his purpose. These were religious and philosophical terms used in common speech. So he explained that Jesus is "the Son of God", "the Lord", "the Saviour of mankind", "the last Adam", "the Firstborn from the dead", and of course he taught the Jews that "Jesus is the Messiah."

In pagan contexts Paul was sensitive to the worldview of the people he was with. Observing the altar to the "unknown God", he declared, "What therefore you worship as unknown, this I proclaim to you" (Acts 17:23). When the jailer asked, "What must I do to be saved?" he replied, "Believe in the Lord Jesus, and you will be saved" (Acts 16:30-31). To people who supposed that he and Barnabas were gods, he spoke of "a living God, who made the heaven and the earth" (Acts 14:15).

Unlike the earlier apostles, Paul had not been present when Christ was ministering in Galilee and Judea. He could not speak as an eyewitness of Jesus's miracles or as a hearer of his teaching. On Paul's earliest mission therefore, he especially valued the company of John Mark.

It was at Mark's home in Jerusalem that Peter and the other disciples had gathered and no doubt shared many reminiscences of days spent with the Master in Galilee or Judea (Acts 12:12). As a boy, Mark may have accompanied them on many occasions, and was perhaps himself the young man who saw what happened in Gethsemane (Mk 14:51). Although he had not continued with the apostles on their first trip, Paul later requested, "Get Mark and bring him with you, for he is very useful to me for ministry" (2 Tim 4:11). It was probably Mark's Gospel, or the notes he was preparing for it, that made him so useful.

On Paul's subsequent journeys, Luke was equally valuable to him as a chronicler. He too possessed much information about Jesus, and at some point probably met Mary his mother and several of his earliest disciples. As Luke prepared his own Gospel, he carefully recorded all they told him, supplementing the details received from Mark.

Paul would encourage every new convert to learn as much as possible from these two Gospel writers. In this way they could pass on "the testimony about Christ" received from the Twelve, and add to it their own testimony of the Saviour's power to save (1 Cor 1:6; 1 Tim 2:6).

Paul's Guidance

It is often difficult for missionaries to know what they should do next. Some may have a plan that must be followed at all costs. Some may have responsibilities that tie them to one place or activity. Some may be directed by authority. Others may feel a little aimless and unsettled. At times we may need a fresh challenge. At other times we may be stressed and over-burdened. We pray for guidance but sometimes suffer a measure of uncertainty. How then did Paul decide where to go and what to do?

We have observed his ambition to proclaim Christ wherever the name of his Saviour was not known. We have seen how he identified the synagogues as an ideal environment for gospel outreach. At the same time he was always sensitive to the leading of the Holy Spirit and to opportunities arising unexpectedly. He did not have a fixed itinerary or a list of places he must cover.

Although he eventually identified Ephesus and Corinth as key centres for widespread diffusion of the message, he did not always make for the largest or most important cities. So far as we know, he did not visit the major provincial capital of Laodicea, for example, or Hierapolis or Philadelphia or Sardis. In general he avoided the rural areas where local languages and dialects would make communication more difficult. When persecution came, he usually moved on to the next place, however small or large it might be, and stayed there if a synagogue could be found. In fact he was very adaptable, sensitive to whatever opportunities might arise, and he expected his Lord to open the right doors at the right times (1 Cor 16:9; 2 Cor 2:12; Col 4:3).

He was guided in various ways. He went to Antioch because Barnabas invited him. He went to Cyprus because Barnabas had lived there and knew it well. He went to the provinces around Cilicia because that was his home territory. He may have headed for Pisidian Antioch to make contact with the family of Sergius Paulus. He went on to Lystra and Derbe to escape stoning in Iconium. He went to Galatia because of a physical illness. He went to Troas because the Holy Spirit prevented him from going to Asia or Bithynia. He went to Macedonia at first because of a vision, and later went back to Macedonia because he wanted to find Titus. He stayed with Aquila and Priscilla because they were of the same trade. He stayed with Lydia and her household because she invited him. He went to Athens because he was driven out of Berea. He went to Ephesus because it was a strategic centre. In various places he would spend a week teaching and encouraging the disciples because they asked him to. He stayed many months in Caesarea because he was under arrest. And he went to Rome because his Lord had assured him, "You must also testify in Rome" (Acts 23:11).

In all this he was responsive to the providential ordering of events. But he was also open to advice and willing to co-operate with others. When the leaders in Jerusalem counselled him, "Do therefore what we tell you," he followed their suggestion (Acts 21:23).

Through long practice Paul had learned to be led by the Holy Spirit. At times he was "forbidden by the Holy Spirit", and at times he was "constrained by the Spirit" (Acts 16:6-7; 20:22). He could tell when the Holy Spirit was witnessing with his spirit about the circumstances he was in (Acts 19:21; 20:23; Rom 8:16).

In all this, he would do nothing without the inner assurance that he was doing the will of God. As a servant of Jesus Christ, he would insist on "doing the will of God from the heart, rendering service with a good will as to the Lord and not to men" (Eph 6:6-7). This is an example that every effective gospel missionary will follow.

The younger men working with Paul would learn all this from him. They would also respect the wisdom he had gained through long experience, and they would look to him personally for a measure of guidance in meeting the needs of widely scattered congregations. We will speak more of this.

Paul's Church Planting Strategy

He proclaimed the gospel in public places

When Paul arrived in a town or city he did not erect a building and invite people to come and hear him there. Like the other apostles, and like Jesus himself, he went out to the people where they were. The good news must be proclaimed in public places.

So we see him in the synagogues of Damascus, Cyprus, Pisidian Antioch, Iconium, Thessalonica, Berea, Corinth, Ephesus and elsewhere (Acts 9:19-20; 13:4-5, 14; 14:1; 17:1, 10; 18:1&4, 19; 19:1&8); in the large house of a Roman governor (13:7); by the city gates of Lystra (14:8-10); beside the river at Philippi (16:13); in the streets and common jail of the same city (16:16-18, 25, 31); in the public square amidst the idols of Athens (17:16-17); in the guild hall of Tyrannus at Ephesus (19:9); on the steps of the military barracks in Jerusalem (21:37-22:1); before the council of Jewish leaders (23:1-6); before the governor and king and their officials in Caesarea (24:10-21; 26:1-29); in a boat on the Mediterranean Sea (27:21-26); in the house of a Maltese official (28:7); and ultimately, according to his wish, before the tribunal of Caesar in Rome.

What do we learn from this? We learn that Paul wanted everyone to hear his message. Because he preached in public places his gospel became known everywhere. It became a talking point in the synagogues and after that in the streets and markets. Everyone's curiosity was aroused. So we read, "The next Sabbath almost the whole city gathered to hear the word of the Lord" (Acts 13:44). He and Silas were accused of turning the world upside down (Acts 17:6). In fact he could confidently declare, "The king knows about these things, and to him I speak boldly. For I am persuaded that none of these things has escaped his notice, for this has not been done in a corner" (Acts 26:26).

The apostle wanted the whole world to know what he stood for. He was happy even in prison, so long as everyone knew why he was there. "It has become known," he said, "throughout the whole imperial guard and to all the rest that my imprisonment is for Christ" (Phil 1:13).

We and Paul have the same commission: "Go into all the world and proclaim the gospel to the whole creation" (Mk 16:15). We cannot do this among our own friends inside our own church buildings. We can only do it in the world outside, where the gospel of Christ is not yet known.

He taught his converts in private homes

Paul's first converts were not strangers to one another. Most of them had attended the synagogue together in the days before their conversion. Having heard him speak in the synagogue, they would frequently adjourn to a house nearby for further discussion. Jason was one who offered hospitality to such enquirers in Thessalonica (Acts 17:6-7).

Friendships would then quickly deepen as they met by chance in the street or market, or in the course of business. The women would begin to visit one another in their homes. With babies and infants around them, they would share personal problems and concerns, and find encouragement and support with one another in good times and in bad. The men would sit together after work in some public courtyard or beside the city walls, and friendships would grow among them too as they talked of the day's events, explained their faith to people they knew, and heard of further remarkable conversions. As darkness fell they would make their way to the house where supper was being prepared.

The followers of Jesus were beginning to form a community of their own in every city. While the gospel was actively proclaimed in public places, Christian fellowship flourished in the comfort of private homes. The poorer Christian families no doubt lived in crowded conditions, but others had larger and better-furnished houses able to accommodate a greater number. Gathering in the guest chamber or courtyard of a reputable citizen would give a measure of respectability to the company, and perhaps some security from common abuse. The poorer people would feel privileged to attend such a place.

In many houses the most spacious area would be the "upper room" above the workshop or stable. We know of one upper room that held at least a hundred and twenty people (Acts 1:13-15). Here the believers would assemble after dark when their day's work was done. One such room had "many lamps", where they were gathered for their common meal, to break bread on the first day of the week (Acts 20:7-8). In country areas there were no doubt many smaller households where believers met together with equal assurance, pleasure and mutual benefit.

In a family home the entire household would naturally be involved in this, along with any visitors who chanced to call. There could be friends, relatives, servants and slaves, travellers, neighbours, clients, tenants, customers and perhaps a number of homeless people who had found shelter there. All of these would have opportunity to meet the assembled believers, to share in their supper, to hear what they were saying and experience something of their love. In such a setting many acquaintances might be drawn to faith who would never trouble to attend a formal lecture or a religious ceremony in a public hall.

The usual plan of public outreach and private fellowship was not a rigid one. Just as believers might encourage one another outside the house, so visitors might hear the gospel within it. A Christian home is always more welcoming than a chapel or a hall. Meeting an acquaintance on the street, it would be much easier to say "Come to supper" than "Come to church", and in those days it meant the same. The meal would not be elaborate, probably consisting of the bread and water or wine used by any ordinary family.

Public proclamation could, of course, bring persecution at any time. The quiet refuge of a Christian home would then be of special value, a place where wounds could be dressed, food provided and decisions prayerfully taken (Acts 16:33-34).

If serious opposition arose, believers could meet there without attracting undue attention. When Peter escaped from prison, "he went to the house of Mary, the mother of John whose other name was Mark, where many were gathered together and were praying." After this, to avoid bringing trouble on them all, he went away quietly to "another place" (Acts 12:12, 17).

In normal circumstances the members of a household would feel great loyalty to the family. Indeed, the security and livelihood of them all depended on the economic, social, political and religious standing of its leading members. But the majority in every household would be from the lower orders, as indeed were the majority of Christians at this time. Any who happened to find themselves in trouble on account of their faith or some other circumstance, would be sure of receiving immediate help and support from other members of the household. This gave the house fellowship an inherent strength and stability wherever the leading members of a family had committed themselves to Christ.

In the great urban centres of the Roman Empire, rich and poor were crowded together within a relatively small area. It would be possible to walk from one side of the city to another and to join a company of believers wherever they happened to be. The location of the meetings could be moved from one house to another without great inconvenience.

Paul himself knew of many such house churches. Wherever Aquila and Priscilla happened to be – in Corinth, Ephesus or Rome – a fellowship was meeting in their home (1 Cor 16:19; Rom 16:3-5). He mentions the household of Stephanas who "have devoted themselves to the service of the saints" (1 Cor 16:15). He sent greetings to "Nympha and the church in her house" (Col 4:15). He wrote to "Philemon our beloved fellow worker and Apphia . . .

and Archippus . . . and the church in your house" (Philem 1-2). In Corinth there were probably several such groups, in various parts of the city, meeting in the homes of Aquila and Priscilla, Stephanas, Titius Justus and perhaps Crispus too. These seem to have combined on occasion, as Paul tells us, in the house of "Gaius, who is host to me and to the whole church" (1 Cor 16:15; Acts 18:7-8; Rom 16:23). He knew of at least three house fellowships in Rome, which together would constitute the church in that city (Rom 16:5, 14-15).

We have seen how, from the earliest days, the believers devoted themselves to the apostles' teaching, fellowship, breaking of bread and prayer. Priority was given to the teaching of the apostles, and we see Paul meeting with them in their homes for this purpose, "teaching everyone with all wisdom, that we may present everyone mature in Christ" (Col 1:28). Their need was not for the same gospel message repeated many times but for "the whole counsel of God" carefully explained from the Law, the prophets, the history of Israel, from the life and ministry of Christ and from the recent experience of his followers (Acts 20:27).

Paul did not neglect to tell them "anything that was profitable" and we see from his letters how comprehensive his teaching was (Acts 20:20). When he wrote to the various churches, he rarely taught them something new. His purpose was to remind them by letter of things he had already told them face to face. So he reassured them, "To write the same things to you is no trouble to me and is safe for you" (Phil 3:1; also 1 Thess 4:1-2; 2 Thess 2:15). Peter's letters served a similar purpose, and so did John's (2 Pet 1:12-15; 1 Jn 2:21, 24).

The apostles were especially concerned for the emotional and spiritual stability of Christian families, and gave specific advice to the varied members of a typical household – masters, servants, wives, husbands, fathers, children (Col 3:18-4:1; Eph 5:22-6:9; 1 Pet 2:18-3:12). To live in harmony together was essential, not merely for the sake of their own happiness, but for the stability and growth of the church itself. The members of a household must deal immediately with any problems that might arise in their relationships with one another. So Paul summed up his advice for them all, "Put on then, as God's chosen ones, holy and beloved, compassionate hearts, kindness, humility, meekness, and patience, bearing with one another and, if one has a complaint against another, forgiving each other; as the Lord has forgiven you, so you also must forgive.

And above all these put on love, which binds everything together in perfect harmony" (Col 3:12-14). In these circumstances, a strong united family would mean a strong united church.

In the relaxed setting of a Christian home, there would be opportunity for everyone present to respond to the teaching, to add a comment or ask a question and discuss what had been said. In our own day we might assume that a sermon or a lecture is the best way to teach God's people. But just as Jesus taught in homes, so did the leaders of the early churches, and just as his teaching was interactive and responsive, so was theirs.

He created communities of believers

Teaching his converts was not Paul's only purpose. He was equally concerned to create a welcoming and supportive community for all who would receive what he taught. He addressed these household fellowships in emotional terms, emphasizing their unity and solidarity, and their distinction from the world around them.

For Paul these men and women were not merely worshippers or communicants or church-goers. He writes to them as a company of people set apart, called, loved, known and valued as brothers and sisters in the family of God. He speaks of the *hagioi*, "the holy ones" in Ephesus, Colossae and Philippi, and the *ekklesia*, "the ones called out" or "summoned" from among the Thessalonians and the Laodiceans. They were special people and together they had a special life to live. He gave them an idealistic vision, to be "blameless and innocent, children of God without blemish in the midst of a crooked and twisted generation, among whom you shine as lights in the world" (Phil 2:15).

However much the world outside is marked with conflict and pain, a Christian home will enjoy peace and loving harmony. None of the household would claim to be perfect, but they were actively striving for perfection in speech, in attitude and in character (Matt 5:48; Phil 3:12). With the Spirit of Christ to help them, their standards would be high. "Love one another with brotherly affection" said Paul. "Outdo one another in showing honour" (Rom 12:10). "Encourage one another and build one another up, just as you are doing" (1 Thess 5:11). To enjoy relationships of this quality was one of the great blessings of the gospel.

Experience shows that people are rarely attracted by new ideas or beliefs but far more often by the positive effect of such ideas or beliefs in the lives of people they know. If Paul's synagogue preaching interested many who heard it, the quality of life in the Christian community must have appealed to far more. Especially so as at this time the conditions of existence and quality of behaviour in the world outside were particularly poor and mean.

In every city the streets were crowded with people longing for a better life. Many were newcomers – strangers, foreigners, orphans, widows, fugitives and refugees, wounded soldiers and disabled seamen, captives or slaves suddenly released to fend for themselves, wives and servants abandoned by armies and trading ventures. All these were hungry, dirty, seeking work and a secure place to sleep at night. Such men and women would be lonely, anxious, sometimes desperate – all yearning for a way to improve their unhappy circumstances. Among them might be educated people of cultured family, who through misfortune had fallen on hard times. If they were Jews they would find their way to the synagogue. If Gentiles, they might head in the same direction, hoping for a little charity or employment.

People like this would be acutely receptive to a message of hope and assurance offered by a community known for its loving kindness and its acceptance of every race and class of person. The friendly intimacy of a family home would be a welcome refuge from the harsh world outside. Its warm teaching about the love of God would appeal immediately to a person feeling profoundly unwanted and unloved. Its trust in a Saviour who could rescue the most miserable for a new and better life must have awakened a similar trust in the hearts of many who had found nothing to hope for in the streets outside.

But caring for these men and women would not be easy. Some of the new converts would have distressing personal problems in need of resolution or repulsive habits capable of disrupting family life. Some had recently suffered tragic and traumatic misfortune and bore the psychological scars of mistreatment. In practice, much of the pastoral care must have devolved upon the women while the men were out at work. They would be nursing the sick, helping the poor, counselling the anxious and distraught, visiting the elderly, giving food and clothing to the needy, providing shelter for the homeless, and offering comfort and advice to other women with difficult husbands, unruly children or inadequate living conditions.

It is likely that compassionate nursing care, using the simple household remedies then available, enabled members of the Christian community to recover from illness and malnourishment much better than the fatalistic pagan populace, and indeed to survive epidemics far more successfully. This may have contributed significantly to their relative numerical growth.[1]

Many writers have noted that the new faith found a response especially among women.[2] Basic Christian teaching on kindness and contentment, and on marriage and divorce, along with the care given to widows and orphans, would give women a security in the church which they had never dreamed of finding in the world. In a poor home committed to Christ, money previously wasted by a husband on drink and dubious entertainments would now go to feeding and clothing the children. In a more comfortable household, the practice of hospitality, and the gathering of believers every evening, would involve the women immediately in the life and leadership of the local fellowship. Here they could participate far more freely than would be allowed in the synagogue. There were endless opportunities for women to be useful and appreciated in the growing Christian communities.

The men moved in a different sphere. Houses in the city were seriously overcrowded, and the husbands and sons would normally spend their leisure hours out of doors. Home for them would be a place to eat and sleep and little more. But in the world outside, a Christian man would have many friends and acquaintances from the days before his conversion. Seeing them as usual each day in the streets and guildhalls, the public baths and sports halls, he would talk with them about daily events and about his own experience of new life. They would listen willingly to a friend or colleague they had liked and respected for many years, or indeed to one who had suddenly changed for the better.

We may be sure that the gospel message was attractive to the populace of a troubled world, but even more attractive would be the community of those who believed it.

---

1. Stark, 88
2. Stark, 95-99

He encouraged spiritual growth

Early Christianity was not a religion as we normally understand the term. It had no temple or ritual or priest or sacrifice. It was simply a company of like-minded friends. Over an evening meal they would discuss the information that came their way from those who had known Jesus personally or were teaching about him in the synagogues or other public places. This was how they met and what they met for.

We may assume that the common meal of the Christian community was not a ritual for selected members. Everyone present in the house would expect to eat and drink with the family, whether they were known as believers or not. The significance of the meal would be explained to any newcomers among them. Guests would join the family in honouring the memory of a crucified Saviour, and so might freely participate. Very few, if any, would refuse this simple politeness, and some may indeed have been drawn to faith through the experience (1 Cor 14:24-25). If anyone was inclined to be divisive or selfish – if anyone ate or drank without honouring Christ and respecting his people – then such a person would be justly rebuked (1 Cor 11:17-21; 27-34).

In such an informal setting there would be freedom for anyone to read the scriptures and comment on the reading, to share some personal experience or testimony, to pray spontaneously, or to sing about Christ and the new life opening up before them. Each would have opportunity to contribute something for the encouragement of all. This was Paul's common experience of such gatherings: "When you come together, each one has a hymn, a lesson, a revelation." If something was said in a foreign language, it would be translated so that all might understand and benefit (1 Cor 14:26-28).

From the start the apostle made it clear that the ministry of the church would be conducted by all its members. They were not passive spectators but active participants in everything it did. They would "instruct one another" (Rom 15:14). They would "care for one another" and "comfort one another" (1 Cor 12:25; 2 Cor 13:11). They would "teach and admonish one another" (Col 3:16). They would sing to one another (Eph 5:19). Each of them would "look not only to his own interests, but also to the interests of others" (Phil 2:4).

With this encouragement and opportunity to participate, a recent convert would not find it hard to confess with his lips what he knew in his heart (Rom 10:9). Each would quickly become involved and useful in the life of the fellowship and its outreach to the wider society. A poor person joining the Christian community would soon find others yet poorer to befriend and help. No one would remain merely a recipient of kindness and compassion but would quickly have opportunity to exercise these qualities of character for the benefit of others. In the face of so many needs, no one who followed Christ could remain selfish or self-centred for very long.

Paul's first converts in each city were already familiar with the Jewish scriptures and had learned from those inspired writings a great deal of wisdom and truth. In every group some would be quick to understand the good news about Jesus and prove capable of instructing others. Young men who had this gift might travel to neighbouring towns and teach there too. But their aim would not be to promote their own ministry. They would be concerned to help each congregation develop its own gifts and teaching ministries. A church would never wish to be dependent on teachers coming from elsewhere. If it is to be healthy, the body of Christ must grow well in every place.

When he entered a town or city, Paul's purpose was to establish a fellowship that would continue to grow once he had left. In each place he stayed long enough to set them an example of consistent Christian holiness – in the workplace, in the streets and in the home. Living among them, he showed them how to build and maintain healthy relationships. Supporting himself with the work of his hands, he demonstrated his principles of honesty, patience and industry. He showed them how to honour one another, to shun impurity of speech or thought, to respect the elders and to care for widows and orphans, eating and drinking in moderation, dealing wisely with children, and avoiding all love of money.

He expected people not merely to understand his teaching but to follow his example, referring to it as "my ways in Christ" (1 Cor 4:17). Knowing that a Christian way of life is more easily caught than taught, he advised them, "What you have learned and received and heard and seen in me – practise these things, and the God of peace will be with you" (Phil 4:9). He established healthy spiritual habits in the Christian community as customs or traditions which would remain with them long after he had gone (Acts 20:18-35). So he reminded them, "Stand firm and hold to the traditions that you were taught by us" (2 Thess 2:15). And again, "I commend you because you remember me in everything and maintain the traditions even as I delivered them to you" (1 Cor 11:2).

The timing of his movements suggests that Paul spent about three months on average in each city.[1] He would move on only when he believed a fellowship was well started or when persecution compelled him to leave. A well-started fellowship would be one whose members understood and rejoiced in the gospel, and who were gathering regularly for teaching, fellowship, breaking of bread and prayer, committed to pleasing their Lord, learning to live holy lives and sharing their faith effectively with the people around them.

But sometimes persecution did force Paul and his companions to leave before their teaching was complete. The new believers must learn for themselves how to apply their faith to the challenges and opportunities of daily life. In these circumstances he remained a little anxious. When forced to leave Thessalonica, he told them how he "endeavoured the more eagerly and with great desire" to see them. He wanted to come to them "again and again" but Satan hindered him. This was why he had to tell them by letter what he would much rather teach them face to face (1 Thess 2:17-18).

He allowed local leaders to emerge naturally

When spiritual ministry is so spontaneous and interactive, the emergence of recognised elders is desirable and indeed essential. This model of leadership was adopted from the Jewish synagogues, where respected elders were always present to care for the community and oversee its meetings. They would be men whose character was "above reproach", tested and accepted by the whole congregation and respected by outsiders. The elders must be able to teach, but of greater importance was their consistency of life. In his advice concerning the recognition of elders, Paul laid far more emphasis on godly character than on social status, academic knowledge or preaching skills (1 Tim 3:1-7; Tit 1:5-9).

The elders must guide, and if necessary, correct and discipline the body of believers. They would need much wisdom to deal with any

---

1. Schnabel, *ECM*, 1307

individuals who proved to be divisive, selfish, dishonest or guilty of sexual offences. False teaching or bad behaviour must be identified and restrained before it could spoil the loving unity and holiness of the congregation or corrupt the truth of the gospel it proclaimed. This is not always a pleasant task, but a necessary one, as we see in Peter's dealings with Ananias and Sapphira, and in Paul's concern for better discipline at Corinth (Acts 5:3; 1 Cor 5:1-2 and 2 Cor 2:6-8).

Others, known as assistants or deacons, were chosen by each congregation to take care of practical matters such as the food allocations for widows (Acts 6:3). But unlike the deacons of today, they had no buildings to maintain or expenses to pay. Any house where the believers met would be the responsibility of the family who lived in it.

Paul expected leadership of this sort to grow spontaneously within each group. He did not bring pastors or ministers from other places to take charge of men and women who were strangers to them. At the start of any new group the natural leader would be the father of the family opening its home and offering a welcome to others. Stephanas would be responsible for the company meeting in his house at Corinth, and the same could be said of Crispus and Gaius in their respective homes. It is significant that only these earliest Corinthian converts were baptized by Paul himself, for they would then be responsible to baptize others who joined them (1 Cor 1:16; 16:15).

The believers associated with these families would meet day by day, learning and teaching, discussing the implications of their faith, praying together and helping one another in various ways. Before long, additional members of the company would also show qualities of leadership. There would be varied gifts and abilities imparted by the Holy Spirit to each person present (1 Cor 12:7, 11). Several might become especially appreciated for their integrity of character, their intelligent understanding and their wise counsel. As spiritual leadership developed in each fellowship, it would become evident to all and then formally recognised by the apostles. So we see Barnabas and Paul revisiting the fellowships they had started during the previous months, and as they did so they "appointed elders for them in every church" (Acts 14:23).

We do not know if the elders at this time were the heads of separate households or if they generally served together in a single congregation. When Paul speaks of "elders in every church" or "elders in every town" he may have been thinking of the various men who opened their homes for fellowship in each place. As these were evidently well-known to each other, he could write a single letter to them all (Tit 1:5; Phil 1:1).

These local leaders carried full responsibility for the spiritual well-being of their people. The apostle could not control them or compel them to do his will; he could only advise and strongly exhort them when necessary. The believers, in their turn, were urged to respect the leaders God had given them and not to make their task more difficult, "for they are keeping watch over your souls, as those who will have to give an account" (Heb 13:17).

As every congregation depended on a Christian home, it was important for the elders and deacons to manage their households well. Paul thought of a local church as the household of God and its leader literally as God's "housekeeper" (Tit 1:7). Such men must have a stable marriage and be respected by their children (1 Tim 3:4-5, 12). They should care properly for their aged relatives (1 Tim 5:4). They should be hospitable and on good terms with their neighbours (1 Tim 3:2, 7).

The leaders worked like other men to provide for themselves and their dependents. In normal circumstances they would not need financial support and would never think of asking for it. But elders who devoted much time to evangelism and teaching might find their business or farm suffering in consequence, and Paul advised that such men should be honoured and assisted if necessary by those who valued their ministry (1 Tim 5:17-18).

The New Testament churches did not have the financial difficulties that we face today. They had no pastor to pay and no church buildings to erect or maintain. To launch a new fellowship required no financial outlay, and this made it easy for groups to gather in even the poorest communities. Indeed the meetings were quite free; it cost nothing to attend. Families with very little to spare would appreciate this economy, fully aware of the painful expense involved in the tithes and offerings of the Jews, the fees of the sorcerers and astrologers, and the costly sacrifices of the pagan temples.

Meeting in their homes, there was never a problem of too little space. If the converts increased in number, then so did the homes. They would simply start an additional house-fellowship in another part of town.

Believers who wished to take the good news to other places were free to do so. They did not need to raise money or persuade a congregation or a society to let them go. They simply went. Nothing in the churches would hinder the spread of the gospel. The Holy Spirit guided their activities, the Lord built his church, and Satan was given no opportunity to prevail against it.

He expected the gospel to spread spontaneously

The New Testament method of church-planting was ideally suited to establish local congregations depending directly on the Lord in their midst. It produced experienced leadership in the shortest possible time. It gave every new believer something useful to do, developing the gifts of the Spirit entrusted to him or her for service to others. Responsibility was thrust upon the churches and upon every member of the churches. They were never dependent on the missionaries. They could be left to grow on their own. And when Paul later went back to revisit them, he went to see how well they were doing without him.

He clearly had high expectations of his converts. If they were truly born again, he expected the Holy Spirit to transform even the weakest and most unstable of characters. Writing to the Thessalonians he declared, "We have confidence in the Lord about you" (2 Thess 3:4). His trust was not in them but in the Lord, that the Lord would complete his work in them. Likewise to the Philippians he could say, "I am sure of this, that he who began a good work in you will carry it on to completion at the Day of Christ Jesus" (Phil 1:6). And when he could no longer be with them in person, he was sure that God himself would be their teacher and their guide.

They did not need any exhortation to share their faith with others. It was a natural part of the new life and the new community they belonged to. So Paul could speak of spiritual shoes as an item of spiritual clothing they would all wear at all times, ready to walk out with the gospel message to people near at hand or far away (Eph 6:15).

The believers still had much to learn and might make many mistakes, but the apostle had shown them the way to work. They were experiencing the power of the Holy Spirit to transform their character. They were growing in understanding and experience. They were exercising the gifts of the Spirit in their fellowship and their outreach. They were praying daily together with one heart and mind. Satan might attack them fiercely through persecution, or through false teachers and internal disagreements, but he could not succeed in dividing them or silencing them. If anything went wrong, or if some particular teaching or advice were needed, the missionaries would be available to help, but so long as all went well they took no further responsibility for the direction or ministry of a local congregation.

Paul's purpose, like that of Jesus, was to launch a movement that would grow and spread spontaneously because it changed people for the better. He did not create an organisation or a denomination. He did not erect or possess any buildings. He did not pay anyone to be a servant of Christ. The only money he ever asked Christians to give went to the relief of the poor in a far country, and he made such a collection only once. But to live this life, and to accomplish this work, cost him all he had.

We have seen all this in the story of Paul's missionary career, and it is time to look now at the last and in some ways the greatest and most ambitious of his gospel strategies.

9

Paul's Final Mission

Paul's Mission to the Roman Empire (Acts 21:17 to 28:30)

In Jerusalem

We left Paul on his way to Jerusalem, accompanied by representatives from the western churches bearing financial gifts for the believers in Judea. The journey itself was uneventful but the closer he came to Jerusalem, the more pressing were the warnings Paul received about serious danger ahead.

This does not seem to have surprised or worried him in the least. It is clear from what he says that he fully expected to be arrested, to stand in danger of his life, and to testify in Rome. This indeed was his desire (Acts 19:21; 20:25; 21:13; 27:23-24). He was entering a new phase of life and was evidently well prepared for it.

On arrival in Jerusalem Paul was warmly welcomed by the church, as were the Gentile converts accompanying him. But religious fanatics among the Jewish populace had become increasingly turbulent in the city, and the church there was under serious threat. Some alleged that Paul himself had been reviling the Jewish faith and teaching Jews to disobey the Law of Moses.

He agreed to show his respect for Jewish tradition by accompanying four men who wished to make a religious vow in the temple and by paying their expenses. Shortly afterwards, however, he was seen in the streets with Trophimus, a Gentile Christian from Ephesus, and falsely accused of taking this man into the inner courts of the temple where Gentiles were not allowed. A violent riot broke out and Paul was seized by the Roman security forces, who in the event probably saved his life. He spoke to the Roman official in Greek, and then at much greater length to the Jewish crowd in Aramaic, telling them the story of his conversion. When the crowd again erupted violently, he was taken away and imprisoned in the Fortress of Antonia adjacent to the temple complex built by King Herod.

Luke had travelled in Paul's company to Jerusalem and now probably made good use of his time by visiting many of the earliest disciples in Judea and perhaps in Galilee, collecting material for his Gospel (Acts 21:15-18). This would supplement the information already received from Mark, and from others he had met earlier in his travels.

In Caesarea

Paul was summoned before a Roman court, attended by the Jewish officials who had accused him, and again he testified concerning his faith in Jesus. A further uproar broke out. A plot to assassinate him was then discovered, and as the controversy seemed likely to be both complex and violent he was taken under armed guard from Jerusalem to the Roman administrative headquarters on the coast at Caesarea. Here he was held in custody at Herod's palace awaiting further enquiry. At Caesarea there was a strong and growing Christian community (Acts 21:8-16).

Paul had been chosen and appointed by Christ as an apostle to the Gentiles (Rom 11:13). His age was now about fifty-two. For twenty years he had travelled rough roads and crossed stormy seas. He had endured hunger, thirst, robbers, sleepless nights, exposure to cold and heat, betrayals, insults and blows, three shipwrecks, several imprisonments, five violent beatings from the Jews, three from the Romans, and one stoning in addition to countless other hardships (2 Cor 11:24-27). He might well be aware that he no longer had the physical strength and stamina to walk the long distances required of a missionary penetrating unreached provinces. That would be a task for younger men.

By this time, as we have seen, the Gentiles of the synagogue communities around the Mediterranean Basin had heard and accepted the gospel. But the world was known to be far bigger than this. The vast majority of Gentiles lived in distant lands with hardly any Jewish settlers and no synagogues. As an evangelist, Paul would certainly wonder how the millions of Gentiles in the wider world might be reached with the good news. Having completed his work in the synagogues, where else might he find Gentiles willing to give him a hearing when he spoke of Christ?

The obvious place would be the Roman administration. Throughout the Empire an immense body of men from many different provinces and diverse cultural origins were employed in offices, barracks, lawcourts, palaces, forts and customs posts. Paul, as a teacher, could not simply enter these places expecting them to give him their attention. But if he were in their midst as a prisoner, he would be called upon to defend and explain himself. And unlike the vast majority of Gentiles in other occupations, these officials would all understand his Greek or perhaps his Latin.

He could be reasonably confident that Roman justice would not condemn him unheard, that he would be respected as an educated man and a Roman citizen, and that the officials themselves would be relatively free from corruption (Acts 22:25; 23:27-30). He knew that a citizen could not be condemned to death except by the imperial court in Rome and that his alleged offences were almost certainly insufficient to merit such a verdict. What is more, as a prisoner under armed guard, he would be protected from the murderous plots of his angry Jewish opponents (Acts 23:26-30). All things considered, it seems very likely that Paul planned this as a deliberate second phase of his outreach to the Gentiles. He had resolved to launch a prison ministry, as a prisoner.

By this time Paul had considerable experience of prisons. The occasion familiar to us at Philippi was only one of several imprisonments during his earlier missionary career. The others are not mentioned in the book of Acts (2 Cor 6:5; 11:23).

He clinched his position by appealing at the earliest opportunity to Caesar (Acts 25:11). As Agrippa observed to the governor, "This man could have been set free if he had not appealed to Caesar" (Acts 26:32). Indeed Paul tells us, "When they had examined me, they wished to set me at liberty" (Acts 28:18). He could have enjoyed immediate release. A ship could be found quite easily in the harbour at Caesarea to carry him far away from the plots and riots of Jerusalem. Paul's desire was not for immediate release but for prolonged imprisonment.

As a place to live, the cell allocated to a Roman citizen in Herod's palace may have been considerably less squalid than many poor homes Paul had visited on his travels. Roman custom allowed his friends to provide him with food, water and other necessities, and to carry news and letters with them whenever they came to see him (Acts 24:23). This meant he could continue to teach and encourage the Christian community and even welcome any interested enquirers who cared to visit him. Natural opportunities would arise for him to explain his faith to other prisoners who might ask him why he was there. He was lightly chained by the wrist to a guard who must of necessity hear his testimony many times (Acts 26:29). Luke notes that when Paul was under military escort a horse was provided for him (Acts 23:24). Despite the lack of stirrups and saddle on a Roman horse, this would be luxury to a man accustomed to walking.

So the apostle became known as "Paul the prisoner" (Acts 23:18). The days went by. He remained in custody at Caesarea for more than two years and during this long period had opportunity for testimony to hundreds of soldiers and officials, to the successive governors Felix and Festus, to Drusilla the Jewish wife of Felix, to King Agrippa and his sister Bernice, and to all the attendants surrounding them (Acts 24:24-27).

He developed a strategy of outreach for these circumstances. When asked to give formal account of himself, he would never attempt a bland display of innocence with a view to regaining his liberty. On the contrary he consistently proclaimed Christ as Saviour, introducing moral issues of personal significance to his hearers, and urging them to believe. As he declared to Agrippa, "I would to God that not only you but also all who hear me this day might become such as I am – except for these chains" (Acts 26:29). He refused absolutely to give money to ease his conditions or to buy his freedom (Acts 24:26).

Paul's ultimate desire was to stand before the court of Caesar in Rome and to explain the truth of the gospel to the most powerful and influential body of men in the world. One of the officials or lawyers associated with this tribunal may have been Theophilus, for whom Luke wrote his impressive account of Jesus's life and the apostles' mission.

From a strategic point of view, Paul would see Rome as a third dynamic base for gospel outreach, along with Ephesus and Corinth. From the Imperial capital the message might be carried to the far northern and western provinces of the Empire, and the missionaries who carried it would be Roman officials won to faith in Christ through his testimony as a prisoner.

Ultimately, if he could then present his case to Caesar in person and to his senators, Paul might hope to gain acceptance for the way of Christ as a legal religion, and so bring a measure of protection from Jewish and pagan persecution for the churches throughout the Empire.

Eventually preparations were made for the expedition under armed escort that would take him to Rome. He would be accompanied by Luke and Aristarchus in the role of servants providing food and other necessities for him (Acts 27:2).

In Rome

After a long voyage and a dramatic shipwreck, the company arrived in Italy. Paul was delighted to see good evidence that the gospel had reached Rome before him and that other evangelists had been active in the synagogues. He enjoyed fellowship with believers who came out of the city to meet him along the road. These were probably a deputation of leaders from the various house fellowships. As Paul would need their help during his imprisonment, their interest and support was a great encouragement to him. When he finally arrived in the great metropolis Paul was given permission "to stay by himself, with the soldier that guarded him" (Acts 28:16). This meant he could look for a house of his own.

Rome at this period was extremely overcrowded. The majority of its inhabitants could only with difficulty rent a small room on an upper floor of some run-down tenement block a long way from any water supply or latrine. The "guesthouse" or "lodging" which Paul now occupied probably belonged to one of the local believers. His earlier letter to the Christian community in Rome shows that he knew at least thirty individuals and groups by name. Among these the first mentioned are Priscilla and Aquila, who had returned to the capital and now had a fellowship meeting in their house (Rom 16:3-5). They may have moved there with the deliberate intention of supporting this new phase of Paul's ministry.

It was a great advantage to him that he had space in his lodgings to entertain companies of visitors. Among them, on several occasions, were "the leaders of the Jews", and their willingness to enter his house probably indicates that it was recognisably Jewish. They would be unlikely to visit a crowded Gentile tenement marked by dubious morals and religious defilement. Paul explained carefully to them how the hope of Israel is fulfilled in the gospel of Jesus.

With time to think and pray, and with news brought to him by faithful friends, Paul seized the moment to write further letters to the churches summarizing his teaching on various subjects of practical importance. He also had many opportunities to explain his faith. Indeed he asked his friends in Ephesus to pray "that words may be given to me in opening my mouth boldly to proclaim the mystery of the gospel, for which I am an ambassador in chains, that I may declare it boldly, as I ought to speak" (Eph 6:19-20). The soldier who was chained to him night and day must have heard and learned a great deal.

There were undoubtedly discomforts, dangers and frustrations in confinement, but Paul had suffered such trials and worse throughout his missionary life. He had learned to be content in all circumstances (Phil 4:11). As a prisoner, however, he was now entirely in the power of other men and subject to their whim – vulnerable to petty refusals and coarse insults from guards and attendants who would enjoy a small measure of authority and freely abuse it. He felt his need of "full courage" to honour Christ when a little compromise, silence or denial might be the easier course. He faced his inevitable humiliations bravely. "It is my eager expectation and hope," he said, "that I will not be at all ashamed" (Phil 1:20). He later urged Timothy, "Do not be ashamed of the testimony about our Lord, nor of me his prisoner" (2 Tim 1:8).

The men and women who supported Paul in his confinement should not be overlooked. To associate oneself with a prisoner would bring many inconveniences, humiliations and perhaps a serious hazard to health. It could be expensive if bribes were required for entry, and dangerous when each visitor ran the risk of arrest and punishment as an accomplice in the prisoner's alleged crimes.

Several of Paul's fellow-workers chose to share his imprisonment for longer or shorter periods, and notable among them were Luke, Aristarchus and Epaphras. For food and other necessities he would be entirely dependent on these men, and they would be his only means of communication with the world outside. The wider Christian community would also play its part by providing bread and other sustenance for him, and perhaps by washing his clothes. They would all follow his circumstances with interest, and no doubt with much prayer. The outcome of his appeal could have serious implications for them all.

When his case was brought before a preliminary tribunal, Paul's concern was not for his own comfort and safety but for the magistrate, secretaries, soldiers, officials and other people present. These were Gentiles who did not attend any synagogue and would never be likely to engage in conversation with a Christian. The best place, and perhaps the only place, to discuss the gospel with them was a law court, and the only way to do this was as a prisoner. These men were paid to hear him and required by law to understand what he said, and even to make a record of it.

Afterwards he wrote to his friends, "I want you to know, brothers, that what has happened to me has really served to advance the gospel, so that it has become known throughout the whole imperial guard and to all the rest that my imprisonment is for Christ. And most of the brothers, having become confident in the Lord by my imprisonment, are much more bold to speak the word without fear" (Phil 1:12-14). There were even some believers now in Caesar's household (Phil 4:22). The gospel was entering new cultures and finding acceptance with people of influence.

Paul's last years

We do not have a clear account of the rest of Paul's life. We do not know if he stood before the Emperor at this time. Innocent of any crime against Roman law, he was probably released for several years of freedom – travelling, preaching, teaching, suffering further persecution, and writing more letters that we still read today. He may have visited Spain according to his wish (Rom 15:24, 28).

Eventually, after more than thirty years of intense activity, Paul is nearing the age of sixty-five or seventy. We may assume he is suffering the usual problems of old age, and for some time he has called himself "Paul, an old man" (Philem 9).

Throughout these years the churches have grown and multiplied wonderfully. But they face increasing pressure. Disowned by the Jewish authorities and resented by the pagan cults, the followers of Jesus still have no legal recognition. It is well known that they do not honour the divine spirit of the Emperor or sacrifice to the gods of the Empire. The authorities, always fearful of what they cannot control, begin to accuse and persecute the local fellowships with increasing violence. Paul is arrested and sent a second time to Rome.

This time he is closely confined and harshly treated. In his cell he has very few visitors. One of them was Onesiphorus, a leading householder from Ephesus, who came to look for him and often refreshed him, as he tells us, not fearful or ashamed to be seen in such a place (2 Tim 1:16-17). Only the bravest and most faithful of his friends would choose to share his captivity in these circumstances. Luke is with him and he hopes Timothy will bring his cloak before winter sets in. But Paul's vision for the world remains undaunted. He is still able to send Tychicus to Ephesus, and more remarkably, he sends Titus to Dalmatia (2 Tim 4:10, 12).

Dalmatia lay in the province of Illyricum, beyond the sphere of Paul's own missionary labours. We have wondered how the gospel might reach that region of very few Jewish settlers and no synagogues. Now we see that the faith of Jesus has taken root even there, and Titus is on his way to teach and encourage communities of believers.

Knowing this, the apostle could cheerfully declare, "I am suffering, bound with chains as a criminal. But the word of God is not bound" (2 Tim 2:9). Deserted by many who might have supported him at his first public hearing, he was content: "The Lord stood by me and strengthened me, so that through me the message might be fully proclaimed and all the Gentiles might hear it" (2 Tim 4:17). In the subsequent history of the Church, many Roman officials and pagan bystanders were won to Christ by persecuted men and women who testified like Paul before governors and tribunals. As a mission strategy it has proved highly effective.[1]

Almost ten years earlier the apostle had received a word from God: "Do not be afraid, Paul; you must stand before Caesar" (Acts 27:24). There is no reason to doubt that this promise was fulfilled. He finally stood before the Emperor Nero, witnessed to him about the Saviour of the world and then sealed his testimony with his blood. The emperor was not persuaded, but other Romans were, and two and a half centuries later a company of church leaders were welcomed into the palace of the Emperor Constantine. He himself, before he died, asked for baptism as a Christian.

---

1. See Robin Daniel, *This Holy Seed* (Tamarisk, Chester 2010), especially 121-132, 162-173.

Nero's power went down with him to the grave but the teaching and example of Paul continue to influence and inspire every generation, and will do so until Christ comes. Finally he could sum up his missionary life in a few simple words. They express not a story of easy success but of intense conflict which he, by the grace of God, had survived: "I have fought the good fight, I have finished the race, I have kept the faith. Henceforth there is laid up for me the crown of righteousness, which the Lord, the righteous judge, will award to me on that Day" (2 Tim 4:7-8).

This brings to an end our brief account of Paul's career. If it has clarified some issues it has also raised many questions. We have looked at some of those questions – the content of his message, the guidance he received and his method of planting churches. Now we will consider his cultural sensitivity, his character as a man of God, his method of leadership and the basis of his financial support.

10
Paul's Cultural Sensitivity

Social distinctions

In the Gentile cities where Paul worked, most people were either rich or poor, and the majority of course were poor. Wealthy families would possess property and employ numerous labourers and servants to take care of their homes, businesses and fields. Many large households were also served by slaves of varied races in circumstances of relative comfort if not liberty. Among the Gentiles themselves there was hardly any middle class, accustomed to earn a moderate independent income, although Jewish craftsmen and traders had often found this a profitable niche as immigrants in the larger urban centres.

As an educated man of correct speech and cultured bearing, from a privileged family with Roman citizenship, Paul would find himself at ease among the social elite. Many of those who responded best to him were in fact people of high social status. We have an impressive list in the book of Acts: a governor in Paphos (13:7), a number of "leading women" in Thessalonica (17:4), some "women of high standing" in Berea (17:12), several intellectuals in Athens (17:34), a synagogue ruler in Corinth (18:8), provincial authorities "who were friends of his" in Ephesus (19:31), a chief official in Malta (28:7). And mentioned in one of his letters there is even a city treasurer (Rom 16:23).

In palaces, courtrooms and prisons he defended himself with confidence before men of refinement and influence – magistrates (Acts 16:38-39), governors (24:10; 25:9), a high priest (23:2), a king (26:1) and probably in due course an emperor (25:12).

The practical issues raised in Paul's correspondence are largely those that concern educated people enjoying financial security – power struggles, boasting, lawsuits, resisting the authorities, invitations to pagan feasts, styles of dress and appearance, choice of food and drink, interpretations of scripture and various philosophical ideas. In the synagogues where he spoke, some members would definitely consider themselves wise, powerful and of noble birth. A number were certainly "rich in this present world" (1 Tim 6:17). They might be a minority but they were the people most likely to welcome Paul and his companions as house-guests.

His readers in general must have been people with a reasonable income, able to "make some contribution for the poor" (Rom 15:26). Indeed he advises them, "Do not be haughty, but associate with the lowly" (Rom 12:16).

In an age when work generally required physical rather than mental expertise, most would be occupied with manual labour of some sort, or with organising others engaged in manual labour. He himself was accustomed to making tents. His advice to them all was, "Aspire to live quietly, and to mind your own affairs, and to work with your hands, as we instructed you, so that you may win the respect of outsiders and be dependent on no one" (1 Thess 4:11-12). Work of this sort could clearly provide a comfortable living.

The evidence available to us in the New Testament therefore suggests that Christianity first became established in the leading families of the major cities rather than through mass-conversion of the poor and destitute. As a missionary, Paul was led to mix with people like himself, and he found many of them willing to accept both himself and his message. Yet when he wrote to the fellowship in Corinth he reminded them, "Not many of you were wise according to worldly standards, not many were powerful, not many were of noble birth" (1 Cor 1:26).

How then did the gospel reach the less privileged majority – the dockers and carters, the brick-layers, cleaners and cooks, the labourers, farmers and fishermen? What about the servants and slaves? How might they become believers in Christ?

Firstly, in the Jewish community itself there would be a proportion of small traders, artisans and unskilled workers – many on the verge of poverty and desperately longing for better days – who would respond well to a message of hope heard in the synagogue.

There would also be beggars of all races, day-labourers, scroungers and thieves hanging around the building, who might receive a greater blessing than they were expecting from those who went in, as did the beggar who hailed Peter and John at the gate of the temple (Acts 3:1-10).

But we may assume that Gentiles from the lower classes would more naturally hear the gospel through the normal relationships of the life they led. A property owner such as Philemon, converted in the synagogue, would be likely to assemble his workers, servants and slaves in a suitable place on his estate to hear whatever Paul or other visiting evangelists might wish to teach them. If the master had become a Christian, then his testimony would soon be heard by his household and by the tradesmen and employees dependent on him.

If some among these craftsmen, labourers, slaves and beggars responded to the good news, they would naturally pass it on to friends and relatives of their own circle. And the vast social gulf that existed between master and servant would by no means exclude personal conversations between a visitor such as Paul and the humbler members of a household. This is well illustrated by the case of Onesimus, a slave who came looking for him in a city far from home to share a personal problem and seek his help.

When he wrote to the churches, Paul had advice for both masters and slaves, and we may assume that both would hear and respect what he said (Eph 6:5-9). James too could envisage a fellowship with room for "a man wearing a gold ring and fine clothing" and also "a poor man in shabby clothing" (Ja 2:2).

The gospel was good news for people of all social levels and the evidence is that all were represented in the church. Some believers in Ephesus had previously been thieves but were now expected to earn an honest income (Eph 4:28). Some in Corinth were slaves hoping to obtain their freedom (1 Cor 7:21). Others had small independent businesses (Acts 16:14; 18:3). But most were probably members of large households, or craftsmen or tradesmen known to those households.

A missionary today will often face the same social complexities as Paul and the other apostles. Concerned for people of all classes, we may nevertheless meet with a better response among men and women of a particular social or educational level. Once the gospel has been accepted by these, it may pass naturally to people of other social, educational and economic levels through the normal relationships of life. This will happen far more easily if our earliest converts are of high status, as Paul's appear to have been.

Before we leave this subject there is a further point to consider. Although Paul did not encourage excessive social ambition (1 Cor 7:17), it seems likely that his message appealed especially to social risers – individuals with drive and initiative who were willing to take risks in order to improve themselves and their future prospects. If converted to Christ, their character would change for the better and so would their social circle.

The danger was that such converts might still attach more importance to their upward mobility than to their Christian commitment. They would be tempted to love money, and also to despise parents and friends occupying the lower social level from which they were eager to escape. Paul could foresee the consequences: "People will be lovers of self, lovers of money, proud, arrogant, abusive, disobedient to their parents . . . treacherous, reckless, swollen with conceit, lovers of pleasure rather than lovers of God" (2 Tim 3:2-4).

The natural desire of men and women for upward mobility may awaken a great interest in the gospel and in the Christian community. This is a good thing and can lead many to faith in Christ. But our responsibility is then to teach them well and ensure that a desire for spiritual progress and effective service to others entirely displaces the more worldly and selfish aspirations of human nature.

Dealing with cultural issues

As far as we can tell from the New Testament records, Paul had no particular interest in the pagan beliefs, practices or customs of the regions he visited. Their temples were visible on every street and their superstitions apparent in every conversation, but he did not embark on a study of pagan culture, nor did he expect his younger co-workers to do so. They did not need to read and learn a great deal of falsehood in order to proclaim the truth.

But the apostle was familiar with the problems and the dangers faced by people from a pagan background, as we see from the early chapters of his letter to Rome, for he had talked personally with many such people and knew from experience how to help them. If other controversies arose on account of local customs or beliefs, he would expect believers from that locality to deal wisely with such matters after they were well established in the basic principles of the faith.

The aspects of culture that most concerned the apostle were those that tended towards racial conflict. He was fully aware of the tensions in the Gentile cities of his day, and especially in the synagogue communities of the Jewish diaspora where he launched his outreach. Greeks would inevitably feel incongruous in a Jewish synagogue, and Jews would feel equally alien in a Gentile city. The Greeks wanted to be accepted as worshippers of God, and the Jews as civilised members of the modern world. Christianity solved the problem for both by denying any significance to ethnic origin. When Paul taught directly from the Greek Septuagint, without reference to Hebrew manuscripts or Aramaic commentaries, he placed all his hearers on an equal linguistic and cultural footing. This must have been a great help to unity and mutual respect among the first generation of Christian converts.

We have seen that Paul's birth and upbringing made him effectively multi-cultural. He was a Jew to the Jews, a Greek to the Greeks, a Syrian to the Syrians, and even a Roman to the Romans. We have seen that he adopted a Latin name, which would lessen the cultural distance between himself and the Gentiles around him. For the same reason, his co-worker Silas became known not by his Aramaic name but by the Latin Silvanus (Acts 18:5; 1 Thess 1:1). The New Testament evidence shows that Paul, like Jesus, usually adapted to the culture around him but sometimes quietly ignored it, and occasionally defied it.

If possible he would always adjust to the people he was with. Among the Jews he would say, "I am a Jew, of the tribe of Benjamin, circumcised on the eighth day, brought up in Jerusalem, educated at the feet of Gamaliel," and even "I am a Pharisee" (Acts 22:3; 23:6). With Gentiles he would affirm, "I am from Tarsus in Cilicia, a Roman citizen of no obscure city" (Acts 21:39). In Jerusalem he takes a vow and shaves his head. In Athens he quotes from philosophers and poets. For Cretans he cites a proverb from Crete. In the Jewish synagogues he reads from the prophets. In pagan Lystra he speaks of the one true God. Paul adapted to these varied cultures for purposes that were important to him – to avoid offence, to win acceptance, and to communicate his message.

But sometimes he would ignore culture. To the people around

him this would be surprising. In prison at Philippi he sings hymns at midnight, which is not normal behaviour for a prisoner. Then he enters the home of the Gentile jailer, which is not normal for a Jew. Everywhere he declares that a condemned criminal is really the Messiah, which is not normal for anyone. He proclaims "Jesus is Lord," knowing that others are saying "Caesar is Lord". He ignores food customs, for *kosher* meat and idol sacrifices are all the same to him. He strolls publicly in the company of Gentiles, uncircumcised and foreign in appearance (Acts 21:29). He is persuading people to worship in a new way, without regard for Jewish ceremony or Roman custom (Acts 16:21; 18:13). Why, in all these cases, does he ignore culture? He does so because he has something better than the culture and is happy for everyone to see it.

On occasion, Paul would go further than this. Sometimes he actively defies culture. To ignore a culture is surprising but to defy a culture may be acutely offensive. He drove out the demon that empowered a girl to tell fortunes (Acts 16:18-19). He dismissed sacrificial animals and flowers as "these futile things" (Acts 14:15). He watched the Ephesians burn their books of magic (Acts 19:19). He spoke to a corrupt governor about righteousness, self-control and judgment to come (Acts 24:25). He accused the high priest of violating the Law (Acts 23:3). He insisted that Jewish and Gentile Christians eat together (Gal 2:11-12). He told the Corinthians to come out of their temples and leave their prostitutes (2 Cor 6:16-17; 1 Cor 6:15). Why, in all these cases did he defy the culture? He did so because the culture had enslaved the people and he wished to set them free.

So we see that Paul, like Jesus, usually accepted the local culture, but sometimes ignored it and occasionally defied it. Yet the really important thing for him was none these. His greatest desire was to introduce a new Christian culture.

For Paul and the other apostles, gospel culture supersedes all local cultures. They taught basic principles of truth and behaviour that override every human worldview and way of life. So Zeus and Hermes can never be worshipped alongside God, for there is no agreement between light and darkness. Fornication and drunkenness are never acceptable in a Christian community, for the fruit of the Spirit must overcome the works of the flesh. A brother will never be caused to stumble by what we eat or drink, for we have learned the meaning of love. Litigation and divorce are not God's way of resolving problems, for he enables us to overlook offences and reach amicable agreement. Racial discrimination has no place in a fellowship of believers, for we are all one in Christ. Masters will never be unjust or violent, and servants will never deceive or steal, for we are all servants of one Lord. Husbands will be kind and considerate, wives loyal and respectful, children helpful and obedient. All will be generous and hospitable, and their home a place of peace and mutual encouragement. The followers of Jesus know the truth, and the truth will set them free from all that is false. Their aim in life is not to become wealthy and powerful but to become wise and good – to be pure and honourable, faithful in little things, loving and compassionate like our Lord himself. This is his will for us all, and it is not negotiable.

Wherever we proclaim the gospel, we are introducing something entirely new to the local culture. If we live as Christ taught us we will always be different from the people around us. They will consider us strange and may soon find cause to mock or insult us. The message of the cross is "a stumbling block to Jews and folly to Gentiles," and some will take offence at what we say, especially if large numbers decide to abandon their old ways and join us (1 Cor 1:23). The early Christians were accused of turning the world upside down. Soon there were riots and they were pelted with stones. We do not go looking for trouble, but we know it is sure to come. "Indeed, all who desire to live a godly life in Christ Jesus will be persecuted" (2 Tim 3:12).

Nevertheless, Paul was concerned to avoid all unnecessary offence. A pagan official in Ephesus testified that in two years the apostle had said nothing rude about their goddess or their sacred places. If someone supposed he had publicly declared "gods made with hands are not gods," they must have been mistaken (Acts 19:26, 37). It is quite possible to proclaim Christ without criticizing traditional beliefs.

A wise evangelist will not engage in argument. It is rare for a person strongly committed to one religion to switch immediately to another. Most first-generation converts are drawn from the uncommitted – lukewarm in their adherence to their previous religion, irregular in their attendance and often somewhat disillusioned and detached from it. In this condition of unease they meet someone offering a more attractive alternative and decide to investigate it.[1]

As a young man, Paul had had been inclined to speak strongly and somewhat aggressively in the synagogues. We read that shortly after his conversion he "increased all the more in strength, and confounded the Jews who lived in Damascus by proving that Jesus was the Christ." The only result, as far as we know, was a plot against his life (Acts 9:22-23). Experience taught him to speak to them more gently and more persuasively. Throughout his later career, "he reasoned" with them, "testified" to them and "tried to persuade" them (Acts 18:4-5). This is a matter of common respect and courtesy, and should be remembered by every evangelist.

So Paul summarizes his approach to culture:

1. "Whether you eat or drink, or whatever you do, *do all to the glory of God.*
2. "*Give no offence* to Jews or to Greeks or to the church of God, just as I try to please everyone in everything I do,
3. "not seeking my own advantage, but that of many, *that they may be saved*" (1 Cor 10:31-33).

With these words the apostle shows us his three great principles in every cultural context: that the character of God should be seen in him, that he give no unnecessary offence, and that the people around him might be saved. How then would this work in practice?

In most places, false religion could simply be ignored. Meat slaughtered at a temple or in honour of an idol could be received and eaten with thanks to God for his provision. But if someone suggested that a particular blessing or curse attached to such meat, it should be avoided. To eat it then would be seen as an act of worship in honour of the idol, which could not be done to the glory of God and might encourage others in idol worship. "Therefore," said Paul, "if food makes my brother stumble, I will never eat meat, lest I make my brother stumble" (1 Cor 8:13). His chief concern was always for others to be saved and to be safe, and he would do nothing that might hinder this.

His work was to teach the culture of the gospel, and this would be most fully experienced and enjoyed in the Christian home.

---

1. Stark, 19

Gospel culture is the same in all the world, for we all have the same New Testament. For this reason, families and congregations separated by thousands of miles are far more similar than anyone would reasonably expect. Although the local culture of Corinth or Lystra would be quite different from that of Syrian Antioch or Jerusalem, there is no evidence that the fellowships in these places adopted different policies on cultural issues or changed their style of meeting to suit local expectations. Paul and the apostles would not encourage them to do so. Indeed, on the one occasion when a local church seemed inclined to follow local customs, Paul three times reminded them of what was done "in all the churches" and urged them to follow suit (1 Cor 7:17; 11:16; 14:33-34).

This meant that that a Christian could travel anywhere in the world and immediately feel at home in any company of believers. If some missiologists are inclined to attach great importance to local cultures, and to subtle strategies of adaptation and contextualisation, they might be led to wonder why the apostles did not do so.

The New Testament shows us a new culture – gospel culture – boldly and joyfully proclaimed, and willingly accepted by a generation dissatisfied with its old beliefs and unhappy in its old ways. We should not be ashamed to offer what is so good, or attempt to hide it behind a facade of worldly behaviour or religious falsehood (Rom 1:16).

Minimizing cultural resistance

Throughout Paul's missionary career we have seen him adopting strategies that minimized cultural resistance. He would focus his attention on places where he was culturally at ease and could expect a positive welcome. In the Jewish synagogues he met Gentiles who had already adopted his own culture to a large degree and would accept him as a teacher worthy of respect. When they responded to the gospel, he expected them to carry it back to their friends and relations in distant provinces where they too would be working within their own culture.

This indeed was the method suggested by Jesus when he sent the man rescued from a legion of demons back to his own people in Gerasa with the news of what God had done for him (Lk 8:39). It was what happened when the Samaritan woman, after meeting the

Messiah at Jacob's well, went and testified to her friends and family in the town of Sychar (Jn 4:39). It was what happened at Pentecost when Jews and proselytes heard the gospel and took it back to the lands they came from. This is the most natural way for good news to spread.

In addition to this, Paul has shown us the key to evangelising provinces and continents beyond the reach of the Jewish diaspora and its synagogue communities. Establishing an active fellowship in a cosmopolitan city, he would then expect its members to follow the natural links they maintained with their homelands, sharing their faith with their own people, with neighbouring people, and with any who might welcome them as friends and fellow-countrymen further afield.

When Paul himself moved into an alien cultural environment, he valued the company of believers familiar with that culture. Planning to visit Corinth he sent ahead of him Timothy and Erastus to prepare the way. Concerned for a distant city, he would send a believer such as Epaphras who had been born and brought up there or somewhere nearby. Paul's mission strategy was highly sensitive to culture, and to illustrate this further we shall consider the case of Titus.

Titus was a Gentile from one of the Greek provinces who met Paul on his travels, heard the gospel and committed himself to Christ. Taking him to Jerusalem, Paul introduced him to the church there as a test-case, a Christian Gentile who was not circumcised, and in Paul's view, had no need of circumcision (Gal 2:1-3).

A few years later, when some leaders in Corinth were critical of Paul, it was Titus he sent to resolve the problem (2 Cor 8:6, 16-17). Timothy had previously attempted this, but being half-Jewish, he was not sure of a good reception. Indeed Paul had to beg the Corinthians, "Put him at ease . . . Let no one despise him" (1 Cor 16:10-11). Titus, however, would be working in his home environment and would be received by the Corinthians as one of their own.

Paul later took Titus with him to the island of Crete, with its Greek culture similar to that of Corinth. Leaving him there, Paul was confident he could establish the church securely: "This is why I left you in Crete, so that you might put in order what was lacking, and appoint elders in every town as I directed you" (Tit 1:5). By entrusting such tasks to his Gentile co-workers, Paul would minimize cultural tension. He knew that men and women will listen best to people like themselves. They will respect those who look the same and speak the same as they do.

The lesson for us is a simple one. We learn from Paul to minimize the cross-cultural strangeness of the gospel. Concerned for an unreached area or people, we will look first for a person who has come out of that area and entered our culture. With prayer we help this friend come to faith in Christ. Then we teach our new disciple well, encouraging him to share his faith with others, until he is ready to take the good news to his own home town in his own language.

We should anticipate that the *first believers* in any culture- or language-group will hear the gospel far from home and then take it back to their own people. This strategy has several advantages.

1. The gospel message enters the community as something discovered by one of their own people, and therefore something appropriate for them. It is not an alien idea introduced by a foreigner, whose motives they would naturally suspect.
2. They will not be distracted by a foreign colour of skin or manner of speech, or by the prospect of foreign money or travel.
3. The facts will be explained in the local dialect, using examples and illustrations that connect with daily life. The issues can be discussed by everyone, including women and children and old people who speak only their local dialect.
4. If the gospel is seen to be good news it will be passed on naturally to friends and relations. It has a spontaneous power to spread throughout the locality.
5. If it is good news it will also be shared with friendly foreigners living among the people or mixing with them in administration or trade. These then have the potential to become missionaries to their own homelands far away.

Once the local community has accepted the gospel, a warm welcome may then be extended to friends of the person who brought it to them. Believers from other places may then be invited to help with teaching and establishing the fellowship.

This is the ideal, but circumstances are sometimes far from ideal. If for some reason we find ourselves located in an unreached area with a culture and language unfamiliar to us, Paul's example would teach us to find someone who will come with us – someone who belongs to that culture and can explain the gospel to the local inhabitants more effectively than we can.

If a people-group has never seen one of their own nationality or tribe converted to Christ, they will often consider such a thing impossible. But if one of their own people stands before them as a convinced and committed Christian, then conversion to Christ immediately becomes a realistic option for them too.

Paul had learned from experience that this is the best strategy for cross-cultural mission. He would see no point in doing things the hard way if there is an easier way. He knew that people will accept the gospel most willingly when it is brought to them by someone from their own culture in their own language. But there is something further to note.

Cross-cultural evangelism

If, for any reason, the easy way was impossible, then Paul was perfectly willing to go the hard way. Although by choice he aimed for the people and places most likely to listen and respond, he would not be constrained by this. He was willing to proclaim and testify to anyone, anywhere, at any time.

We have seen that he did not go to the city of Athens in order to launch a mission to idol-worshippers and philosophers. He went to Athens simply to escape danger in Berea. He was waiting there for Silas and Timothy (Acts 17:16). Among the sophisticated Athenians he was culturally out of his depth. Most of them thought he was talking nonsense. "Some said, 'What does this babbler wish to say?' Others said, 'He seems to be a preacher of foreign divinities' – because he was preaching Jesus and the resurrection." They asked him to present his teaching again, and when he did, some mocked, some wanted to hear more, and finally "a few men joined him and believed" (Acts 17:18, 34). It was not a great success. But despite this, he was determined to preach in season and out of season, to proclaim the truth whether or not people would listen (2 Tim 4:2).

If we hear of a region with no known believers, and none from that region converted elsewhere, then we may be led to go and learn their language and win their confidence and so lead some to Christ. This may be a slow process but it can be done. Many times, in fact, it has been done. By the grace of God, missionaries have crossed culture and won to Christ the firstfruits of a tribe or nation which had never before heard the gospel. We honour such men and women. They have done it the hard way and their Lord will reward them for their faith and their obedience.

In cross-cultural situations like this – in Athens, Lystra, Philippi and in other pagan environments – we have seen the difficulties that Paul faced. But he proclaimed Christ anyway. From the barrack steps in Jerusalem, amidst a rioting crowd in Ephesus, on a ship in a stormy sea, in the house of an official in Malta, on the road to Rome, he was always speaking about Christ. He would not be silenced. Nevertheless, as we have seen, the key to really effective cross-cultural mission lay with converts who had crossed from one culture to another before they heard the gospel, and then took it back to their own people in their own tongue.

Making full use of cultural skills

Our study of scripture has shown that there is much less cross-cultural mission in the New Testament than we might expect. Both Jesus and Paul habitually worked in a cultural context familiar to them, among people who looked like them, who spoke their language, and accepted them as leading men from their own community. Yet both were willing to speak to outsiders when the opportunity arose, and both trained a company of evangelists who would carry the gospel message far further than they could carry it themselves.

Finally we should note that although he was multi-cultural like many people of his day, Paul saw a great need to help those who were mono-cultural. He was concerned to help Jews accept Gentiles, as we see in his discussion with the leaders at Jerusalem (Acts 15:2-4). And he was concerned to help Gentiles understand Jews, as we see in his letter to the fellowship at Rome (Rom 11:13). His multi-cultural background enabled him to bring the two together, ignoring deeply-rooted racial prejudices and demolishing "the dividing wall of hostility" (Eph 2:14).

Paul was especially concerned to build relationships of love and respect within the congregations where believers of diverse culture were represented. He insisted that all should be accepted in the fellowship, but equally importantly, that all should participate in a way that is understandable.

The early Christians spoke many different languages. In the house meetings of the Jerusalem church for example, the local families would speak Aramaic and visitors would speak Greek. They would need much patience and gracious sensitivity to make sure that everyone could understand and take part. In the great cosmopolitan cities of Ephesus and Corinth there might be a dozen or more languages represented when the believers gathered together. If all spoke their own dialect, confusion would surely reign.

Perhaps for this reason, Paul insisted that if someone wished to say something in a language not understood by others, interpretation was essential: "If any speak in a language, let there be only two or at most three, and each in turn, and let someone interpret. But if there is no one to interpret, let each of them keep silent in church and speak to himself and to God" (1 Cor 14:27-28).

Paul himself would naturally prefer to speak his own dialect of Cilician Aramaic, but who would understand him in Corinth or Thessalonica? In these circumstances he chose to exercise his mind and speak Greek for the benefit of all. And he took care to explain. "There are doubtless many different voices in the world, and none is without meaning, but if I do not know the meaning of the voice, I will be a foreigner to the speaker and the speaker a foreigner to me" (1 Cor 14:10-11). He was always concerned to reduce the "foreignness" of the gospel, as much inside the church as outside it. We will consider this further in due course (see Additional Notes: Various kinds of languages).

Paul's vision for the church and for mission required believers of diverse cultures to mix freely. Without this, the gospel could not easily spread into new areas. If we have learned anything at all from his example we will value the presence in our churches of visitors from other places and make them especially welcome. They may not feel quite at home in our culture, and they may not speak our language very well, but as they grow in their faith among us they may become our best missionaries. They understand other cultures and speak other languages that are essential for proclaiming the good news to the ends of the earth.

11

Paul's Missionary Character

His spiritual maturity

The character of a missionary is far more important than his knowledge of languages or his natural eloquence. However brilliant his ministry may be, a weak or worldly character will sooner or later do great damage – causing new converts to stumble, seekers to turn away in disgust, and congregations to fall apart. Dishonesty in finance or unfaithfulness in marriage may begin with a very small compromise and end by destroying a ministry and a life.

It was not Paul's teaching alone that so profoundly influenced the people around him. Above all, it was his example. He showed how a true follower of Christ will live – in self-discipline, in loving kindness, with a clear conscience, an assured faith, a wise perspective on life, good stewardship of money, speaking the truth in love and avoiding every appearance of evil. "Brothers," he said, "join in imitating me, and keep your eyes on those who walk according to the example you have in us" (Phil 3:17).

The apostle never lowered his standards. He disciplined himself to be the man he wanted to be. "Every athlete exercises self-control in all things," he observed. "So I do not run aimlessly; I do not box as one beating the air. I discipline my body and keep it under control, lest after preaching to others I myself should be disqualified" (1 Cor 9:25-27).

More than thirty times in his letters Paul uses the word "always". That is a measure of the importance he gave to consistency. We will never have Paul's effectiveness as a teacher without his consistency as a man. So he reminded Timothy, "You have closely followed my teaching, my conduct, my aim in life, my faith, my patience, my love, my *steadfastness*" (2 Tim 3:10). Then his advice to Timothy and us is this: "As for you, *continue* in what you have learned and have firmly believed" (v.14).

Paul's ministry depended on the guidance and blessing of God's Spirit. He knew his need to be filled with the Spirit at all times, and so took great care never to grieve or quench the Spirit (Eph 5:18; 4:30; 1 Thess 5:19). To become mature in Christ was essential for him and for all his co-workers (Phil 3:15). A mature person is one who has grown to full stature and developed his full potential, and he expected this of himself and all his converts (Col 1:28; Col 4:12).

Through good times and bad, a strong and dependable character will never fail to be a blessing to others in some way. To work alongside a man or woman of profound and godly character fills us with confidence and high expectation of what our Lord will do through our fellowship together.

It was Paul's character that made him such a great missionary. He uttered no empty boast when he said, "I know that when I come to you I will come in the fullness of the blessing of Christ" (Rom 15:29). He knew from experience that this blessing never for a moment left him.

His personal credibility

Along with his strength of character, Paul had credibility as a missionary who had prepared himself well and acquired the skills needed for his task. Having studied the scriptures, he knew them by heart and understood their meaning. He had learned how to teach clearly and earnestly without deceit or exaggeration. He spoke several languages fluently and correctly. Through wide experience, he knew how to speak appropriately to people of all types. Earning his living with useful work, he was not dependent on others for his needs.

Everything about Paul showed him to be genuine. Suffering so greatly for the cause of his mission, he could never be suspected of pursuing it for personal advantage. Adapting so patiently to the people around him, he could never be accused of glorifying himself. With no sign of wealth about him, he was clearly not doing it for the money. Everyone could see this. The only reason he proclaimed his message was that he believed it to be the truth. And his determination to do so at such personal cost showed how important he considered it to be.

Paul did not seek credibility by offering material benefits, by omitting hard truths, by asking people to speak well of him or by praising himself and his achievements.

He was a man worthy of respect and anyone who met him would quickly recognise this. It is important for every missionary to have credibility. A man or woman who cannot quickly win the respect of strangers will not be effective in gospel ministry.

His love for his converts

We should not think of Paul as a cold academic who ignored suffering and felt no pain. He was a sensitive and emotional man. He felt things deeply and did not hide it – partly because this was in his nature but also because he knew the importance of positive relationships. His converts would need to feel accepted and loved in the new community of faith, and he in turn must gain their affection if he wished them to heed what he said. He reminded one group of his earliest days with them: "We were gentle among you, like a mother taking care of her little children. We longed for you so much that we were ready to share with you not only the gospel of God but also our own selves, because you had become very dear to us" (1 Thess 2:7-8).

Paul was a warm-hearted and devoted friend. Separated from those who were dear to him he wrote, "my brothers, whom I love and long for, my joy and crown" (Phil 4:1). Others he hoped to visit soon, "so that by God's will I may come to you with joy and be refreshed in your company" (Rom 15:32). To one he said, "I have derived much joy and comfort from your love, my brother" (Philem 7). But he could be very hurt if, after his great affection for these friends, they refused their love to him. "I will most gladly spend all I have and myself as well for your sake," he said. But then, "If I love you more, will you love me less?" (2 Cor 12:15).

Paul's letters are full of joy and rejoicing, but also of anxiety and longing. Concerned about the fellowship in Philippi, he sent Epaphroditus for news of them, "so that I may be less anxious" (Phil 2:28). To others in Galatia he wrote, "my little children, for whom I am again in the anguish of childbirth until Christ is formed in you"

(Gal 4:19). And he tells us about "the daily pressure on me of my anxiety for all the churches" (2 Cor 11:28).

Just as the love of Jesus drew people to him, so did the love of Paul. Boarding a ship on one occasion, "there was much weeping on the part of all; they embraced Paul and kissed him"(Acts 20:37). His example would be contagious, but he feared that after he had gone his converts might cool in their affections for one another. So he reminded them, "Love one another with brotherly affection. Outdo one another in showing honour." (Rom 12:10). And again, "Let all that you do be done in love," "bearing with one another in love, eager to maintain the unity of the Spirit in the bond of peace" (1 Cor 16:14; Eph 4:2-3). When one of them has confessed to wrong-doing, "I beg you all to reaffirm your love for him" so he will not be "overwhelmed by excessive sorrow" (2 Cor 2:8-9).

Love is the first fruit of the Holy Spirit, and as missionaries we must learn to express warm affection in ways appropriate for the culture we are in (Gal 5:22). The world is desperately in need of unselfish love, and many people live and die unloved. A genuinely loving person will be welcome wherever he or she may go.

His servant spirit

Many people in Paul's day possessed the same natural advantages that he did. Many had his education; many were multi-cultural from childhood; many were highly intelligent; many had travelled widely and seen the world. But none made better use of their natural advantages than him.

In every multi-cultural person there is great potential, but without disciplined effort, responsive sensitivity and compassionate love, this potential will remain largely unfulfilled and useless.

It is not easy to shift quickly from one culture to another, always discerning the kind of person we are with, adjusting what we do and say to meet their needs and expectations. It takes much effort to say the same thing several times in several languages so that everyone grasps the meaning. It requires great sensitivity to do a job one way today and another way tomorrow for the sake of people with different preferences. Without a loving heart we cannot do it.

From his own experience Paul could say, "the love of Christ compels us" (2 Cor 5:14). It was love that moved him to have this sensitivity and to make this effort. It was love that enabled him to be a servant.

"Though I am free from all," he said, "I have made myself *a servant to all*, that I might win more of them." So he tells us that among the Jews he followed Jewish customs in order to win Jews to faith in Christ. With the proselytes (who kept the Law) he kept the Law in order to win proselytes. With worshippers of God (who did not keep the Law) he ignored the Law in order to win worshippers of God (1 Cor 9:19-21). His thoughts were always focussed on the needs of the people he was with. He would even become "weak", avoiding food and drink that might possibly tempt others and so cause harm, in order to keep them safe from such temptation (1 Cor 9:22; 2 Cor 11:29).

But he never lost sight of his ultimate purpose: "I do it all for the sake of the gospel, that I may share with them in its blessings" (1 Cor 9:23). His aim, as we have seen, was that they might be saved (1 Cor 10:33).

Just as Jesus took the form of a servant, so did Paul, and that meant putting the needs and concerns of others first. Every true missionary of the gospel will learn to have this disciplined sensitivity and so become "a good servant of Christ Jesus" (1 Tim 4:6).

His constant prayer

Paul's letters give us many insights into his life of prayer, not as a religious duty but as a simple conversation with his Lord that continued night and day wherever he happened to be. When good news came, it did not merely make him happy; it made him thankful, for his Lord had done good things. When trouble came, he asked his Lord immediately to work it out for the best. When faced with uncertainty, he committed it to his Lord and waited for clear guidance. There were several reasons for Paul's constant desire to pray.

1. He prayed because he lived in the presence of God. It was entirely natural to share every experience with the One who had loved and saved him and now worked with him (1 Cor 3:9). He knew how little he could accomplish on his own, for his personal ability was quite inadequate to influence and change people for eternity. Only through the conviction of the Holy Spirit could a man or

woman be born again. Only through the power of the Spirit could a selfish person be filled with "love, joy, peace, patience, kindness, goodness, faithfulness, gentleness and self-control" (Gal 5:22-23). The things that Paul could not do, he simply asked his Lord to do.

2. He prayed because he cared so deeply about people – especially for those who were far away, because prayer was almost his only way of helping them. Writing to friends he had left unexpectedly, he told them, "We always pray for you" (2 Thess 1:11). To others he had never met he said, "From the day we heard, we have not ceased to pray for you" (Col 1:9).

3. He prayed because he had made a habit of prayer. He could urge his converts to "be constant in prayer" because that was his own experience (Rom 12:12). To Timothy he said, "I remember you constantly in my prayers night and day" (2 Tim 1:3). This was both a pleasure and a discipline requiring thought and time, and often hard work – thinking, remembering and asking God about specific details, individuals and circumstances. Because he was accustomed to work hard in his prayers for others he could urge them, "Strive together with me in your prayers to God on my behalf" (Rom 15:30).

4. He prayed because the Holy Spirit led him to pray and guided him in his prayer. He was sensitive to the witness of the Spirit with his spirit as he prayed (Eph 6:18). In his letters we see how detailed were his prayers for individuals and churches but sometimes he would confess, "we do not know what to pray for as we ought, but the Spirit himself intercedes for us with groanings too deep for words" (Rom 8:26). Such prayers would correspond with the will of God himself.

5. He prayed because prayer brought him great comfort. Having placed his circumstances in the hands of his Lord, he no longer had need to worry. From experience he could say, "The Lord is at hand; do not be anxious about anything, but in everything by prayer and supplication with thanksgiving let your requests be made known to God. And the *peace of God*, which surpasses all understanding, will guard your hearts and your minds in Christ Jesus" (Phil 4:5-7).

Everything that Paul achieved in life came in answer to his prayers. A

PAUL'S MISSIONARY CHARACTER

missionary who prays constantly is one who will see God constantly at work.

His devotion to Christ

With his family background and personal abilities, Paul could have become a great man of the world – a famous rabbi among the Pharisees, or a great political leader of his people. Engaging in business he could have enjoyed a life of luxury and ease. Writing Jewish commentaries or histories, he could have been renowned among the scholars of his people. But he gave it all up in order to be a servant of Christ. "For his sake," he said, "I have suffered the loss of all things" (Phil 3:8).

He gained nothing for himself from the beatings, shipwrecks, imprisonments, dangers, toils and hardships, sleepless nights, hunger, thirst and cold (2 Cor 11:24-27). He bore it all for the sake of others. "I rejoice in my sufferings for your sake," he told them, "and in my flesh I am filling up what is lacking in Christ's afflictions for the sake of his body, that is, the church" (Col 1:24).

All that happened to him he accepted for the sake of his Lord. "For the sake of Christ, then, I am content with weaknesses, insults, hardships, persecutions, and calamities" (2 Cor 12:10).

In hard times he had learned how to endure cheerfully: "I have learned the secret of facing plenty and hunger, abundance and need. I can do all things through him who strengthens me" (Phil 4:12-13). And he was happy with his lot: "I have learned in whatever situation I am to be content" (Phil 4:11)

Paul was so sure of rising from the dead that he risked his life daily (1 Cor 15:31). "I am ready," he said, "not only to be imprisoned but even to die in Jerusalem for the name of the Lord Jesus" (Acts 21:13). On one occasion he was pelted with stones in Lystra, dragged out of the city and left for dead. Regaining his senses, he did not try to escape or hide but went back into the city and spent the night there, determined not to leave his converts frightened and discouraged by what had happened (Acts 14:20). Later he returned to the same place, "strengthening the souls of the disciples, encouraging them to continue in the faith, and saying that through many tribulations we must enter the kingdom of God" (Acts 14:22). It was among this group of believers that he found

Timothy and recruited him for his mission (Acts 16:1-2).

Paul's consistent desire was simply to please his Lord Jesus Christ – not to please himself, nor his friends, nor his co-workers, nor his converts, nor the churches he had planted. And the same was true of the men who worked alongside him: "So whether we are at home or away, we make it our aim to please him" (2 Cor 5:9). They were all labouring "not by the way of eye-service, as people-pleasers, but as servants of Christ, doing the will of God from the heart" (Eph 6:6).

As missionaries of the gospel we may find that people do not appreciate us. This will not worry us unduly if our greatest desire is to please our Master and to hear his voice saying, "Well done, good and faithful servant" (Matt 25:21).

His great vision

Finally we should note that Paul was a great leader because he had a *great passion*. He was not distracted by temporary comforts, ambitions or rewards. "One thing I do," he said. "Forgetting what lies behind and straining forward to what lies ahead, I press on toward the goal for the prize of the upward call of God in Christ Jesus" (Phil 3:13-14).

Throughout his life he was a man with *great energy*. People will follow an energetic leader. A missionary, even if his physical powers wane, must take care that he never loses his spiritual energy.

He knew he was entrusted with a *great task*: "In Christ God was reconciling the world to himself, not counting their trespasses against them, and entrusting *to us* the message of reconciliation" (2 Cor 5:19).

He was inspired by a *great vision*, a world vision – for the gospel to reach every tribe and tongue, "as indeed in the whole world it is bearing fruit and growing" (Col 1:6).

Paul inspired his recruits to risk all and give all for the sake of their mission. He offered them no salary, no house, no comforts. They would expect persecution, shipwreck, prison, stones and beatings, and still they were willing to go with him. Why? Because he inspired them with his vision. They could see it was a great vision, a true vision, and an effective vision for transforming men and women. It would change the world.

We may feel that Paul was unique, and perhaps fear that we

could never be like him. But he was surrounded by ordinary people quite similar to ourselves – Timothy, Luke, Priscilla and Aquila, Lydia, Barnabas and many others. Perhaps we can relate to them more easily. So how did these men and women respond to Paul, and how did others respond to them? That is our subject as we turn our attention to his converts and the team of missionaries he recruited from among them.

12

Paul's Missionary Team

Apostles and Evangelists

The word missionary is derived from the Latin *missio*, which means "sending". It is not found in most English translations of the scriptures but other words have a similar meaning. In the New Testament we read about people who were sent long distances as pioneer missionaries. They are called "apostles". Others involved in mission are called "evangelists".

There is a difference between an apostle and an evangelist. The Greek word "apostle" has two elements: *apo* meaning "from", and *stellō* meaning "to send". So an apostle is a person "sent from" somewhere to somewhere else. He is sent on a mission.

The word "evangelist" also has two elements: *eu* meaning "good", and *angelos* meaning "messenger". So an evangelist is a "messenger of good", that is a person who brings good news.

The difference between an apostle and an evangelist is shown in the meaning of the two words. And we have people engaged in both these ministries today. We often call them missionaries.

The early apostles were sent to places far away, and their journeys occupied many months. They were commissioned by Jesus to make disciples in every nation, and it takes time to make a disciple. When Paul and Barnabas were sent out from Antioch they travelled far by land and sea, and were away for several years. They made disciples in many places, and the people they discipled established churches.

Apostles have many tasks to fulfil – proclaiming the gospel, answering objections, leading people to personal faith, teaching the scriptures, helping believers grow to maturity, caring for those in need, resolving problems, rebuking errors and hypocrisies, comforting the downhearted, encouraging the emergence of local leaders, and praying constantly for the believers near at hand and far away. They may also, like Paul, interact with officials and governments in order to secure freedom for the gospel and the churches. Some today might need to translate the Bible, make recordings, write tracts or produce videos. An apostle must have many skills and know how to meet many needs. Some may be involved in medical work, literacy, agriculture, or employment co-operatives. The aim of all this activity is to make disciples in far away places and to plant churches that will grow and flourish there.

An evangelist has a simpler task. He is someone who announces good news. He proclaims a welcome message. He can do this quite quickly. An evangelist is a sower of seed and a fisher of men. He does not generally start churches. He does not remain in one place as a shepherd caring for a flock. Philip, for example, was an evangelist. From Jerusalem he went down to Samaria and proclaimed Christ there; he spoke to an Ethiopian on a desert road; then he was found in Azotus (Acts 8). But he did not stay to establish a congregation in any of these places.

There is another difference between apostles and evangelists, and it concerns their financial support. An apostle may look for employment in places where he settles (as Paul did making tents), and he may receive hospitality or gifts from believers who value his work. An evangelist, on the other hand, does not generally travel so far and is not away for so long. He will usually have a home and a regular job, assisting in his local church and going out to proclaim the good news in his spare time.

Missionary Recruits

When writing his book of Acts, Luke naturally focused his attention on the missionary team to which he himself belonged. We may assume there were similar teams in other parts of the world. While Paul and his friends were heading west, others would be pioneering to the north, south and east, and probably achieving as much as he did, if not more.

Paul's team began with just three members, and grew quite slowly. Mark, indeed, went home at an early stage. On Paul's second trip he and Silas were joined by Timothy and Luke. To launch a mission in a new area has never required a complex organisation or a large number of people. Jesus sent his disciples two by two, and this is usually quite sufficient for mutual encouragement and prayer. In fact a larger number may overcrowd a place with strangers and reduce the effectiveness of their witness.

But the success of Paul's mission in Asia and Europe greatly increased the amount of work to be done. There was an urgency about it. New converts needed to be taught, leaders recognised, problems resolved and outreach to surrounding areas co-ordinated. As we have seen, Paul felt the burden of "the daily pressure on me of my anxiety for all the churches" (2 Cor 11:28).

But he did not send back to the well-established congregations of Antioch or Jerusalem for missionary reinforcements. He did not ask for additional Jewish evangelists or teachers from the older churches. Nor did he ask for volunteers from the newer churches. He made no appeals for missionary recruits or for their financial support. From among his own converts he simply invited suitable men to join him. And they would trust God to meet their needs in the same way that he met Paul's.

For training these men, we may be surprised to see the apostle using the same methods as Jesus. He was always in the company of a small group of disciples. They must be with him before he could send them out to preach. They heard him speaking in the synagogue. They watched him making tents to earn his keep. They went with him teaching from house to house. Early in his ministry we read of "his disciples", and wherever he won converts they became his disciples (Acts 9:25; 14:21; 20:1 etc.).

Living and working with them day by day, he would observe with interest the spiritual progress of each one. His men were known, tested, and approved before being sent on assignments requiring much patience, discernment and self-discipline. He did not give responsibility to new converts or to immature believers. With good reason he could write to his friends, "Timothy's proven worth you know" (Phil 2:22).

When he left Silas in Berea, or Titus in Crete, and when he sent Timothy to Thessalonica, or Erastus to Corinth, the young missionaries were not obliged to work out a new method or to wonder how they might apply missionary theories. They had seen the expert at work and they knew how he did it.

They had heard him explaining the scriptures, answering questions, discussing the gospel of Christ with Jews, Gentiles, young, old, rich, poor, educated and uneducated. They had seen him dealing with moral problems and religious controversies in the churches. They had walked long distances with him, prayed with him, slept in the same uncomfortable places and suffered the same threats and insults. They had learned from experience how to draw on the power of the Holy Spirit for the love, joy, peace and patience they would need, and how to have victory over personal temptation, frustration and discouragement.

The young missionaries had learned what it meant to be accountable to their Lord and to his people for godly behaviour and true teaching, "acceptable to God and approved by men" (Rom 14:18). Each of them knew how to serve "as one approved, a worker who has no need to be ashamed, rightly handling the word of truth" (2 Tim 2:15). As Paul practised exactly what he preached, he had taught them to follow his example. "Be imitators of me," he said, "as I am of Christ" (1 Cor 11:1). It was an example they could pass on along with his teaching, and which would influence an ever-widening circle. "What you have heard from me in the presence of many witnesses," he said, "entrust to faithful men who will be able to teach others also" (2 Tim 2:2).

This is how Paul recruited and trained workers for the harvest. He was particularly interested in the missionary potential of Gentile converts, who might become evangelists to their own people. We know the names of several but there were undoubtedly more. Titus, as we have seen, was Greek although we do not know his home town. Timothy was half Greek from Lystra in southern Galatia. Epaphras was from Colossae in the province of Asia, Sopater from Berea in Macedonia, Aristarchus and Secundus from Thessalonica in Macedonia. Gaius was from Derbe (or more likely from Douberus in Macedonia). Erastus was a Gentile but we do not know his place of origin. Tychicus and Trophimus were from Ephesus. Epaphroditus was a Macedonian from Philippi (Acts 19:29; 20:4; Phil 2:25).

It is interesting to see from their place of origin that these men all came from busy ports or cities on caravan routes. They would be familiar with travellers and probably well accustomed to travelling. People from foreign lands would not seem strange to them, and a long journey on foot or by sailing ship would not be a new experience. As they must travel far from home, we may assume they were young single men and free of family commitments. They were strong and fit, and able to endure hardship (2 Tim 2:3).

The men who worked with Paul could live quite cheaply. Walking from town to town, they would usually stay overnight with Christian families and so had minimal travel and accommodation expenses. To pay their way they might share in household chores or perhaps help with the family business for a few days or weeks.

If they decided to marry, this would signal a change of focus and ministry. They would then be likely to settle in one place and find employment to support a wife and children and elderly relatives (1 Tim 5:8). Here they would play a full part in their local fellowship and perhaps take shorter trips for ministry elsewhere. If they had been trained as apostles, they would certainly know how to be effective as evangelists.

It is likely that many of the elders and deacons in the churches were men who had been apostolic missionaries in their youth. They would understand and appreciate the work of gospel outreach and keenly support the next generation of missionaries. One such was Philip, who in his youth had preached extensively in Samaria, as we have seen, before following a desert road to meet an Ethiopian. Later he married and raised four daughters. His home in Caesarea became a place of Christian hospitality where travelling missionaries were warmly welcomed (Acts 21:8-9).

The Ministry of Women

The daughters of Philip were unusually perceptive and skilled in making known the word of God. But they were not the only women with a valued and highly effective spiritual ministry.

Paul had always been aware of the strong role played by women in the early Christian movement. In his young days as a persecuting Pharisee he had recognised the significant contribution of the women to the stability and the growth of the church. Most persecutors would assume that silencing the men would end the movement, but he arrested and imprisoned "both men and women". Three times this is emphasized by Paul himself and by Luke in the book of Acts (Acts 8:3; 9:2; 22:4).

Most of the apostles, apart from Paul and Barnabas, were married. On one occasion Paul asked, "Do we not have the right to take along a believing wife, as do the other apostles and the brothers of the Lord and Cephas [Peter]?" (1 Cor 9:5). Paul clearly expected the wife of an apostle to travel with him, and they would share the apostolic ministry. Wherever the couple might happen to be, she would naturally speak to the women, as he would speak to the men. In each local fellowship, the women would come to her with their problems, as the men came to her husband. Together the couple would discuss many matters relating to the outreach and the developing leadership of the churches, and pray with one heart and mind about it all.

If this is correct, it may seem strange that we do not find any women mentioned among Paul's missionary recruits in training or in service. We do not find him sending women to solve problems or appoint leaders or teach the word of God. There could be several reasons for this.

Firstly, he was aware of the serious physical dangers involved in apostolic ministry at this time. It would be hazardous for single ladies to travel long distances alone, or even in company. As a man he had suffered many hardships, and several times barely escaped with his life, but a woman would find it arduous in the extreme to walk hundreds of miles on rough roads, and might not easily survive stoning or shipwreck. She would be far more vulnerable than a man to robbery, assault or abduction. Pioneer mission was extremely tough and Paul would not ask a women to face such physical dangers.

Secondly, knowing the culture of both the synagogue and the pagan world, Paul could appreciate the enormous difficulty a Christian woman would face in trying to influence a company of traditional Jewish elders or to subdue a clique of arrogant super-apostles such as those in Corinth.

Thirdly, as an unmarried man with many enemies he would be concerned to avoid all opportunity for scandal and wicked accusation. His position, and that of the young men with him, would become extremely weak if they were seen in the company of young single women. A missionary may be entirely pure in heart and mind, but the worldly people around him will delight to think the worst of him.

Despite these obvious difficulties, it is clear that women played a highly significant part in the mission of the early church. A number are mentioned by name in the New Testament, and especially in Paul's letters.

The majority of these were probably single ladies, widowed perhaps at a relatively young age, as were many women at that time. First among them is Lydia, whose importance we have already noted. Chloe and "her people" are also mentioned (1 Cor 1:11). A warm commendation is given to Euodia and Syntyche as Paul recalls how they have "laboured side by side with me in the gospel" (Phil 4:2-3). Tryphaena and Tryphosa are "working hard for the Lord" (Rom 16:12). Persis and Mary are women especially praised for their hard work and for many things they have done (Rom 16:6, 12). There were no doubt others whose names we do not know. They all appear to be serving Christ in the context of a local fellowship.

Among them Phoebe deserves a special mention. She was a Gentile whose name is associated with the goddess Artemis. When Paul writes of her she is on her way to Rome from the port of Cenchreae near Corinth. He says, "I commend to you our sister Phoebe, a servant of the church at Cenchreae, that you may welcome her in the Lord in a way worthy of the saints, and help her in whatever she may need from you, for she has been a patroness of many and of myself as well" (Rom 16:1-2).

As a "patroness", Phoebe must have been a wealthy lady, respected in the wider community and known for her interest in the welfare of others. Her home in Cenchreae would be a place of fellowship for the believers there, and of hospitality to missionaries on their way to and from Corinth. She had helped Paul himself and was probably carrying his letter to Rome, for which she deserves our thanks. On such a journey, she would certainly have an escort of several trusted servants, and perhaps a male relative, a son or a brother, to deal with unpleasant dock officials and sea captains.

Phoebe had made herself extremely useful as a "patroness". But what else might a Christian woman do in the service of her Lord? In a world where the majority of people were suffering poverty, illness or abuse, a woman would have countless opportunities to help where help was desperately needed. She would then naturally explain how she had learned this happy way of life from Jesus who had done so much for her. In the synagogue, of course, she would meet with many ladies in need of the gospel, and many children too, and by inviting them home or offering some practical service would find opportunities to share her faith.

While the men were at work all day in the markets or fields, or travelling with consignments of goods to foreign parts, the upkeep and management of a Christian home would be the responsibility of the wives, mothers and unmarried daughters who lived there.

Larger households would have many visitors and perhaps a regular meeting for fellowship, and the lady of the house would be responsible for the well-being of everyone who came under her roof. She would have travellers, beggars, friends and relatives to look after, and servants to train and supervise. All these would know she was a follower of Jesus and would learn from her what that meant. New converts with all manner of problems would appear on her doorstep, and she would find ways to care for them, to meet their most urgent needs and explain to them whatever they needed to know.

Female servants and other women associated with the household would be busy indoors, as were their husbands outdoors, and might sing softly about their Saviour as they went about their tasks. They might offer a word of testimony on occasion and perhaps pause to pray with any who needed prayer. Whatever her station in life a woman would have many natural opportunities to help others and to share the gospel as she did so. Her ministry would be unending.

With the blessing of a stable marriage, Christian women would normally have more children than their pagan neighbours, and would raise their boys and girls with much more thought and care. Within a generation or two, the Christian community became well-known for its willingness to raise daughters (when pagans destroyed many baby girls at birth) and to nurse the sick (when pagans quickly abandoned them to their fate).[1] The positive relationships and quality of life that so attracted outsiders to them should be credited especially to the women who had the vision, the self-discipline and the compassionate love to forge a new way of living for their families, and to make unhappy strangers welcome in their midst.

We have seen the importance of homes and households in the life and mission of the early church. In reality, there was nowhere else for believers to meet and nowhere else for missionaries to stay overnight on their long journeys. In most cases the public inns were little more than brothels, offering obscene entertainments and drunken revelry,

---

1. Stark, 83, 97

where a man was very likely to be set upon and robbed. Public houses would be avoided, in any case, by a Jew travelling in Gentile territory, for every utensil and furnishing would be ritually unclean. Indeed, there was a long tradition of hospitality for Jewish travellers in Jewish homes and synagogues; no one would expect a Jewish believer to seek shelter in an inn.

For these many reasons hospitality was a virtue required of every Christian. Any summary of basic teaching would include a line such as "Show hospitality to one another without grumbling" or "Contribute to the needs of the saints and seek to show hospitality" or "Do not neglect to show hospitality to strangers" (1 Pet 4:9; Rom 12:13; Heb 13:2). Indeed it was a requirement for an elder to be hospitable (1 Tim 3:2). When Paul planned a visit to Colossae, he expected Philemon to prepare a guest room for him (Philem 22).

In the event it was probably Philemon's wife Apphia who prepared the room, and who effectively ran the household while her husband was engaged in business elsewhere. Paul knew the value of such women. In his mind a godly widow would be one who had "shown hospitality" (1 Tim 5:10). And he sent special greetings to the mother of Rufus, "who has been a mother to me as well" (Rom 16:13).

We have spoken several times of Priscilla and her husband, and the good use she made of her home. We have thought of Lydia's household in Philippi. We have seen how the earliest Jerusalem congregation met in the house of Mary the mother of Mark. In Christian history the importance of the women who opened their homes for Christian fellowship can hardly be overestimated. Without the faithful dedication of these women to the cause of the gospel, the Christian communities could not have survived.

Missionary Leadership

When Barnabas and Paul launched their first mission from Antioch, they were sent out by the Holy Spirit and the church (Acts 13:1-4). But once they had left the church, it was the Spirit alone who would guide them and provide for them. There was no mission committee or council to direct them, no contract signed, no promise of continuous financial support, no demand for accountability.

The freedom to follow his Lord's personal leading was precious to Paul. It was something he would not relinquish for any man or group of men. He identified himself as "Paul, an apostle – not from men nor through man, but through Jesus Christ and God the Father" (Gal 1:1). Like him, the missionaries he trained were dependent on God, and they established churches dependent on God.

We must not conclude, however, that any of them acted independently. There are no independent missionaries in the New Testament, and no independent churches. Every missionary is part of the body of Christ, and so is every church. Jesus Christ has only one body, and no part of that body can say to another part, "I do not need you" (1 Cor 12:21).

Like other Christians, missionaries have diversity of character and calling. "There are various types of gift . . . various forms of service . . . various ways of working, but it is the same God who works everything for everyone" (1 Cor 12:4-6). When several are working together, each will contribute what he or she can do best. Luke, for example, will have a different role from Silas or Timothy. Priscilla's contribution will differ from that of Phoebe or Lydia. But no part of a body can work effectively on its own.

Although New Testament mission was never controlled by a society or a superintendent, it was not without leadership. Wherever he happened to be, Paul received news of the churches as travellers came and went, and his many years of experience enabled him to respond wisely to each new circumstance. If a problem arose he would send someone to deal with it. If a door opened he would find someone to enter it. In this way the needs of all the churches were properly met and the work of outreach to new areas efficiently planned.

Paul had a distinct style of leadership. He thought of himself not as a director or president but as a father. Indeed he was a spiritual father to the churches and also to the young missionaries who went to help them – they were all his spiritual children. To the Corinthians he wrote, "I became your *father* in Christ Jesus through the gospel," but also "I sent you Timothy, my beloved and faithful *child* in the Lord" (1 Cor 4:15, 17). All would give Paul the honour and respect due to a good father. If they failed to do so, it would be to their shame.

When Paul's fellow-workers were sent on their various assignments, he never required them to do anything against their will but always sought their cheerful agreement. Telling the Corinthians how he had encouraged Titus to visit them, he said,

"Thanks be to God, who put into the heart of Titus the same earnest care I have for you. For he not only accepted our appeal, but being himself very earnest he is going to you of his own accord" (2 Cor 8:6, 16-17). A little earlier the apostle had strongly urged Apollos to visit the same fellowship, "but it was not at all his will to come now. He will come when he has opportunity" (1 Cor 16:12).

It is clear that Paul's leadership relied on personal encouragement, patience and prayer rather than authority or command. Affection and confidence are evident in many of his references to his fellow-workers, and each of these men had found him worthy of their utmost respect.

In his team, missionaries of varied races worked together, demonstrating the truth that "here there is no distinction between Greek and Jew, circumcised and uncircumcised, barbarian, Scythian, slave and free: but Christ is all and in all" (Col 3:11). Though often separated for long periods with inadequate means of communication, their commitment to one another and to their common purpose did not waver.

This loyalty and affection was a fruit of the Holy Spirit. It came through respect well earned and service willingly given, for they were not compelled to co-operate by the rules of a mission society or church denomination. They were all dedicated to serving Christ. They had the spiritual maturity and consistent character to do so in difficult circumstances for long periods of time.

Missionaries and Churches

Paul was not in the least possessive. He never attempted to start a denomination of his own or to create a network of churches separate from other churches. He did not launch his own missionary society or require his team to work with him alone and no one else. In his letters he took pains to emphasize that he was appointed by Christ as a servant to the *whole* Church and as an apostle to *all* the Gentiles (Col 1:24-25; Rom 15:16). He was not a minister or a member of a particular congregation or collection of congregations. He was a member of the universal body of Christ, a servant to all his people everywhere and an evangelist to any who had never heard the gospel (Tit 1:1; Rom 1:14).

There never was a "Church of Paul". When he visited a synagogue or a house he spoke of Christ and won his hearers to Christ. "For what we proclaim," he said, "is not ourselves but Jesus Christ as Lord, with ourselves as your servants for Jesus' sake" (2 Cor 4:5). To his mind the church was "God's field, God's building" (1 Cor 3:9). For this reason he expected his converts to mix freely with the converts of other missionaries. He and Apollos and Peter and many others were working together for one spiritual harvest, for one spiritual household. They were not in competition (1 Cor 1:10-15).

If false teaching was found in a local fellowship, Paul would oppose and correct the teaching (Gal 2:11-12). If a false teacher proved stubborn and divisive, the believers were counselled to avoid him (Rom 16:17; Tit 3:10). But Paul's great concern was to prevent and heal divisions rather than to cause them (1 Cor 1:10; 12:25). The same was true of the missionaries he had trained. They were ambassadors of Christ, servants of all the churches and heralds to the world (1 Tim 1:3-4; 2 Tim 2:24-26).

Paul and his team did not present themselves as representatives of a foreign organisation, appointed and financed by people far away. Wherever they went, they simply belonged to the church in that place. In fact their relationship with converts won in a new area was probably much closer than their relationship with the churches where they were originally converted or baptized or had served in past years. This profoundly influenced their own outlook and that of their converts. The gospel drew people together wherever it was proclaimed because those who received it would immediately join the company of those who brought it to them. They formed a new congregation in which there were no distinctions of race or origin and no other organisational commitments to separate one believer from another.

Whenever Paul wished to communicate with a fellowship, he did not write to its leaders but to all the believers in that place. He was not establishing hierarchies of authority and control but encouraging all to take spiritual responsibility. The relationship between missionaries and churches was based on love and mutual respect. Neither had any authority over the other to compel conformity or obedience. Paul depended entirely on persuasion and prayer to win over anyone inclined to differ from him. By addressing the entire fellowship he would hope for a consensus to see the wisdom of what he said, so that any individual inclined to take a different view would be held in check by the members of his own congregation.

It was common for a believer, when he travelled, to carry a letter of approval from a person who would be known and respected in the place he was going to. The letter would be signed and probably sealed to prevent forgery (2 Thess 3:17). This was necessary because false teachers frequently sought to introduce strange ideas and practices into the churches, and in some cases could be hard to identify (Acts 20:28-30; 2 Cor 11:12-14; Rev 2:2).

Missionaries would carry such letters so that local leaders could introduce them immediately to the fellowship without needing to test the soundness of their character and doctrine. When Apollos went to Corinth, he took with him a letter from Aquila and Priscilla who were well-known to the fellowship there (Acts 18:27). When Phoebe went to Rome, Paul himself sent a letter of commendation with her (Rom 16:1). When the churches of Macedonia and Achaia sent men with gifts to Jerusalem, Paul offered to write a letter for each of them (1 Cor 16:3). Whenever Timothy or Titus visited a congregation, they would be placed in a strong position by showing the letter they carried from Paul referring to them as his fellow-workers, to be received as he himself would be received (1 Cor 16:10).

When Paul sent missionaries to visit local fellowships, their purpose was not to take over the leadership but to support the local leaders and help them resolve any problems that may have arisen. There would be a free exchange of ideas, just as Paul himself had discussed matters of mutual concern with the leaders in Jerusalem and Antioch in order to reach agreement about the best course of action.

The visitor would be especially concerned to identify faithful men capable of teaching others, and then provide such men with the information and stimulus to do so effectively (2 Tim 2:2). If the believers were suffering persecution, he would encourage them to stand firm in the faith (1 Thess 3:2-3). If they were inclined towards false teaching, he would remind them of truths they already knew (1 Cor 4:17; 1 Tim 1:3-4). If they had not yet appointed leaders, he would help them to do so (Tit 1:5). If they were failing to support their leaders, he would ensure they did so (1 Tim 5:17; Heb 13:17). If a local leader was suspected of misconduct, he would investigate the matter carefully. In such circumstances Paul advised, "Do not admit a charge against an elder except on the evidence of two or three witnesses. As for those who persist in sin, rebuke them in the presence of all, so that the rest may stand in fear" (1 Tim 5:19-20).

Financial Support

Free of charge

Missionaries, like other people, need to eat, and to sleep safely at night, and often to pay for transport as they travel. How then did Paul and his team finance their mission?

We have seen how the apostle supported himself for a period in Corinth and in Ephesus. He did the same in Thessalonica and later wrote to his friends there, "You remember, brothers, our labour and toil: we worked night and day, that we might not be a burden to any of you, while we proclaimed to you the gospel of God" (1 Thess 2:9).

Financial independence was for Paul a matter of principle, as he tells us, "that in my preaching I may present the gospel free of charge" (1 Cor 9:18). He refused absolutely to accept money from anyone to whom he was ministering, "for we are not, like so many, peddlers of God's word, but as men of sincerity, as commissioned by God, in the sight of God we speak in Christ" (2 Cor 2:17). He did not want anyone to think he was only preaching for the sake of money. He did not want anyone to miss out on the message because they could not afford to pay for it. He did not want anyone to feel burdened financially by his presence. He did not want anyone to gain control over him. So he insisted, "I coveted no one's silver or gold or clothing" (Acts 20:33).

In normal circumstances a Jewish rabbi would live by his craft or trade, and Paul would naturally comply with this cultural expectation among the Jews. With Gentiles too, his occupation gave him credibility; they would hardly respect an idle and impoverished rabbi dependent on their charity.

His work supported not just himself but also his team, and anything left over would go to friends who were ill or elderly or otherwise in need. So he said, "You yourselves know that these hands have supplied my own needs and the needs of my companions. In all things I have shown you that by working hard in this way we must help the weak, remembering the words of the Lord Jesus, how he said, 'It is more blessed to give than to receive'" (Acts 20:34-35).

In all this he was concerned to set a good example, perhaps aware that some believers were inclined to laziness or slackness in their work: "For you yourselves know how you ought to imitate us, because we were not idle when we were with you, nor did we eat anyone's bread without paying for it, but with toil and labour we worked night and day, that we might not be a burden to any of you." (2 Thess 3:7-8). This was not merely an ideal for some; it was a requirement for all. Indeed, he said, "If anyone is not willing to work, let him not eat" (2 Thess 3:10).

Some might think that as a qualified teacher Paul had the right to expect payment for his teaching. "Nevertheless," he insisted, "we have not made use of this right" (1 Cor 9:12). Some might argue from the Law of Moses that "you shall not muzzle an ox when it treads out the grain." Others might contend that Jesus sent out his disciples with no bread or money, and some might even recall that "the Lord commanded that those who proclaim the gospel should get their living by the gospel." But Paul insisted, "I have made no use of any of these rights, nor am I writing these things to secure any such provision" (1 Cor 9:9, 14-15). On the contrary, "We endure anything rather than put an obstacle in the way of the gospel of Christ" (1 Cor 9:12).

At times the apostle was definitely "in need" (Phil 4:11-12). Even when working for his living, his income was barely sufficient. In Corinth, for example, "When I was with you and was in need, I did not burden anyone" (2 Cor 11:9). At such moments it would be possible to ask for money but he refused to do so.

Paul's fellow-workers always followed the same principle. So he challenged the Corinthians, "Did I take advantage of you through any of those whom I sent to you? . . . Did Titus take advantage of you?" (2 Cor 12:17-18). They must acknowledge that Titus had asked them for nothing. The young missionaries working with Paul took care, as he did, to avoid giving any impression that they wanted money or that their dependence was on people rather than on their Lord.

Helping them on their way

In such circumstances we might wonder how these men obtained the necessities of life. How did they survive? For months or years they would be away from home, so who would provide for them?

It is clear that Paul and his co-workers had no promise or pledge of support from anyone. The fellowship in Syrian Antioch, from where he started, never sent him a regular sum. Nor, as we shall see, did any other congregation.

Even if his friends in Antioch had thought of sending him money, there would be no simple means of delivering it. A bag of coins might be carried over land and sea by a reliable man, if he would guard it with his life, and if he knew where to find the person he should take it to. Paul himself was once accompanied by such couriers bearing gifts from the Gentile churches to Jerusalem. But that was a unique occasion; it was not normal. How then would a pioneer missionary obtain his support?

We have observed the warmth of hospitality in Christian homes. Before the missionaries travelled, they would simply ask if believers were known in the next town along the road. If so, they could be sure of a warm welcome after a long day's walk. Introducing themselves to the household with letters of approval from church leaders or from Paul himself, they would join the family for their evening meal and stay overnight.

If possible, they would repay the kindness of their host by helping the family in any way they could. Some might know how to make or mend household items; others might work a few hours in the family business. Their knowledge of the world and its languages might assist the children's education. Some, like Luke the physician, might have skills that were urgently needed and greatly appreciated.

In the evening, friends and neighbours would come in, and the visitors would teach the word of God to the assembled company. If their stay lasted more than a night or two, they would get to know each member of the household, including the servants and employees, and find opportunity to advise, encourage and pray with them all. In such close and intimate circumstances they would be a blessing to many.

Although the missionaries would accept no payment from those to whom they ministered, the time would soon come for them to move on. Perhaps some members of the household had come to faith through their witness; others had learned things of value from their teaching. As they set off for distant provinces, it would be natural for their friends to express appreciation, and so help them on their way. Luke recalled how this happened in Malta: "They also honoured us greatly, and when we were about to sail, they put on board whatever we needed" (Acts 28:10).

When writing to the churches about his co-workers, Paul encouraged such support for missionaries preparing to travel on to other places. He wrote to the Corinthians, when Timothy was about to leave them, "Help him on his way in peace, that he may return to me" (1 Cor 16:11). To Titus in Crete he said, "Do your best to speed Zenas the lawyer and Apollos on their way; see that they lack nothing" (Tit 3:13).

In fact Paul had come to expect that pioneer missionaries would be sent out with sufficient for their immediate needs. To Rome he wrote, "I hope to see you in passing as I go to Spain, and to be helped on my journey there by you, once I have enjoyed your company for a while" (Rom 15:24). Such gifts were not payment for blessings received but a helping hand for the missionary to take the same blessings to others far away.

This was the experience of the other apostles too. John, for example, wrote to a friend about some strangers travelling to further provinces: "You will do well to send them on their journey in a manner worthy of God. For they have gone out for the sake of the Name, accepting nothing from the Gentiles. Therefore we ought to support people like these, that we may be fellow workers for the truth" (3 Jn 6-8). Here again we note that these missionaries would accept nothing from the people to whom they were ministering. But as they set out on their journey, Christian friends would make sure they lacked for nothing.

In none of these cases, however, do we read of any promise or commitment to continue sending money to the missionaries after they had gone. How then would they be supported during the latter stages of their journey and once they reached their destination? How would they survive among people who were not believers and would not be keen to welcome them?

A generous church

We have seen that Paul earned his living in some places, enjoyed hospitality in others, and was sent on his way elsewhere with supplies for the journey. Apart from this, so far as we know, he was supported entirely by gifts sent to him by one group of people. This was the fellowship in Philippi, in the province of Macedonia. Now, what was special about this fellowship?

We know of one Christian in Philippi who undoubtedly had

access to financial resources. The book of Acts mentions very few of Paul's converts by name, but Lydia was one of them, and therefore a person of particular significance. She is carefully described as "a seller of purple cloth", and this was a costly high-status commodity. She must have had links with markets and tradesmen in many places – with people, in other words, who were accustomed to sending and receiving money safely and efficiently. It seems likely that the mission to the Gentiles owes far more to this one woman than has been generally appreciated.

The Philippian gifts may have been from Lydia herself, or from others influenced by her, or most likely both. They sent support to Paul several times in Thessalonica and in Corinth, and again when he was in prison at Rome (2 Cor 11:9; Phil 4:14-18). But no other church did so. Indeed he wrote to them, "You Philippians yourselves know that in the beginning of the gospel, when I left Macedonia, no church entered into partnership with me in giving and receiving, except you only" (Phil 4:15).

But why were these gifts sent? They were sent not for the benefit of Paul but for the benefit of people waiting to hear what Paul could tell them. They were sent so he could put down his needle and thread and go out to proclaim the good news. For this reason, the generosity of the Philippians was called "fellowship [or partnership] in the gospel" (Phil 1:5).

Nevertheless, it is clear that the Philippians and other Macedonian Christians were not excessively wealthy. At times indeed they suffered "extreme poverty" (2 Cor 8:1-2). And we should note that they were not providing for one of their own kind or for the son of a local family. In helping Paul, these inhabitants of a Roman city in Macedonia were supporting a Cilician Jew, educated in Jerusalem, from a congregation in Syria, and labouring in Greece and Italy. It was a truly international vision.

Paul's chief pleasure in receiving support from Philippi was the proof it furnished of their spiritual growth, demonstrated in their desire to give. And when he sent thanks to them, he was careful to avoid implying he would like more. "Not that I seek the gift," he said. "I am well supplied" (Phil 4:17-18).

How was he well supplied? Staying in a place for a period of months, he would work with his hands. Travelling on, he would receive supplies for the journey. Entering a Christian home, he

149

would enjoy hospitality. From his own experience he could assure his friends, "My God shall supply all your need according to his riches in glory in Christ Jesus" (Phil 4:19).

In one way or another his Lord would provide for him. It was a hand-to-mouth existence, and as Paul might say, from God's hand to his mouth. It forced him to live by faith, in direct dependence on One who answers prayer. "We are always of good courage," he declared, "for we walk by faith, not by sight . . . We make it our aim to please him" (2 Cor 5:7-9).

Paul must have heard what Jesus said about God's provision for such a person: "Anyone who has left home or brothers or sisters or mother or father or children or lands, for my sake and for the gospel, will receive far more in this present time – a hundred times more houses and brothers and sisters and mothers and children and lands – with persecutions too, and in the age to come eternal life" (Mk 10:29-30). That was exactly his experience. Wherever he went he gained brothers and sisters who believed his message and welcomed him into their family. There is probably no one in human history who has been made more welcome in more homes than the apostle Paul.

Having looked at many aspects of Paul's missionary career, we are now in a position to summarize his basic strategy:

1. He identified a clear and simple message to proclaim.
2. He trained missionaries through practical experience.
3. He looked for strategic places where people would give him a hearing.
4. He lived by faith without financial obligation to anyone.
5. He proclaimed his message in public places.
6. He taught his converts thoroughly in private homes.
7. He let local leadership develop naturally in each local fellowship.

The question that now concerns us is whether we might follow the same strategy today. Some people would suggest that the New Testament provides us with a practical manual of mission methods. Others would reply that the New Testament only describes how mission was done a long time ago and offers very little help or guidance for mission in the modern world.

13

The Value of Old and New

Understanding Jewish Scripture

It is not easy for us to understand the Bible as the early Christians did. Many people do not read it in the way its writers intended. The reason is that the writers and most of their early readers were Jewish, or strongly influenced by the culture of the Jews. They had a particular way of writing and reading scripture.

Jewish people have always lived in the light of great events from the past. Judaism as a religion arose from Yahweh's dealings with mankind in history, and a large part of Jewish religion consists of re-enacting those events, remembering what Yahweh has done.

In Jewish theology, truths are revealed through incidents. A defining experience is given by God on one occasion so that all generations may learn from it and act in the light of it. An event such as the Passover, or the crossing of the Red Sea, or the gift of manna, or the fall of Jericho, or the exile in Babylon, or the marriage of Hosea, or the testing of Job will have ongoing significance for every subsequent generation.

As a well-known rabbi explains, "Things did not merely *happen* to the ancient Israelites. Events were shaped, reformed, and interpreted by them, made into the raw materials for a renewal of the life of the group. The reason is that the ancient Israelites regarded their history as important and significant, as teaching lessons."[1]

Because of this, "Great events called forth, and continue to call forth, a singular two-part response among Jews: first, to provide a

---

1. Rabbi Jacob Neusner, *Time and Eternity* (Encino, Dickenson, 1975), 16

written record of those events; second, to reflect in a religious spirit on their meaning."[1] For this reason, "Loyalty to the norms and thoughts conveyed in the event is as essential as the reality of the event."[2]

So the Israelites were taught to remember. The Hebrew verb *zākar* (remember) occurs more than two hundred times in the Old Testament. The Jewish faith was built upon the memory of Yahweh's dealings with his people. It grew as a response to significant events, and each event in their history added a facet to their communal faith. Yahweh told them to remember how he had rested on the seventh day, how they were once slaves, how they were led through the wilderness, how they rebelled against him, how they crossed the Jordan, what happened to Pharaoh and to all Egypt, what happened to Miriam, what was revealed to Moses, what Balak did and what Balaam did. Each of these events was a defining moment that revealed an essential truth. As the moment is remembered and celebrated, the truth is reinforced and taught, and so it continues to influence subsequent generations. In short then, we might say that each event sets a precedent and so establishes a principle.

The apostle Paul was, of course, a Jewish rabbi trained in the exposition of scripture. He taught his disciples the significance of Old Testament events – and not only his Jewish converts but also the Gentiles who met with them. So he wrote to the Corinthians about the Israelites in the wilderness: "These things took place as examples *for us* . . . They were written down for *our* instruction, on whom the end of the ages has come" (1 Cor 10:6, 11). To the believers in Rome he wrote about Abraham: "The words 'it was counted to him' were not written for his sake alone, *but for ours also*" (Rom 4:23-24). Indeed, Paul affirmed, "Whatever was written in former days was written for *our* instruction, that through endurance and through the encouragement of the Scriptures *we* might have hope" (Rom 15:4). The dealings of Yahweh with his ancient people were of significance to generations far distant in space and time and culture, because each incident revealed something about the character and the will of the Lord.

But significant events did not cease with the closure of the Old

---

1. Rabbi Jacob Neusner, *The Way of the Torah: An Introduction to Judaism* (2nd edn., Encino, Dickenson, 1974), 3
2. Rabbi Abraham Joshua Heschel, *God in Search of Man* (Farrar, Strauss and Giroux, 1955), 217

Testament. The earliest Christians were also Israelites. Things did not merely happen to them; all that happened was significant. Indeed, the Gospel writers were recording the "foundation events" of a new covenant far surpassing the old in grace and glory. To Jewish disciples, every experience in the ministry of Jesus and in the early church would be profoundly meaningful. Everything that happened would reveal something of the mind and will of the Lord.

So we are shown some highly significant events in the earthly life of Jesus. He was born in one particular town, he grew up in another, he came out of Egypt, he went through the waters, he was tempted in the wilderness, he rode a donkey to Jerusalem, he cleaned out the temple, he stilled a storm and he fed a multitude, he gave sight to Bartimaeus and life to Lazarus. His Jewish followers did not fail to observe that the fig tree was withered from the roots up and the temple veil torn from the top down. There was a meaning to be understood in all these things.

Every day the disciples were watching carefully. Peter learned something as he walked on the water and then sank; he learned something more as he hauled in a miraculous catch of fish; he learned something else when the Master stooped to wash his disciples' feet. Each of these was a unique event, but each has a universal implication as a revelation of God. That is why sermons are still preached about these incidents, drawing out applications of relevance to congregations in every age and every culture.

Sometimes the meaning of an event escaped the disciples' notice, and so Jesus asked them, "Do you not remember the five loaves for the five thousand, and how many baskets you gathered?" (Matt 16:9). There was a significance in the number of baskets, a significance they had missed.

Like the disciples, we are required to remember these things. At least sixty times in the New Testament we find reference to remembering. Jesus advises his hearers to remember Lot's wife (Lk 17:32). He says every generation will remember the woman who broke a flask for him (Mk 14:9). Taking bread and wine he bids them, "Do this in remembrance of me" (Lk 22:19) There was significance in Lot's wife, in the woman's gift and in the loaf and the cup that remained long after the event.

Then the book of Acts shows us significant moments in the life of the early church. Tongues of fire at Pentecost, Peter's vision of animals in a sheet, signs confirming the gift of the Spirit to the Samaritans and Romans, the death of Ananias and Sapphira, the conversion of Saul. Each of these incidents was unique, but each has touched generations far distant in time and place. We may all identify with those biblical characters at their point of need or failure, their personal faith or sin, and the consequences that follow for time and eternity.

As we read the Gospels, Acts and Letters, we should be aware that these are Jewish writings about Jewish people. The writers were all steeped in Jewish culture, including Luke as we have seen. Their Jewish readers would understand the practical implications of what they wrote – the principles established by the precedents.

When Mark recalls that Jesus sent his disciples two by two, he expects us to notice and learn from this, as did Barnabas who asked Paul to join him, and Paul himself inviting Silas. When Matthew describes how Jesus trained his disciples by living and working with them, he expects us to appreciate the value of this method. When Luke records how the early Christians devoted themselves to teaching, fellowship, breaking of bread and prayer, he expects us to admire this prototype of all church life. When we see how many of the early converts responded to the gospel far from home, we may identify this as a key to effective mission. When we find Paul addressing people who had already crossed culture and would give him a ready hearing, we may suppose this a wise plan to adopt. As the earliest churches had free participation in open meetings, we may see good reason to do likewise. When we observe how they proclaimed the gospel in public places and met for fellowship in private homes, we may decide to follow their example. As they were led by unpaid local men, we may see wisdom in this form of leadership. As their missionaries lived by faith without asking for money, we may resolve to do the same.

In their Passover liturgy, Jewish communities recite the *Haggadah*, declaring, "It was not only our ancestors whom God redeemed from Egypt . . . It was us." The text states, "In every generation each one should feel as if he or she personally came out of Egypt."[1] With this

---

1. "A Passover Haggadah" at http://bparnes.com/haggadah/seder.pdf (accessed 13 June 2012). See also Rabbi Jill Jacobs, "I Was Redeemed From Egypt: Re-enacting the Exodus in every generation" at www.myjewishlearning.com (accessed 23 April 2012).

cultural heritage a Christian might similarly affirm, "It was not only our ancestors who were baptized with the Holy Spirit at Pentecost . . . It was us!" Or if we are Gentiles, "It was not only Cornelius and his household who were grafted into the spiritual olive tree of Israel at Caesarea . . . It was us!" For we are the spiritual descendants and heirs of those who were present then.

A modern rabbi has said, "Every Jew must imagine him or herself, at every moment, always, as if he or she were standing at Sinai to receive the Torah."[1] In the same way a Christian might imagine himself or herself seated among the disciples at the Last Supper, or standing on the Mount of Olives as Jesus ascends to the Father, or setting out with Paul and Barnabas on their mission from Antioch. We are part of what happened then. And for this reason each of us may read a letter from one of the apostles as a personal message of comfort or advice.

The early readers of the New Testament would not view it simply as a historical record of what people had once done, or even what God had led them to do. It was a revelation of *what God wanted done*, and as such it was timeless. The apostles saw "the mighty works of God", observing how "the hand of the Lord was with them," describing "all that God had done through them" (Acts 2:11; 11:21; 15:4). The churches would remember the events of those days and live in the context of those days all their lives.

Some missionaries, for this reason, will seek to follow the methods of Jesus and his apostles as closely as possible. Others, however, will point out that we work in cultures quite different from theirs, with the benefit of technologies unknown to them. This, of course, raises a further question: Are we not free to adopt more modern and efficient methods, better suited to our own time and place?

Technologies and Strategies

Helpful technologies

We have looked at the mission strategies of Christ, and of Paul and the other apostles, and we have seen how successful they were. But we may not be convinced that their methods will work so well today.

---

1. Rabbi Ronald Aigen, *Wellsprings of Freedom: The Renew Our Days Haggadah* (Congregation Dorshei Emet, Quebec, Canada).

Times have changed and the world moves on. So we may wonder: Why should we go back to methods that are two thousand years out of date?

Granted that we have the same gospel message to proclaim, it may not be sensible or even possible to follow the same strategies in proclaiming it. If we go to a synagogue and preach about Jesus today, we will not receive the same response as Paul did. If we wait for people to enter our culture before telling them the good news, we may wait a long time. If we try to re-create the churches of first century Judea or Macedonia in the modern cities of the developing world, or in the arid stretches of the desert waste, we might find we are deluding ourselves with an impossible romantic dream. Surely we will condemn ourselves to failure. We will become old-fashioned, irrelevant and ineffective in a world that demands novelty, style, progress and sophisticated presentation.

Jesus and his early followers had no access to technologies now familiar to us. They had no printed books, electronic keyboards, public address systems . . . no video projectors, radio, television, compact discs or DVDs . . . no telephones, no internet, no cars or planes or other means of rapid transport. They did not have an effective range of medicines for healing or preventing disease. They had no access to money for the purchase of land or investment in agricultural, industrial, social or medical projects. Should we conclude that Jesus, Paul and the early churches would have shunned and refused these benefits if they had been available? And would we be wrong to make use of them simply because they did not have them? For most people the answer is clear. Technological progress and material resources are a gift from God and we should make full use of them.

Does that mean we can learn nothing of value from the New Testament about mission strategies? Do the Jewish scriptures provide no help or guidance for gospel outreach in a modern world preoccupied with the latest news and all that money can buy?

Then even if we do see value in the methods of Jesus and his apostles, how can we possibly apply them in a day when most mission societies are using different methods – methods that their churches and denominations have been developing for a hundred years or more? These are serious questions and must be answered carefully.

Firstly, we should remember that the earliest Christians pioneered at least one major technological innovation. For hundreds of years the Jewish scriptures had been written on long scrolls rolled around handles, which were extremely cumbersome. But almost from the start, the followers of Jesus copied their Gospels and Letters on to pages of paper or skin and then sewed the pages together inside wooden covers. A book of this nature had several advantages. It was compact and durable and would survive rough usage on long journeys. The pages could be written on both sides, and additional pages could easily be inserted. Above all, a book with pages made it easy for the reader to locate a particular passage or to compare several passages in different parts of the book. At a later date the invention of the printing press made it possible for people all over the world to read the word of God in their own language.

Technology has always assisted us in our task, and we can be thankful for it. We should learn to make good use of it. Of course, the world will use technology to make money, and Satan will use technology to corrupt morals and distract people from the truth, but we may also find the Holy Spirit using technology to reach large numbers of people with the gospel more quickly than in past times. Computers assist us in the work of Bible translation. The internet enables seekers to find what they are looking for. Audio recordings take God's word to people whose language we do not know. Videos can lead families and villages to faith in Christ.

But in addition to technology we need wisdom. This is where Jesus and the apostles can help us. Human needs and human nature change very little from age to age, and the gospel does not change at all. In most cases the people we meet have the same problems as the people Jesus met. That is why we can so easily preach the gospel from the Gospels, reading about an incident in the life of our Lord and identifying the truths and principles revealed there. What is more, the human issues we face in mission are often the same as those faced by the apostles – loneliness, guilt, fear, greed, ambition, prejudice, mistrust of foreigners, love of power or money. That is why their writings are so helpful to us.

From the New Testament accounts we have seen how Jesus trained his disciples for world mission, responding to the culture of his day and introducing a new culture of his own. We noticed how the gospel was proclaimed by the apostles in public places and how its first converts had crossed from one culture to another before they heard it. We saw how Paul identified environments where the good news might be heard willingly, and from there taken into the wider world. We have looked at his message, his guidance, his character, credibility and leadership. We have seen how he chose and trained co-workers and how their work was financed. We observed how the earliest believers were drawn together, visiting one another, caring for one another, meeting informally in their homes for teaching, fellowship, breaking of bread and prayer. We saw how the Holy Spirit gave to each of them some particular ability or insight or ministry for the common good as they met together day by day. We observed how leadership developed naturally within each group as gifted people gained knowledge and experience, and learned how to help others.

All these things can be done in places that lack technology. They can also be done in places with highly advanced technologies.

Technology is a tool that we may be glad to use if we have it. It is often very expensive. It may serve us, but it should never control us. We should not suppose it is essential or even particularly important. A minimum of technology will provide scriptures to read or hear, and often there is need for no more than this.

In reality all we require in order to plant a church is two or three believers and a shady tree – somewhere we can sit quietly together. This costs nothing at all. We do not need any money to start a church.

Dangerous technologies

It is easy to love the things that money can buy, and we know how well the advertising industry tempts and entices us to buy them. This is the world we live in, but we are warned, "Do not love the world or the things in the world." Why do we have this warning? What is the problem? "For all that is in the world – the desires of the flesh and the desires of the eyes and pride in possessions – is not from the Father but is from the world. And the world is passing away along with its desires, but whoever does the will of God lives forever" (1 Jn 2:15-17).

The greatest blessings of God can never be purchased with money. No one can buy forgiveness. No one can pay for eternal life. No one can install a technology to inspire faith or guarantee spiritual growth. For a thirsty soul, the water of life is without price. The gifts and the fruit of the Spirit are free. "The wind blows where it wishes, and you hear its sound, but you do not know where it comes from or where it goes. So it is with everyone who is born of the Spirit" (Jn 3:8).

A spiritual man is worth far more than a technological man, and it costs no money to be a spiritual man. A Christian whose heart is filled with the Spirit will achieve far more for eternity than one whose house and pockets are filled with electronic gadgets. A well-known leader needed to hear the truth about this: "May your silver perish with you, because you thought you could obtain the gift of God with money!" (Acts 8:20).

The fact that a particular technology is available does not guarantee it will be helpful. "All things are allowable," said the apostle, "but not all things are helpful. All things are allowable, but not all things build up" (1 Cor 10:23). Some of the things we buy for our church or mission may actually do more harm than good.

Technology, indeed, may be the greatest hindrance to outreach and church growth. Some satellite television channels teach doctrines that are plainly false, arousing unrealistic expectations in the slums and shanty towns, causing disillusionment and a hardening of heart against the gospel. Tele-evangelists, strutting and ranting on a glittering stage, offer a poor example to a persecuted house fellowship in Libya or a family of subsistence farmers in southern Sudan. Glamorous singers, mega-church services and wealthy foreign preachers (male and female) will embarrass and mislead a conventional Muslim community in the Atlas mountains. Such channels offer a model of Christianity quite alien to the needs of those who watch them. Other viewers, dazzled by the display, will dream of emigrating to America or some other place, and so abandon their own people. Too often these broadcasts fail to add converts to the churches, and indeed draw people away from the churches by offering a more entertaining form of Christianity and confusing believers who had previously taken the New Testament as their guide. At times these insensitive displays of Christian bravado have antagonized local religious leaders and brought severe persecution upon the churches.

In our own congregations too, technology may dominate proceedings – a service led by a computer, hymns chosen in advance and displayed on a screen, a sermon configured in colours with bullet points and pictures. The preacher has a microphone and a powerful sound system; he is a performer with an audience for only he is able to speak. Believers in such places may never have experienced the joy of an open meeting where "each one has a hymn, a lesson, a revelation" (1 Cor 14:26). There is no freedom for the Holy Spirit to give every member of the body something to contribute for the encouragement of all. Scripture says, "To each is given the manifestation of the Spirit for the common good" (1 Cor 12:7). But what benefit is this, if technology stifles and quenches the Spirit?

Outside the church, technology may easily separate us from the people we are trying to reach. We have seen how Jesus was a friend of sinners and tax-collectors. He cared for them and they followed him. We have seen how Paul lived among the people, sharing not only the gospel of God but also his own life because they were so dear to him. A missionary who rides a bicycle, stays in local homes and speaks quietly about his experience of Christ is likely to make more genuine converts than one who rides in a big car, checks into luxury hotels and addresses stadiums through loud speakers. We may try both these methods, and in time we will see the results.

It is clear that technology may be either a hindrance or a help, and our greatest concern must be to use it wisely. May God give us the gift of discernment!

Many of the older and cheaper technologies, in particular, have great value for genuinely spiritual work. Many people around the world still listen to small radios powered by cheap batteries. A mobile phone will enable us to encourage others every day and keep in close contact with friends seeking the truth. Printed Bibles, books and correspondence courses will serve us well as we proclaim the gospel and teach believers. Recordings of scripture, testimony and teaching in audio and video may bring understanding and encouragement to people living far from Christian fellowship. It is not just technology that we need but *appropriate* technology, used creatively and with much spiritual wisdom.

Even satellite television can serve us well, if programmes are designed to meet the needs of the most needy rather than the wishes of the most wealthy. But producing a programme is only the first stage of a media ministry. Every responsive viewer must be introduced to a trustworthy local fellowship, and encouraged to play a full part in its spiritual life. Every believer needs to be active in the body of Christ, asking and answering questions, learning patience and love, and developing spiritual gifts for the benefit of others. We all need Christian fellowship and should never allow technology to hinder it.

Global Culture, Gospel Culture and Local Culture

Many of our current mission methods were inherited from the days when most tribes and peoples on the planet remained deeply rooted in their place of birth. Missionaries had to go to them, learn their language and adapt to their culture. In many places this is still necessary, and such work must be done. But the modern world grows increasingly like the Roman Empire. Men and women are travelling more widely, entering new cultural environments and learning other languages – as they did in first-century Corinth, Ephesus and Rome.

The Romans had learned a great deal from the Greeks, and added many practical applications of their own. Throughout its domains the Empire introduced a sophisticated high-status culture possessing the knowledge and technology, the universal languages of education and the political power to achieve great things. People of many different local cultures were keen to enter and gain acceptance in this global culture, and large numbers moved, by choice or by necessity, to the cities where it was most strongly represented. The future lay with Rome and they wanted to be part of it.

The modern world is very similar. In addition to many local cultures, we have a high-status global culture with advanced knowledge and technology, universal educated languages and political power. This attracts individuals and families ambitious to improve their circumstances. They are moving especially to the cities. Such people may function in one culture at work and another at home, one culture on the farm and another in the market, one in the classroom and another in the dormitory. They have become bi-cultural or multi-cultural. As time passes, their children are likely to drift away from their parents' cultural roots to identify with their own vision of world culture representing modernity, prosperity and progress.

We have seen how travellers and immigrants were drawn to the Christian communities of the first century. One probable reason for this was their perception that the followers of Jesus, drawn from many local cultures, were now functioning in the global culture that represented the future for them all. People may be attracted to us for the same reason, thinking that evangelical Christianity represents modernity, progress and prosperity – a global movement in a global world and a means of access to global culture. They come to us with a desire for change.

This creates a problem for us, because the changes we are proposing may not be the ones they are expecting. As evangelical missionaries we are offering gospel culture and perhaps some elements of global culture, whilst their desire may be for global culture in its entirely with no thought of the gospel.

Global culture is most evident in advertising hoardings, television channels, magazines and shop fronts. It shows everyone wearing the same clothes, drinking the same fizzy drinks, watching the same films, listening to the same kind of music. It promotes alcohol, cosmetics, gambling and sex. It influences what people sing about, talk about and think about, and especially how they spend their money. It is promoted in mass media driven by commercial interests and entertainment industries which are secular, often immoral, and in general portray a corrupt and perverted form of Christianity.

Introducing this global culture has never been our goal as missionaries of the gospel. The churches of the first century did not attempt to make people citizens of Rome but earnestly desired them to become children of God. New converts were not introduced to the theatres, the contests and races in the arena, or the politics of the Roman state. Joining the Christian community meant adopting not global culture but gospel culture and there is a great difference between the two. Global culture is very visible but gospel culture is largely invisible. Global culture is now brilliantly advertised wherever electricity can take it, but gospel culture remains largely unknown to the modern world. Many Christians indeed would have difficulty defining it. So what exactly is gospel culture?

Like any other culture, gospel culture is reflected in the things we sing about, talk about and think about, and in how we spend our money. It profoundly affects our relationships, our priorities and our lifestyle. It is evident in the books we read, the films we watch, the music we listen to, our forms of greeting, our food and drink, our use of time and our circle of friends. But it is far more a question of what we *are* than what we *do*. Gospel culture is a matter of personal character. To us, inner purity is more important than outward show. Happy relationships matter to us more than money or status. We are concerned for others rather than ourselves. We prefer a small honest income to a large dishonest income. We keep our word, our appointments and our temper. We are patient, truthful, and willing to forgive. We love our enemies and the enemies of our people. We pray for guidance and blessing in all we undertake. Our aim is to follow Jesus, doing what he calls us to do. We have become one global family. But entrance to this family is through personal faith in him – faith that transforms character, priorities and eternal destiny.

This is gospel culture. It may surprise and perhaps impress people who are seeking global culture in the great cities of our day. It can lead them to faith and to fellowship with the global people of God. But it is quite different from the global culture publicised and financed by international business interests.

The implications of this are profound. Firstly, we must recognize that the growth of a global culture can greatly assist us in our task of world mission, because it awakens an almost universal desire for change. In general we should consider it a help rather than a hindrance.

But secondly and crucially, we see many people totally confused, failing to understand the difference between global culture and gospel culture. One such was Demas, of whom Paul sadly observed, "Demas, in love with this present world, has deserted me and gone to Thessalonica" (2 Tim 4:10). Wherever people have access to both cultures, we will need to clarify the difference between them.

This is not always easy. When viewers are repelled – or fascinated – by the glamour of evangelical television, this may be a response not to the gospel but to the global culture of those attempting to present the gospel. When parents are angry at the conversion of a son or daughter this may reflect a fear not of the gospel but of global culture mistakenly associated with the gospel.

On the other hand, when a holistic ministry is warmly welcomed as a provider of *global culture*, it may be resented or dismissed for insisting on gospel culture. When newcomers are attracted by our *global technology*, they may quickly lose interest in us and our beliefs when they obtain the technology, or fail to obtain it from us.

A devotion to global culture may lead a man who speaks other languages to declare he can only preach in English. Or it may cause a multi-lingual church to sing nothing but American choruses. But a faith expressed only in a global language, and never in the heart-language of the street and home, is unlikely to become deeply rooted in the character or the family. If evangelical believers associate the gospel with global culture, we should not be surprised when the world outside is so thoroughly confused.

Our wisest course may be to treat global culture like a supermarket, selecting from the shelves only those items that we definitely need and can afford to buy – not simply because they are available or attractive or exciting but because they will be *helpful* in leading people to faith and maturity in Jesus Christ. The choices we make will be guided by the high ideals of the gospel culture learned from him.

Thirdly and finally, although global culture may attract many, it remains unattainable to most. The majority of people in the world are still working on the land inherited from their fathers, too old to learn global languages, too poor to afford the latest technologies, and in many cases quite happy as they are.

To be sure, we will encourage our multi-cultural urban converts to take the gospel back to the towns and villages that gave them birth. But they must think carefully how to do this. There is a cultural heritage among their people which is loved and valued. Local customs and dialects will not simply fade away. Into this context they will want to introduce the fullness of gospel culture, but along with it only as much global culture and technology as will really benefit their people. If they can sow the right cultural seeds, there will be a great harvest among them of hymns, poetry, parables and testimonies, forms of greeting, humour, sympathy and wisdom – owing most to gospel culture, much to local culture and perhaps a little to global culture.

The confusion will become easier to unravel if we always remember the apostle's words: "Do not be conformed to this world, but be transformed by the renewal of your mind, so that by testing you may discern what is the will of God, what is good, acceptable and perfect" (Rom 12:2).

In this chapter we have looked at the old and the new in world mission. We have considered the use of inspired scripture and appropriate technology, and then assessed the relative value of global and gospel cultures. But many other practical issues arise to challenge and shape the strategies we adopt. These we must now investigate.

14

Missionary Methods Then and Now

"Tent-making"

We have seen that Paul was a tent-maker by profession and supported himself when necessary with this craft. If a missionary today is led to settle for a period in one place he or she may take up secular work and accept the designation "tent-maker". But what exactly does this mean?

In the New Testament we find there were two types of "tent-maker". Paul was a "tent-maker" and so were Aquila and Priscilla, yet Paul's commitment to "tent-making" was quite different from theirs. Aquila and Priscilla were excellent business people who served the Lord in their spare time and opened their home for Christian fellowship. But Paul was called to be an apostle, that is a missionary who travels widely and plants churches in many places. He worked with his hands only when necessity compelled him to.

These two types of "tent-maker" each have a vital role to play, and we need both today. Following the example of Aquila and Priscilla, a teacher or doctor or engineer may settle in a place where the name of Christ is not known and pursue a professional career there. Similarly, a salesman or taxi-driver or cleaner may take a job among people who have never heard the gospel and earn his living there. An initiative like this can provide many opportunities for witness. It will set an excellent example of honest and consistent work for new believers and may also provide a home or a workplace where they can safely meet.

But others, like Paul, are called to apostolic mission. They must remain free to travel anywhere, proclaiming the gospel, correcting errors, resolving problems, teaching the whole counsel of God. The law or custom of the land may require them to have a secular job, and if that is the case they must do it to the best of their ability. But if someone is called to an apostolic work, he or she must fulfill that calling and not become tied permanently to a secular business in a specific place. They should never become so dependent on an income, or obligated to an employer or to customers or employees, that they cannot quickly leave their secular work when the Holy Spirit calls them away to proclaim the gospel and teach the churches in other places.

Experience shows that some jobs offer more flexibility than others. Peter left his nets because he could not be both a fisherman and an apostle. Matthew left his accounts for he could not be both a tax-collector and a missionary. But Paul, as a craftsman, could pick up his needle wherever he found work, and put it down as easily. He could work whenever he needed money, proclaiming the word of God in his spare time. And he could travel widely to preach and teach whenever he was well supplied.

Paul had this freedom because Aquila and Priscilla understood and supported his call to pioneer mission. In time of persecution the presence of an apostle in their workshop was a danger to their business, and Paul willingly acknowledged his debt to them. He said, "Greet Prisca and Aquila, my fellow workers in Christ Jesus, who risked their lives for me" (Rom 16:3-4). We should honour and value people with secular jobs who provide a home or employment or financial support for our apostolic missionaries and so enable them to preach the gospel where the name of Christ is not known.

Strategic Leadership

We have seen how Jesus and the apostles trained leaders in the real world rather than the classroom. Does this mean we should never build Bible colleges or seminaries, never read books or write essays, never award diplomas and degrees?

The value of practical experience cannot be denied, and the method of the Master cannot be bettered for the development of character and skill in communicating with all kinds of people. But specialist knowledge is also of great worth. Paul was able to expound the scriptures and refute the errors of the Jews because he had sat at the feet of Gamaliel. And he could do so far more effectively than Peter or Barnabas who had not.

In the course of life some of us may be called to interact with the top leaders of universities, businesses and nations. Others may have opportunity to discuss controversial issues with scientists, economists and politicians. To develop the intellectual ability of missionaries and church leaders, and to provide them with accurate information, must surely be a contribution of great value to the churches in any country.

A Bible college or seminary is a place for exchanging ideas, sharing experiences, imparting knowledge and stimulating intelligent study of the scriptures. It will attract teachers who are godly, experienced, and well-informed. They will learn from one another and from their students. Travelling widely they will take with them a wealth of personal understanding enriched by recent testimonies and fresh experiences, enabling them to advise and encourage church leaders in many places.

Through mentors worthy of respect, students will be stimulated to think carefully, study diligently, and serve Christ faithfully. Bible college graduates will be equipped to engage in discussion with graduates from institutions with very different worldviews, and so introduce the gospel to a wide range of influential people. Potential church leaders will be stimulated to teach their congregations and their youth effectively so that all will know what they believe, and why, and be able to proclaim, defend and apply their biblical faith in a world that often opposes it. Missionaries will see exactly what the Bible says about cross-cultural outreach, and learn from the experience of people in many different places. Translators will discover how to understand biblical texts and accurately express their meaning in other languages. All this shows the benefit of time well spent at a good Bible college or seminary.

But we should not exaggerate the importance of academic achievement in preparation for spiritual ministry. Certainly, a leader or elder in any church must be able "to give instruction in sound doctrine and also to refute those who contradict it" (Tit 1:9). But he will not always need a diploma or degree in order to do this. We have seen the value of Paul's training at the feet of Gamaliel, yet he never required all missionaries or church leaders to spend three years at his own feet before starting their ministry. No one in the New Testament was ever disqualified for leadership in church or mission by the lack of a diploma or degree.

In fact Jesus warned against pompous titles that can make us proud. "You are not to be called rabbi," he said, "for you have one teacher, and you are all brothers" (Matt 23:8). There was, however, one title that he did approve. When he chose some of his followers for missionary training he named them "apostles" (Lk 6:13).

We have seen that an apostle is someone sent on a mission. His task is not to rise to high status and authority in a comfortable place, but to walk long dusty roads and cross wild stormy seas with the gospel message and "to suffer dishonour for the name" (Acts 5:41). This is what it meant for Paul to be an apostle: "For I think that God has exhibited us apostles as last of all, like men sentenced to death . . . We are fools for Christ's sake . . . We are weak . . . You are held in honour, but we in disrepute. To the present hour we hunger and thirst, we are poorly dressed and buffeted and homeless, and we labour, working with our own hands. When reviled, we bless; when persecuted, we endure; when slandered, we entreat. We have become, and are still, like the scum of the world, the refuse of all things" (1 Cor 4:9-13). That is the life of an apostle.

In the New Testament we have seen that those who gave up their secular work and devoted their time and energy to spiritual ministry were all pioneer missionaries, carrying the gospel to unreached places and establishing groups of new converts. We must admit that most of our full-time paid workers today are pastors, conducting worship services in long-established churches for people who have been Christians many years. And we might wonder: Is this the reason why the world still waits to hear the gospel?

Jesus will not return until every tribe and people has had opportunity to hear the truth and to share in his great salvation. "This gospel of the kingdom," he declared, "will be proclaimed throughout the whole world as a testimony to all nations, and then the end will come" (Matt 24:14). At the present moment almost seven thousand tribes and peoples have not yet heard and understood the gospel, and some of these groups are many thousands strong. Together they form 42% of the world's population.[1] What can we do about this?

---

1. Source of data: www.joshuaproject.net/great-commission-statistics.php (accessed 2nd March 2012).

Are there seven thousand pastors and ministers in our nation? What might happen if the members of their churches said to them, "We can take care of ourselves. Go out and find those who have never heard! Go and tell them about Jesus!"? Could the gospel reach the whole world in our generation? And if it did, might we see our Saviour return in our lifetime?

Preparing for Persecution

Overcoming ignorance

Jesus devoted his life to helping other people, yet he was despised and hated and finally crucified. To despise and hate a good man is never rational or reasonable. It can only be perverse and senseless. But Jesus had to face it. And so would his disciples. He prepared them carefully for persecution, and he warned them, "If they persecuted me, they will also persecute you" (Jn 15:20). Having seen what happened to their Lord, they would never expect the people around them to be reasonable and rational. The Twelve would devote their lives to loving and serving others, and for this they too would be despised and hated.

They had learned from their Master to do good in exchange for evil. He had taught them, "Love your enemies and pray for those who persecute you" (Matt 5:44). As he was stretched upon the cross they saw him do exactly that. He did more than turn the other cheek. When the soldiers had nailed one hand, he let them nail the other. He did more than give them his shirt. When they had taken his tunic, he let them take his life. And he cried, "Father, forgive them, for they don't know what they're doing" (Lk 23:34).

In many parts of the world, we must prepare our converts for persecution and teach them to count it all joy for the sake of Christ (Ja 1:2; 1 Pet 4:13). Persecution may take one of two forms – by government authorities on the one hand, or by individuals or crowds on the other. In most cases it was limited then, as now, to lies and rumours circulated around the streets and markets. The Christians were different from everyone else, and the difference would be exaggerated by those who resented it. Children from Christian families would suffer bullying and insults. Their parents would face unfriendliness and petty discrimination in shops, at work and in social life.

Most of this prejudice stemmed from ignorance – from things said by people who did not know them at all. It could be overcome only by friendliness, kindness, honesty, and by winning the trust and respect of some, at least, of the people around them. "Repay no one evil for evil," Paul advised, "but take care to do what is honourable in the sight of all. If possible, so far as it depends on you, live peaceably with all" (Rom 12:17-18).

A person respected by his neighbours and workmates may soon have opportunity to explain the purpose of his life. "Have no fear of them, nor be troubled," said Peter, "but in your hearts honour Christ the Lord as holy, always being prepared to make a defence to anyone who asks you for a reason for the hope that is in you; yet do it with gentleness and respect, keeping a clear conscience, so that, when you are slandered, those who revile your good behaviour in Christ may be put to shame (1 Pet 3:14-16).

Every genuine believer will be proud to bear the name of Jesus, and to suffer for him if necessary. So Peter encouraged them, "Rejoice insofar as you share Christ's sufferings, that you may also rejoice and be glad when his glory is revealed. If you are insulted for the name of Christ, you are blessed, because the Spirit of glory and of God rests upon you. But let none of you suffer as a murderer or a thief or an evildoer or as a meddler. Yet if anyone suffers as a Christian, let him not be ashamed, but let him glorify God in that name" (1 Pet 4:13-16).

Opportunities for witness

We naturally shrink from persecution. We do not like to talk about it. It can bring terrible suffering and leave physical and mental scars that never entirely heal. It may cause some to hide their faith and others to deny it, and may seriously obstruct the work of God (Lk 11:52). But persecution, while it closes certain doors to the gospel, may open others.

A thief and a centurion, who had not known Christ in the streets of Jerusalem, encountered him as he hung in extreme pain on the cross. A jailer, unaware of what Paul said by the river at Philippi, was powerfully converted by his testimony after a severe beating in prison. Persecution may lead us into places we would never normally go. As Jesus had told his disciples, "They will lay their hands on you and persecute you, delivering you up to the synagogues and prisons, and you will be brought before kings and governors for my name's sake."

He assured them that, far from being intimidated and silenced, "this will be your opportunity to bear witness" (Lk 21:12-13). Standing before the council of Jewish elders, Peter and John took their opportunity, declaring, "We cannot but speak of what we have seen and heard" (Acts 4:20). After their release they prayed not for peace and safety but for courage to speak again: "And now, Lord, look upon their threats and grant to your servants to continue to speak your word with all boldness" (Acts 4:29).

The New Testament gives us much practical guidance about responding to persecution from established authorities. First of all, we have the example of Jesus. When arrested and interrogated he spoke willingly about his own ministry, but never once betrayed others. When asked about his disciples and his teaching he told the high priest about his teaching but nothing about his disciples (Jn 18:19-21). He demanded of the soldiers, "If you seek me, let these men go" (Jn 18:8).

When questioned by the Roman governor, his concern was not for his safety but for his testimony. He spoke not about his innocence but about his kingdom, about the purpose of his birth, his witness to the truth, and then about authority from God and guilt before God. The soldiers and officials all heard the words of this remarkable prisoner, "who in his testimony before Pontius Pilate made the good confession" (1 Tim 6:13).

In lawcourts and tribunals there will be no need for methodical lectures or subtle diplomacy. The gospel of eternal life through faith in Christ will pour from a faithful heart whenever a judge or accuser will listen. Jesus had told his disciples, "Settle it therefore in your minds not to meditate beforehand how to answer, for I will give you words and wisdom that none of your adversaries will be able to resist or contradict" (Lk 21:14-15). We have seen how well they learned this lesson and how perfectly the promise was fulfilled.

Just as Jesus had prepared his followers for persecution, so did Paul. His converts quickly learned from his example to seize every opportunity when a governor or king or a public crowd seemed disposed to listen. He was aware of the astonishing spiritual power in a bold declaration from a person in danger of his life. As a bigoted Pharisee he had encountered Stephen, a man full of faith and of the Holy Spirit, whose martyrdom he saw and heard and never forgot. Many years later Paul himself – bruised, bloody and bound with two chains – told a riotous crowd about Stephen (Acts 22:20). To stand in chains might seem weak and humiliating, but Paul had learned from Stephen how the weak may win the victory and overcome the strong. Before long he was standing before the council of Jewish leaders and the high priest, and then before a governor and a king. These were his greatest opportunities to bear witness.

Whenever possible on such occasions, he would give his personal testimony. And he refused to be intimidated. As a trained rabbi he knew exactly when Jewish leaders were exceeding their authority, and he insisted that they treat him fairly according to their Law (Acts 23:3-5). He was familiar with Roman regulations and knew his rights as a Roman citizen. He spoke respectfully to soldiers and officials, calmly insisting that they do their duty according to the law of Rome (Acts 16:37; 22:25; 25:11).

Like Jesus and his apostles we may be persecuted either by government officials or by aggressive individuals, factions or crowds. When questioned by lawful authority, our priority will usually be calm testimony concerning our faith in Christ. But when attacked by violent mobs, testimony may not be possible (although both Stephen and Paul attempted it). In these circumstances our wiser course may be to move elsewhere, hoping to return at a later date. So Jesus instructed his disciples, "When they persecute you in one town, flee to the next" (Matt 10:23). After Paul was stoned in Lystra, he moved on to Derbe, and later came back to Lystra (Acts 14:19-21).

Partners in mistreatment

Knowing how quickly the world may turn against the truth, an apostolic missionary will rarely, if ever, invest in property he cannot easily take with him. But pioneer missionaries are not alone in facing troubles of this sort. Any company of believers may suffer persecution, and will not find it so easy to move house and work in search of security elsewhere.

On one occasion we read of Sosthenes in Corinth, who was beaten by a mob and lost his position as ruler of the synagogue. Shortly afterwards we find a believer named Sosthenes with Paul in Ephesus (Acts 18:17; 1 Cor 1:1). If this is the same man, he must have moved away for a time. But most would not be free to do so. Farmers, tradesmen and administrators will be tied to their workplace and their family home.

In such circumstances we must be wise as serpents and harmless as doves. At Thessalonica a number of believers meeting in the house of Jason were dragged before the authorities. After Jason had paid a sum of money as security for their good behaviour, they might possibly continue to meet in his house. But they would surely do so discreetly, and perhaps secretly, to avoid provoking further violence (Acts 17:5-9).

The antagonism which the early Christians faced in the world must have greatly strengthened their affection and love for one another. The more rudely they were treated in the streets and lawcourts, the more deeply they would appreciate the warm welcome and happy friendship they found in every Christian home.

The believers in each place were accustomed to support any of their number who fell foul of the authorities or the mob, "sometimes being publicly exposed to reproach and affliction, and sometimes being partners with those so treated" (Heb 10:33). Each day they would take food to the common jail, providing blankets or clothing for their friends inside, "for you had compassion on those in prison" (Heb 10:34a; also 13:3). We have seen how the Philippians sent help to Paul in captivity and how a friend would often choose to share his confinement (Phil 4:18; Col 4:10; 2 Tim 4:11).

The early Christian communities followed a general pattern of public outreach and private fellowship, but in a context of severe persecution, the distinction between public and private might need to be more carefully defined in order to protect the congregation from spies, informers and trouble-makers. The Christian home will then become a haven and refuge for genuine believers – a safe place where they can be sure of comfort, encouragement and teaching, free from all fear of betrayal. Meanwhile the gospel can be discussed with outsiders elsewhere – in cafés, parks, markets and in their own homes – until they are ready to affirm their wholehearted commitment to Christ through baptism and be welcomed into the household of faith.

In his letters to the seven churches of Asia, Jesus gave seven promises for those who overcome (Rev 2 and 3). We should know and teach these promises for they are a great encouragement in the art of overcoming. When joy is set before us we can more easily endure the cross, despising the shame (Heb 12:2). From Paul we learn how to overcome evil with good, leaving all thought of vengeance to God (Rom 12:17-21). From Peter we learn to entrust our lives to a faithful Creator while doing good (1 Pet 4:12-19). From John, whose brother was killed by the sword, we learn to overcome the world not by violence but by faith (1 Jn 5:4). Every day we may overcome persecution, as Jesus did, by loving our friends, forgiving our enemies, and leading thieves and soldiers with us into paradise.

In the end, of course, we are fragile people. Our bodies are made from dust and to dust they will return. Persecution may hasten that process a little but cannot for a moment delay the resurrection and transformation of our mortal remains when Christ returns. "So is it with the resurrection of the dead. What is sown is perishable; what is raised is imperishable. It is sown in dishonor; it is raised in glory. It is sown in weakness; it is raised in power. It is sown a natural body; it is raised a spiritual body . . . Just as we have borne the image of the man of dust, we shall also bear the image of the man of heaven" (1 Cor 15:42-44, 49).

Indeed, the more we have suffered for Christ in this age, the more wonderful will be the moment when we hear his voice and awake to find ourselves among our dearest friends and family in the new heaven and earth. "For this light momentary affliction is preparing for us an eternal weight of glory beyond all comparison, as we look not to the things that are seen but to the things that are unseen. For the things that are seen are transient, but the things that are unseen are eternal" (2 Cor 4:17-18).

Holistic Ministries

The greatest need of mankind

The New Testament missionaries were not indifferent to the unhappy circumstances of the people around them. Wherever they went they saw men and women with distressing handicaps and painful diseases, and they saw destitute children begging for the necessities of life.

Jesus himself was deeply concerned for the sick and disabled, and we will discuss his healing ministry in due course. We know that compassion moved him to expel demons, to restore many who were blind and paralysed, and sometimes even to raise the dead. He was also concerned for the hungry. Twice he provided food for a hungry crowd. He was especially concerned for people in poverty, and he urged the rich young ruler to give all he had to the poor. With his approval Zacchaeus gave half his assets to the poor. And Jesus reminded his followers, "You always have the poor with you, and whenever you want, you can do good for them" (Mk 14:7).

He was concerned for all these, and he told his disciples, "When you give a feast, invite the poor, the disabled, the lame, the blind" (Lk 14:13). But we read that when Jesus wept, it was not for the sick or the poor that he wept. He wept for a man who had died (Jn 11:35).

Jesus never for one moment forgot that mankind has a more serious problem than disease and hunger and poverty. The most traumatic horror we all face is death – our own death and the death of our loved ones.

Death is an enemy to us all, and it will defeat us all. We fear it and the power it has over us. If some scientist offered us a way to live for ever, we would pay anything for it. If there were some place where people never die, we would give all we possess to go there. We hate the idea that we will cease to exist. We hate the idea that when the heart stops the light goes out – the end has come and it's all over. Yet time is running out for each of us. The minutes and the hours tick by. Every grey hair, every aching joint, every loss of memory shows we are in decline. Our eyesight and our hearing become weaker and remind us that soon we will not see or hear at all. The greatest longing of all mankind is to live and not die. We are desperate for eternal life.

But here is the most astonishing thing. Eternal life is exactly what Jesus offers to each one of us. And he alone can do so. He can give us life because he has defeated death. On the cross he suffered in our place, "so that by the grace of God he might taste death for everyone" (Heb 2:9). For this reason he can "deliver all those who through fear of death were subject to lifelong slavery" (Heb 2:15).

His work in dying for us was a greater work than healing us or feeding us. By dying for us, he has saved us from our greatest distress: "that whoever believes in him should not perish but have eternal life" (Jn 3:16). In rising from the dead, he has shown that for him and for those who are his, death is not the end. He himself is the first of a new generation who will live forever, "the firstfruits of those who have fallen asleep" (1 Cor 15:20).

To a frail human being, growing older and weaker every day, the gift of eternal life is the greatest of all possible gifts. Jesus never advertised a healing ministry, because he had something more wonderful to offer. He did not continue multiplying loaves and fishes, because he had a greater gift in store. He did not say, "Come to me for healing." He did not say, "Come to me for food and clothes." He said, "Come to me . . . and you will find rest for your souls" (Matt 11:28-29). A soul can only be at rest when it is free from the tyranny of death.

The gift our Saviour offers is life for ever in a world restored to glory, in a world as perfect as it was in Eden. There we shall live, and never face sickness or death again. "Death shall be no more, neither shall there be mourning, nor crying, nor pain any more, for the former things have passed away" (Rev 21:4). This is not fiction; it is fact, and we will be there. So will our loved ones who put their trust in Jesus. We will see them again, not old or sick but in the prime of life. The meek will inherit the earth. We will have endless days to accomplish all the things we have longed to do. No one will ever be poor or blind or diseased or disabled again.

This is the gift of God who alone can give it. "By grace you have been saved through faith. And this is not your own doing; it is the gift of God" (Eph 2:8; also Rom 6:23). But we see that this gift is not for everyone. It is for those who are "saved through faith". A person who has faith is someone who knows what they believe – that is, someone who understands.

When people came to Jesus he wanted them to understand: "Crowds gathered to him again. And again, as was his custom, he *taught* them" (Mk 10:1). He offered them his gift. He showed them how to have eternal life, and how to start living that life. But the people needed to understand what he was saying, and to believe in him. Without this understanding and belief, eternal life would remain beyond their grasp. "So he went throughout all Galilee, *teaching* in their synagogues and *proclaiming* the gospel of the kingdom" (Matt 4:23). He said, "Let us go on to the next towns, that I may *preach* there also, for that is why I came out" (Mk 1:38).

He proclaimed a message that brought *eternal life*. To the people around him this was something completely new. Some asked him, "What shall I do to inherit eternal life?" (Lk 10:25). To them he explained as much as they could understand. Others heard but would not accept what he said. To them he replied, "You refuse to come to me that you may have *life*" (Jn 5:40). But some heard and believed, declaring, "You have the words of eternal life" (Jn 6:68). They had entered by "the narrow gate . . . that leads to *life*" (Matt 7:14). They were a small minority but they had understood.

It is this message of eternal life that we are called to proclaim in all the world. Never has there been such good news as this. For God's plan "has now been revealed through the appearing of our Saviour Christ Jesus, who abolished death and *brought life and immortality to light through the gospel*" (2 Tim 1:10)." So the angel told Peter and John, "Go and stand in the temple and speak to the people all the words of this *Life*" (Acts 5:20).

Jesus came so that people everywhere might call out to him and receive the life he offers. "But how can they call on him in whom they have not believed? And how can they believe in him of whom they have never heard? And how can they hear without someone proclaiming it? And how can they proclaim unless they are sent?" (Rom 10:14-15). It is our privilege to go, and our privilege to send those who will go.

That is the message and mission of the gospel. We must now consider how it affected those who heard and received it.

The poor among the saints

When the Holy Spirit started to work in the hearts of those who heard this good news, they were born again and became men and women of great kindness and sympathy. In the history of the world, the followers of Jesus have led the way in all manner of caring ministries and institutions. These are the fruit of Christian character generated by the Holy Spirit and the teaching of the New Testament.

The word "holistic" may be relatively new, but Christians have always been concerned for the whole person – body and soul. From earliest days, the Jerusalem fellowship provided food for its widows (Acts 6:1). Luke describes how Dorcas was "full of good works and acts of charity", and how she made clothes for the widows among the Christians at Joppa (Acts 9:36, 39). James taught compassion for widows and orphans and for any believer who was "poorly clothed and lacking in daily food" (Ja 1:27; 2:15). Paul agreed with the church leaders at Jerusalem in his eagerness to "remember the poor"

(Gal 2:10). Timothy had instructions about regular provision for widows in the churches (1 Tim 5:3-16). The fellowships in Galatia, Macedonia and Achaia sent famine relief to "the poor among the saints" in Judea (Rom 15:26).

In all these cases we notice something interesting. The early Christians were taking great care of the poor in their own community of believers, but we do not read that they attempted to supply food or clothing or financial assistance to those outside their fellowship. We do not see the apostles initiating holistic ministries for the benefit of idol worshippers, magicians or philosophers. In their relations with those outside, their priority was proclaiming the message of eternal life. Other ministries might relieve hardship a little – and for a time – but eternal life would solve every problem for ever.

To illustrate this further, we may take the case of Luke. Although Luke was "the beloved physician" (Col 4:14), we do not read of him settling anywhere to conduct a medical ministry. This was not because he had hardened his heart or considered such a ministry valueless, but because he had a higher priority. He knew that if many people could hear and accept the truth about Christ, then many churches could be launched to care for the sick. No doubt Paul and others had reason to be grateful for Luke's medical help, and perhaps Luke passed on his knowledge of herbal infusions and ointments to friends as he travelled, but he was not a "medical missionary". There is no sign that he offered healing as a form of holistic mission. He was far more concerned to write and distribute an account of the healing ministry of Jesus than to engage in a healing ministry of his own. And in the history of the world, Luke's Gospel has proved far more important than his knowledge of physical illnesses and remedies.

Pioneer missionaries and holistic churches

By definition, an apostle or missionary is someone sent on a mission. He is called to a travelling ministry, proclaiming his message, teaching new believers, starting healthy churches and restoring weak churches. But he does not stay long enough in any place to organise and manage clinics, hospitals, schools, orphanages or social rehabilitation centres. His calling is to transform the character and eternal destiny of men and women, not to initiate agricultural projects or seed banks or sources of clean water.

But in each locality the men and women who put their faith in

Christ, and experience this transformation of character and destiny, may find the Holy Spirit leading them to undertake many such initiatives. The pioneer missionary proclaims his message, and the church he plants will then consider the physical needs of the believers and the people around them.

This is a general principle. But we cannot completely separate church from mission. We should not assume that "proclamation" is a task for the missionary alone, and that "caring" is a task for the church alone. Just as every believer has opportunities to proclaim the gospel, so we may be sure that every missionary has bandaged wounds, offered medicines, provided food and clothing for the poor, and helped when necessary with education and employment.

Christian love often requires an apostolic missionary to care for people with physical and material needs. But this practical help should never distract him from his ministry of the word. When the widows in Jerusalem needed attention the apostles said, "Therefore, brothers, pick out from among you seven men of good repute, full of the Spirit and of wisdom, whom we will appoint to this duty. But we will devote ourselves to prayer and to the ministry of the word" (Acts 6:3-4).

With these things in mind, we should encourage the churches in holistic ministry. We should also encourage them to send out missionaries proclaiming the gospel of eternal life through personal faith in Jesus. Such missionaries will plant churches of converts transformed by the Holy Spirit. These converts and these churches may then be led to start holistic ministries of great benefit to the local believers, to the neighbourhood around them, and ultimately to the whole nation.

Institutional work

It is after the gospel has been proclaimed, and converts well established in the faith, that orphanages, hospitals and other institutional ministries may be successfully undertaken by the churches. Many mature believers will then be at hand to support the project financially and to staff the institution.

But holistic ministries launched in unreached areas, or in places where the churches are weak, may have great difficulty in raising funds and finding suitable staff. They may be compelled to employ unbelievers and to receive money from unbelievers. This seriously undermines their gospel witness. It blurs the distinction between those who believe and those who do not believe. And it devalues the truth that will separate one from another for eternity. As ambassadors for Christ we should avoid being "unequally yoked with unbelievers" (2 Cor 6:14). The example of Jesus and his apostles, if followed carefully, would save us from many difficulties of this nature.

We should also note that institutions run by foreigners, and supported by foreign money, will not easily lead local people to faith in Christ or create active indigenous churches. The fruit of the gospel will be sweet to those who taste it, but if they can enjoy the fruit produced by other people they may see no need to produce their own. They will enjoy the holistic benefits of the gospel without the hard work of personal commitment to Christ.

Indeed, a holistic strategy may easily benefit the body without touching the soul. The five thousand whom Christ fed were happy to eat the loaves and fishes but never understood the call to trust and follow him. They were pleased with a small gift and never took the greater gift he offered. They never grasped the *meaning* of the miracle. So he told them, "Truly, truly, I say to you, you are seeking me, not because you saw signs, but because you ate your fill of the loaves. Do not labour for the food that perishes, but for the food that endures to eternal life, which the Son of Man will give to you" (Jn 6:26-27).

Relief work

It is often suggested that holistic outreach could be a key to the opening of resistant nations and hostile minds to the love of God and the truth of the gospel. A Christian doctor, for example, on account of his medical skill, may be welcomed in regions closed to an evangelist, and find opportunities there to testify about Jesus.

There is truth in this. As God leads, such initiatives must be commended and supported. Wherever a seed is planted it may take root. "There are varieties of gifts . . . varieties of service . . . varieties of activities," and God inspires them all (1 Cor 12:4-6).

But experience shows that clinics, hospitals and public health campaigns give birth less frequently than hoped to spiritually healthy churches. While a medical work may open doors for the doctor's medicines and surgical skill, it has not so often opened hearts and minds to the need for repentance and faith in Christ. The digging of wells, introduction of new crops, vaccination of livestock and creation of work co-operatives are all initiatives of value and should be encouraged. But we have not seen many strong congregations launched in unreached areas through such enterprises. We may find schools a great benefit to the churches, providing opportunities of progress and subsequent employment for children from homes that are truly or nominally Christian. But rarely do we find many pupils from families following other religions converted to Christ through these schools. All this is cause for regret.

More urgent than any of these is relief work among refugees and disaster victims. The importance of this work is obvious to all. But with attention focused on material needs, it is not easy to awaken a hunger for the greater gift of eternal life. Many times we have longed for spiritual as well as material receptivity in such a context.

This is not to say we should abandon these works of compassion, support and development. If the Spirit leads us to do these things, we should engage in them with energy and dedication as an important ministry of the churches. But we should not confuse these holistic initiatives with gospel mission.

Indeed, the offer of short-term material benefit may distract a person from long-term spiritual concerns, and even harden his or her heart against the gospel. It is the word of God, heard and believed, that saves for eternity. In the parable of Jesus, "the sower sows *the word*." The ones who benefit are those who "hear the word and accept it." But when the word is not deeply rooted, "the cares of the world and the deceitfulness of riches and *the desires for other things* enter in and choke the word, and it proves unfruitful" (Mk 4:14).

Miraculous Healing

The healing ministry of Jesus

In the ministry of Jesus and his apostles we read about extraordinary miracles of healing. If we are seeking guidance in the New Testament concerning mission strategy, it is essential to enquire whether miraculous healing should play a part in our outreach today.

We should not underestimate the healing ministry of Jesus. When he had taught the crowds, he also healed their diseases and disabilities. "He went throughout all Galilee, teaching in their synagogues and proclaiming the gospel of the kingdom and healing every disease and every affliction among the people" (Matt 4:23).

No one else has ever miraculously healed as many people as Jesus did in three short years, for these were complete and genuine miracles of healing. "He went about doing good and healing all who were oppressed by the devil, for God was with him" (Acts 10:38).

Jesus healed people for two reasons. Firstly, because he had compassion on them: "When he went ashore he saw a great crowd, and he had compassion on them and healed their sick" (Matt 14:14).

And secondly, he knew his generation was seeking a sign. His healing miracles proved he was the long-awaited Messiah, and that with his coming the kingdom of God had come. So we read that "many of the people believed in him. They said, 'When the Christ appears, will he do more signs than this man has done?'" (Jn 7:31; see also Lk 7:18-23). One eye-witness declared, "Jesus did many other signs in the presence of the disciples, which are not written in this book; but these are written so that you may believe that Jesus is the Christ, the Son of God, and that by believing you may have life in his name" (Jn 20:30-31). His miracles proved who he was.

Of course Jesus was and is unique – the only-begotten Son of God. He alone possessed authority on earth to forgive sins, to still the storm, to multiply loaves and fishes, to walk on water. He did not need to pray for the sick, as we do, asking his Father to heal them. He himself had the power to heal. He could heal anyone at any time. He could heal them all, whatever their disease or disability might be. This is repeatedly emphasized in the gospel records. He "healed *all* who were sick." (Matt 8:16). "He healed them *all*" (Matt 12:15). "He laid his hands on *every one of them* and healed them" (Lk 4:40).

Now what would this mean to the people who watched it happen? They knew well enough that death is caused by disease, deformity and decay, and that every generation since Adam has suffered these terrible afflictions – for the wages of sin is death (Jn 9:2; Rom 5:14; 6:23; 1 Cor 15:22). But now, with their own eyes they saw the authority of Jesus to take away sin and the deadly consequences of sin. It was truly the dawning of a new age.

In his commission to his disciples Jesus told them "that repentance and forgiveness of sins should be proclaimed in his name to all nations" (Lk 24:47). English translations usually speak about "forgiveness of sin". To forgive can mean simply to ignore or overlook an offence but the Greek *aphesis* means much more than this. It describes "remission" or "removal" of sin. To remit someone's sin is to release them from it – to set them free. This is what Jesus did.

When he healed a paralysed man, saying "Rise, pick up your bed and go home," Jesus showed his "authority on earth to take away sins" (Matt 9:6). By remitting this paralysed man's sin, Jesus rescued him from death and its deadly companions – disease, deformity and decay.

Yet we know that his three short years of ministry did not remove death and disease entirely from the world – or even permanently from that man. The miracles Jesus did in one small place were "signs" or tokens of a work he will complete when he returns in power and glory to remove sin and every consequence of sin from all the earth forever (2 Pet 3:13). John the Baptist foresaw this when he declared, "Behold, the Lamb of God, *who takes away the sin of the world*!" (Jn 1:29).

This is what we understand by salvation. This is why we call him our Saviour. We have seen the salvation of the Lord, and yet with patience we wait for his salvation (Rom 13:11; 1 Pet 1:5).

The healing ministry of the apostles

As Jesus is unique, we might suppose that his power to heal any disease at any time would be possessed by him alone and no one else. But scripture shows him giving this same power to his disciples. He did so on two occasions. "He called to him his twelve disciples and gave them authority over unclean spirits, to cast them out, and to heal *every disease and every affliction*," and even to raise the dead (Matt 10:1, 8). A little later, when the Seventy-two were sent out, they too had power to heal (Lk 10:9).

But only twice did Jesus send out a company of followers to teach and heal. Apart from these two missions, we do not read of the disciples healing people. Indeed, a man whose son had a demon complained to Jesus, "I brought him to your disciples, and they could not heal him." The disciples asked, "Why could we not cast it out?" Jesus replied that with prayer and faith it might be possible. But he did not then encourage his disciples to continue with a healing ministry (Matt 17:16, 19; Mk 9:29).

Some months later, after his ascension, the apostles received the power of the Holy Spirit to testify in Jerusalem. Once again we see they were able to heal *everyone*. "The people also gathered from the towns around Jerusalem, bringing the sick and those afflicted with unclean spirits, and *they were all healed*" (Acts 5:16).

Miraculous healings continued as the Christian communities grew. Peter prayed for several believers who were ill and for one who had died, and they were restored to health (Acts 9:32-41). Philip's ministry in Samaria was confirmed with miracles (Acts 8:5-7). And miracles were done through Paul, especially in Ephesus, and also in Iconium, Lystra, Corinth and Malta, and probably in some other places too (Acts 19:11-12; 14:8-10; 28:8-9). Paul himself describes these miraculous healings as "signs" (Rom 15:18-19; 2 Cor 12:12). They were signs to the Gentiles that his message was true, and signs to the Jews that salvation had come to the Gentiles (Acts 14:3; 15:12).

But Paul could not always heal everyone everywhere. He advised Timothy, "No longer drink only water, but use a little wine for the sake of your stomach and your frequent ailments" (1 Tim 5:23). Paul could not heal Timothy's frequent ailments; the leaders of the churches could not heal them; Timothy himself could not heal them. Epaphroditus, another of his co-workers, was ill for a period of time and indeed was close to death (Phil 2:26-27). A little later, Paul tells us, "I left Trophimus, who was ill, at Miletus" (2 Tim 4:20). Paul's prayers had not restored his friend to health, so he must travel on without him. The apostle himself suffered a period of illness early in his ministry, as he reminded his friends in Galatia: "It was because of a bodily ailment that I preached the gospel to you at first, and though my condition was a trial to you, you did not scorn or despise me" (Gal 4:13-14).

Paul never boasted of a healing ministry. He never claimed to have a gift of healing. In fact he preferred to boast of his weakness, showing how a man who was ill and afflicted could serve as a missionary of the gospel by the grace of God. "A thorn was given me in the flesh," he said, "a messenger of Satan to harass me, to keep me from becoming conceited. Three times I pleaded with the Lord about this, that it should leave me. But he said to me, 'My grace is sufficient for you, for my power is made perfect in weakness'" (2 Cor 12:7-9).

Healing ministry today

All this is true to life, matching our own experience. Sometimes God answers prayer wonderfully and we are quickly healed. Sometimes he lets our healing take the slower course of natural recovery through the body's defences or through medicine. Sometimes he allows the body to suffer and even to die, awaiting the resurrection day for its healing when Christ returns to restore all things.

If people around us are suffering, we are right to pray for them. We have the advice of James on this point: "Is anyone among you sick? Let him call for the elders of the church, and let them pray over him, anointing him with oil in the name of the Lord. And the prayer of faith will save the one who is sick, and the Lord will raise him up. And if he has committed sins, he will be forgiven. Therefore, confess your sins to one another and pray for one another, that you may be healed" (Ja 5:14-16). The oil used for this purpose in James's day would probably contain powdered herbs, roots or bark with recognised healing properties. Our Father will answer such prayer as this, for we ask in Jesus' name, desiring that his will be done, and we know that he will heal – immediately, or gradually, or when Christ comes.

In the fellowship at Corinth, and perhaps in other places too, there were believers with a special ability to heal, perhaps through nursing care and medicine, perhaps simply through prayer, but most likely through both. This was Christ's gift to the church as a blessing for his body (1 Cor 12:9). There may be such people in our congregations today, and we should value them highly and thank God for them.

But we must always be absolutely honest. We should not claim that a person is miraculously healed if they are not. We should not say they are in perfect health if they merely feel a little better. We should not report a miracle if the healing is natural. We should not imply that everyone is healed when most are not. We cannot glorify God by telling lies. Scripture warns us, "Do not boast and be false to the truth" (Ja 3:14).

In all this we should not pretend that we can do exactly what Jesus did, for that would make him as limited as we are. No doubt we would love to see everyone healed miraculously, completely and instantly, as they were when he laid his hands on them. That would be wonderful. But today we must admit that things are different. If someone somewhere could heal everyone miraculously, completely and instantly, we would hear of villages, towns and cities where nobody is ill and nobody dies. But such a ministry has been entrusted to no one except Jesus himself – and for a brief time his earliest apostles and evangelists; then they too, like everyone else, eventually grew old and died.

Since then no one has ever been able to heal "every disease and every affliction among the people". We will not see this on earth again until Jesus returns to raise the dead and make all things new. Then we will have an end to death and mourning and crying and pain. Then we will inherit the kingdom prepared for us from the foundation of the world (Rev 21:4; Matt 25:34). This is the hope that inspires us and the gospel we proclaim.

Further observations

Before we leave this subject, there are three more things to note. Firstly, we see in the book of Acts that the places where the apostles healed many people were places where pagan sorcerers were also famous for a healing ministry (Jerusalem, Samaria, Ephesus and Corinth).

Missionary experience shows that this is often the case today. Where occult miracles are common, Christian miracles are frequently reported. The reason for this may be unclear. In some cases the populace may be unduly eager to identify a miracle where no genuine miracle has occurred. Or indeed God may lovingly reveal himself to people in each place according to their culture – through meaningful dreams or scientific evidence or warm relationships, or indeed supernatural miracles – matching and surpassing whichever of these is most valued in that particular culture.

But the fact that signs and wonders can be accomplished by satanic powers complicates the issue (2 Thess 2:9). We cannot accept every miracle as proof that the one who performs it is teaching the truth. In the last days, Jesus warns us, "False christs and false prophets will arise and perform great signs and wonders, so as to lead astray, if possible, even the elect" (Matt 24:24).

Finally, there remains a practical question. If we cannot now do the miracles that Jesus and his apostles did, how can we presume to follow their example in other aspects of our mission to the world?

A careful study of scripture shows that signs and wonders did not open doors for gospel proclamation but rather followed after it, confirming the message in certain times and places (Mk 16:20). We see that Jesus had called his disciples *before* he did any miraculous signs (Jn 2:2, 11). It was his teaching rather than his miracles that worried his enemies and convinced his hearers (Lk 23:5; 20:21). He rebuked those who required signs and wonders in order to believe (Jn 4:48). "The kingdom of God," he said, "is not coming with signs to be observed" (Lk 17:20). He had no confidence in people whose faith depended on miracles: he "did not entrust himself to them" (Jn 2:24). And in the end his miracles of healing counted for nothing with the crowds who demanded his death (Mk 15:11-14).

After this the book of Acts shows that in every city people accepted the apostles' message *before* any signs or wonders took place to confirm it. In many places converts were multiplied and fellowships started without any reference to miracles at all. No miraculous healings are reported, for example, in Syrian Antioch, Pisidian Antioch, Athens, Berea, Caesarea, Colossae, Derbe, Philippi, Rome, Thessalonica, Tyre, or in the provinces of Galatia, Syria or Cilicia, or on the island of Crete. This does not prove that no miracles occurred in these places, but if they did they were not considered worthy of mention. It was the teaching and the testimony of the apostles, rather than miraculous healing, that led people to faith in Jesus. Paul tells us that, in his experience, "faith comes from hearing, and hearing through the word of Christ" (Rom 10:17).

Cross-cultural Mission Today

Opportunities for outreach

We have seen that the early Christians met for fellowship in private homes and proclaimed the gospel in public places. In many parts of the world, however, our circumstances are now quite different from those in New Testament times.

In large areas of Africa, for example, many people are Christian in name. They have attended church services all their lives. Despite this they may show no evidence of being born again or filled with the Spirit of holiness and the character of Christ. Their lifestyle speaks of other beliefs, choices and priorities. We call them nominal Christians.

In such a context the church building has become, in effect, a public place where unconverted men and women will give us a hearing. This may be our most accessible mission field. Indeed, these churches could be for us what the synagogues were for the apostle

187

Paul. With earnest prayer, serious preaching and honest testimony we may speak freely to nominal Christians, urging them to lay aside every weight and sin which clings so closely and turn in faith to Christ as Saviour and Lord (Heb 12:1).

In this way, by the grace of God, we may see passive and static congregations transformed into active growing fellowships, attracting worldly people to Christ. Thieves and drunkards will become men and women of integrity. Fetishes and spells will be renounced in the name of Jesus. Sexual irresponsibility will be halted and marriages preserved. Quarrels and lawsuits will be forgotten, and loving kindness become a reality in daily life. The need in such places is not for revival but for conversion and salvation, for rescue indeed from the deeply-rooted power of evil.

But that is not all. In nations with a long Christian history, every local church may enjoy a recognised and respected status in its own neighbourhood. This offers wonderful opportunities for gospel outreach. By visiting door-to-door, we may find many homes and hearts open to the love of God and the message of Life.

Our church compound could then begin to fulfil its true potential, with a programme of education and development bringing crowds of children through our gates each week, or a regular health and maternity clinic attracting many men and women to our premises. In this way too, our property would become a public place, a community centre where the gospel can be freely and willingly heard. Families introduced to the Christian community in this way might soon become some of its strongest and most effective members when drawn to personal faith in Christ.

At the same time we may find strangers at our gate in need of help. Refugees in large numbers pass from one country to another in time of conflict or famine and then come to the churches for assistance. Some have suffered greatly and may be hungry or in need of medical attention. Others cross the border in search of work. Some are students in our colleges and universities.

Experience shows that individuals moving from one country to another, or even from one region to another, are usually more open to the gospel than those who remain among their own people. Lonely, uncertain, suffering from culture shock, perhaps in search of work or a place to live, these men and women are in need of a friend. A Christian family or fellowship can easily provide this friendship and in due course lead them to faith in Christ.

We know that some immigrant communities are carefully watched and guarded by their own religious devotees, but among them are usually a substantial number who dislike this form of religious bullying, and in private will be glad to escape it.

Newcomers in a foreign city will be especially pleased to find people from their own country living there – cooking their own food and speaking their own language – and may willingly hear what they say about Jesus. Indeed an expatriate fellowship may grow far more quickly than a similar group in its own homeland.

After some months of steady growth in understanding and in character, these disciples may eventually return to the land of their birth to share their faith with their own people in their own language. Then in due course we may be invited to help them disciple believers in some of the most difficult and unreached parts of the world and to encourage the growth of indigenous fellowships there.

This is a strategy we have seen in the New Testament; we see it in Africa and elsewhere today, and we know how effective it can be. This method of mission does not require us to raise support, to leave our family, to learn a new language or to disrupt our children's education. It has many advantages.

Wherever we make contact with people – at work, at school, door to door, in a shop, in hospital, in our church compound – they will appreciate an invitation to supper in our home with a company of our friends. A Christian household is still the best place in the world for teaching, fellowship, breaking of bread and prayer. In an open meeting with free informal interaction, individuals can ask questions, request prayer for urgent needs, deal seriously with personal issues, confess what they have done or failed to do, find hope for their present circumstances, and perhaps in some cases declare for the first time that they have really put their trust in Christ to save and sanctify. Before long they will have learned from experience how to pray for others and to help and encourage them.

In all this we see how well the strategies of the New Testament may work in contexts far removed in space and time from the world of the apostles.

Pioneering unreached people

We have considered the great potential for gospel outreach in a nation or a continent with a strong Christian heritage. Indeed there are many wonderful opportunities for mission among people who are Christian in name. But there are also some particular difficulties.

Although we may benefit from the immediate respect and appreciation of thousands who will hear us gladly, we may also suffer from their mistaken assumptions concerning what we will say and do. They already have a perception of "church" and "mission", and may become annoyed with us if we do not meet their expectations. Others, thinking that they know all about Christianity – and disliking what they know – may be prejudiced against us from the start.

Secondly, we are aware that traditions can be deeply rooted. In some places, churches and missions have been using methods developed and established over many generations. If an alternative strategy is proposed, this may cause a measure of tension and distress which does more harm than good. Indeed, if long-established missions and churches are working effectively for the cause of the gospel, we are bound to honour them for their work and thank God for them. If they proclaim the true gospel, we must respect their arrangements and not trouble or upset them (Rom 13:7; Lk 9:49-50).

But the world is a large place. Paul might go in one direction and Barnabas in another, and so the message would travel twice as far (Acts 15:39-40). We do not need to work where others are working. Thousands of tribes and peoples are still waiting to hear the gospel. Sections of our great inner cities have no active gospel fellowships. Immigrants and travellers are coming to us from many places where evangelists cannot go.

Unreached people are by definition ignorant of mission procedures and church traditions, and in this respect our work is much simpler if we proclaim Christ where he is not known. This indeed was Paul's ambition, as he tells us, "lest I build on someone else's foundation" (Rom 15:20). Like him, we have the opportunity to make a fresh start, to lay new spiritual foundations, to think carefully about our strategy and launch our work in the best possible way. And we can do this where no one else is working.

What then is our strategy for introducing the good news to an unreached area, or an unreached culture or language group? First of all, we must do some research. There may be some among these unreached people who are especially likely to welcome us and respond to what we say.

This is not always easy to predict. Jesus found the villages more responsive than the towns, whereas Paul ignored the countryside and headed for the cities. There may be particular regions, parts of the city, immigrant communities, trade or craft or ethnic groups that are especially open to the gospel, whilst others are less responsive. In some places educated people with good jobs will show most interest; elsewhere the less educated or the unemployed. It may be younger people, or older people; those who are sick or those who are well; those who have comfortable homes, or those who have no homes at all. We can only discover this by enquiry and experiment, by talking with many types of people, and by asking friends who live among them.

Then we must discover where and when such people might give us their best attention. There may be certain times of day or particular places where our message will be willingly heard. It may be in a café or a social club, a cultural association or a charity, a classroom or clinic or workshop, or beside a well or spring of water, at a market stall or taxi rank, at lunchtime in a public park, or on our neighbours' doorsteps in the evening after work. Some individuals may have been listening to Christian radio, or studying correspondence courses, and perhaps even requested a visit. If so, they will be expecting us and pleased to see us.

In some places we may be advised to approach the local authorities and obtain permission to teach the word of God. Elsewhere we may simply speak with anyone who seems interested. On occasion Paul asked for such permission (Acts 21:39). He would expect it as a matter of course in the synagogues (Acts 13:15). But Jesus never asked permission from anyone. As for Peter and John, they spoke even when the authorities forbade them (Acts 5:28-29). In such matters, we must prayerfully seek guidance in choosing the best strategy for each place.

But one thing is more certain. The gospel generally finds its best response among people unhappy with their circumstances. We have seen how Jesus was appreciated by the sick and the outcasts of society. Although most of his followers were neither especially poor nor rich, the majority were profoundly unhappy with the political and religious condition of their nation. They were longing for God to visit and redeem his people. Paul too was well received by synagogue worshippers far from home, somewhat dissatisfied with traditional religion and desiring to better themselves in this world and the next. As we prepare for mission we will be wise to look especially for unhappy people, frustrated people, ambitious people – men and women and youth who are eager to improve their circumstances and themselves. People of this kind are usually the leaders in any cultural or religious innovation, and when they hear the gospel they may receive it gladly.

It is also worth remembering that strangers will welcome us most warmly when we are introduced by someone they already know and respect – someone who has credibility. Indeed, gospel witness is usually most effective when the first Christian they meet is one of their own people speaking their own dialect. In pioneer mission we should always, if possible, take such a person with us.

Finally, it is important to be very gentle with people who have lived all their lives in ignorance. Although Jesus and Paul both argued with the Jews (because the Jews were stubbornly rejecting the grace of God), both were very gentle with people following other religions – the woman of Samaria, the man with a legion of demons, the Canaanite woman, the Athenians and the Iconians. If I am an evangelist among people who have already heard the gospel many times and still fail to respond, I should confront and challenge them. But if I am a cross-cultural missionary among people who have never had a chance to hear, I should persuade them gently and patiently and with much prayer until finally they put their trust in Jesus. They will be won not by condemnation but by love.

Starting churches

In the New Testament we do not find missionaries planting churches. They simply proclaimed the gospel and encouraged their converts to start their own churches.

When one or two have confessed their faith in Christ we can begin to read the New Testament systematically with these new disciples – one of the Gospels to start with, then perhaps the first letter of Peter, and of John, and Acts, followed by the rest. There are 260 chapters in the New Testament. If we read together and discuss one chapter every day – during the lunch break or in the evening after supper –

each of them will get to know and understand the whole book in less than nine months.

In the scriptures our disciples will see for themselves what a Christian is, and how a fellowship can start and grow. But there are certain things they will not find in the New Testament.

1. There were no church buildings. Fellowships of believers flourished for two and a half centuries without any religious buildings. When Paul introduced the gospel to a city, he did not construct a chapel, or rent a hall, or provide benches and a pulpit and a sound system and musical instruments.

He did not even ask believers to come to his own house lest they become dependent on him. Only when he was in chains and forbidden to go out did they come to his house (Acts 28:16-17).

The apostle did not establish a mission compound or an office or clinic or school. In fact he avoided anything that would require him to remain permanently in one town, paying for properties and running programmes. He simply proclaimed the gospel in public places wherever people would listen. Then he went with his disciples to their own homes or workshops, teaching them "in public and from house to house" (Acts 20:20).

2. There were no paid ministers. The believers did not have a pastor or reverend or priest receiving a salary in order to minister to his congregation. The churches were led, as we have seen, by local men with secular occupations.

The question of whether we should have female priests or pastors would never have arisen if we had followed the example of the early churches, for they had no priests or pastors at all. In each fellowship the elders would ensure that the teaching was sound and behaviour consistent. And their wives would play a full part in this, especially in matters concerning the women (Tit 2:4-5).

3. They did not meet for worship as we normally understand it today. The early Christians met, as we have seen, for teaching, fellowship, breaking of bread and prayer.

In Troas, for example, they "gathered together to break bread" – that is, to share a simple meal (Acts 20:7). As they ate they remembered their Saviour. Then they heard what Paul would teach them. In loving fellowship they helped a young man who was hurt. Then they surely prayed together, and especially for the apostle embarking on his journey. So we see that their meeting was devoted to the four things that Jesus had shown his disciples during their last supper together.

4. They did not have denominations. There could be several house fellowships in a city but the believers in each city were always united as one church. Paul speaks of "the church of the Thessalonians", "the church of the Laodiceans" and "the church of God that is in Corinth". In a province with several cities there would naturally be a church in each city, so we have "the churches of Galatia", "the churches of Macedonia", "the churches of Asia" and "the churches of Judea".

The believers in these places were not divided among competing denominations like those we have today. When some claimed, "I am of Paul," or "I am of Apollos," or "I am of Cephas," the apostle rebuked this unhealthy tendency to division (1 Cor 1:10-13). When other teachers came trying to separate Jews from Gentiles, he worked hard to maintain the unity of the Spirit in the bond of peace (Eph 4:1-6). Christ has only one body. He has only one bride. "What therefore God has joined together, no human being should separate" (Matt 19:6).

5. They were never dependent on a foreigner. It is often said that churches started by missionaries must *become* self-governing, self-supporting and self-propagating. This has never been easy. We cause our converts great difficulty if we begin to work one way and then tell them to continue in a different way. The New Testament churches did not discuss ways to become self-governing, self-supporting or self-propagating. They had no reason to think of self at all. They were indigenous from the start and never needed to shift from one system to another. They never did anything they could not arrange and afford themselves.

We will be wise to learn from this. In the homes where we meet, nothing will be provided except the furnishings possessed by the family who live there and something simple to eat and drink for the common meal. Even Bibles and hymnbooks are best purchased by each believer, saving and sacrificing to obtain the spiritual nourishment they desire. There will be no need for financial support and no thought of the missionary supplying it.

Encouraging church growth

When we lead people to faith in Christ we must trust in the power of the Holy Spirit, as Paul did, to transform idol-worshippers, sorcerers, drunkards and adulterers into true disciples of Jesus – washed, sanctified and justified in his name (1 Cor 6:9-11). Growing rapidly in understanding and character, their personal testimony of salvation from shame and sorrow will inspire and strengthen others setting out on that same path.

As our fellowship increases in number, we may feel anxious when newly converted people speak to the company lest they say something wrong. But it is through the sharing of ideas that wrong ideas can be identified and corrected. This indeed is one of the great benefits of an open meeting with free participation. Whenever a new believer shares questions and discoveries from the scriptures, he or she develops the ability to teach and encourage others. Such gifts are God-given but they must have opportunity to grow. If a missionary waits until his converts become mature before permitting them to speak, he may wait a long time. And in the end he will have a church of immature people dependent on his own continued ministry.

We have seen that New Testament Christianity was a missionary movement with missionary leadership and vision. It did not create local congregations merely so that each congregation could run a programme for its own benefit and enjoyment. In every house fellowship, it was normal for neighbours, visitors, travellers and immigrants from elsewhere to hear the gospel, learn the whole counsel of God and be thoroughly prepared to carry what they heard and learned to the ends of the earth.

Our brothers and sisters in Christ will learn from us how to be evangelists and missionaries. As we take them to visit homes and workshops, speaking freely about our Saviour, reading the scriptures at every opportunity, giving thanks to God and praying constantly together, new believers will acquire the habit of doing the same. Some will become natural leaders, setting a spiritual example to everyone and guiding the growth of the fellowship. Some may be called to travel far away and help establish groups of believers in distant places. Others will take a leading part in the holistic ministries of the fellowship, caring for the widows and orphans and people in need. All this can be seen in the New Testament.

When it is time for us to move on to other places, we must leave the congregation in the care of their own Lord, trusting they will love one another patiently, counsel one another wisely, teach the truth faithfully, and proclaim the gospel boldly to their own people and to the strangers all around them.

Eventually, of course, someone may come and assert that we were naïve to copy what was done in New Testament times. They will say that churches and missions in other places are far more modern and sophisticated. Then the leaders of each local fellowship must seek the Lord in prayer and choose the way ahead for their own group. Some may decide to join a famous denomination, apply for financial assistance and adopt expensive modern methods. Others may prefer to continue as they are, seeing a greater wisdom in the strategies chosen by Christ and his apostles.

As missionaries we cannot direct such decisions taken by the churches. We have done what we can for them, giving them the best possible start before turning our attention to other unreached fields. We will still be available to advise and to pray, but not to direct and control. The local leaders will seek guidance from God, and we must trust him to guide them. For each of these leaders, "it is before his own master that he stands or falls. And he will be upheld, for the Lord is able to make him stand" (Rom 14:4).

15
Our Glorious Hope and Expectation

We began our study with the great enterprise entrusted by Jesus to his disciples – the call to proclaim the gospel to every nation. Then we looked at some of the difficulties we face in doing this today. Having raised some hard questions, we then began our search for answers.

Examining the life and ministry of Jesus himself, we saw what a wonderful missionary he was, with his concern for others, his prayerful spirit, his perseverance and self-sacrifice and his warm-hearted fellowship with those who believed his word. We saw how he made friends with the people around him, went out to where they were and taught them what they needed to know. We noticed how he respected the culture of his day, yet at times ignored it, and occasionally defied it. We watched him trusting his Father to protect and provide, always desiring to do his Father's will. We saw how he launched a movement inspired by a great vision and high ideals.

Then we enquired how he prepared his disciples for their future work – inviting them to live with him and assist him in his mission. Choosing his men carefully, he helped them grow in spiritual maturity and character, training them through practical experience with all kinds of people, and showing them how to trust their heavenly Father for every need. When they were ready he sent them on a short-term mission, then afterwards discussed it with them, answering their questions and teaching them more.

At Pentecost we witnessed the greatest of all missionary events as visitors from many nations heard the gospel in their own languages and returned home to share it with their people. We watched the believers day by day proclaiming their Saviour in the temple and gathering in their homes for teaching, fellowship, breaking of bread and prayer. We met some Gentiles far from home – an Ethiopian, a Roman, several from northern Africa and Turkey – who heard the gospel in a foreign language and could then take it to their own people in their own tongue. We saw how the Twelve set out to fulfil their apostolic calling – in Jerusalem, in all Judea, Samaria and ultimately to the ends of the earth.

We saw how Paul grasped the strategic value of a synagogue in every town where Gentiles and Jews would give him their full attention and naturally pass on what they heard. We followed his travels, his perseverance, his clear proclamation, his faithful testimony and persuasive discussion, leading men and women to faith in Christ. We saw his converts transformed in character and purpose through the power of the Holy Spirit. We noted his special interest in the great commercial ports of Corinth and Ephesus, whose constant flow of travellers, adapting rapidly to the culture and language of modernity, might carry the good news throughout the Mediterranean basin.

We considered the content of Paul's message, his guidance, his proclamation in public places, his teaching in believers' homes, his encouragement for the growth of local fellowships and his support for local leaders. We saw how sensitive he was to culture, and how careful to avoid giving offence, yet willing to ignore culture when necessary, and occasionally to defy it. We took note of his personal credibility, his servant spirit, his love for his disciples, his faithfulness in prayer, his devotion to Christ, his great vision and his readiness to testify to great and small at risk of his life. We saw the high expectations he had for his converts, and his confidence that they would grow in maturity and continue his mission after he had left them.

We discussed Paul's leadership in relation to other missionaries and church leaders. We observed how he dealt with money, supporting himself by the work of his hands, never accepting payment from people to whom he was ministering. We saw how he recruited missionaries from among his own converts and sent them to help their own people and other people far away. We saw how he valued the warm hospitality of Christian homes and honoured the godly women who managed them. Then we surveyed his last great mission to the Gentiles as a prisoner of the Roman Empire and a witness to the soldiers, attendants, governors and ultimately the Emperor himself.

From this vantage point we turned our attention to some crucial issues facing us today – technologies both helpful and unhelpful, the role of global and gospel culture, different types of "tent-making", strategic leadership, financial policies, missionary support, holistic ministries, miraculous healing and the complex challenges of persecution. We saw the potential for mission in our homes and church compounds, and considered how to approach unreached people and places and start vigorous spiritual fellowships among them.

We live in days of change and opportunity. In some places, as doors close to traditional mission methods, others are opening for creative and imaginative strategies. Every day the modern world becomes more like the Roman Empire. Ordinary people are travelling widely, entering new cultures, learning new languages and settling among us. They do this for reasons of work, education, health, tourism, and in some cases as refugees. Our modern cities closely resemble Corinth and Ephesus, each of them a strategic location for outreach to visitors, travellers and immigrants. In our churches we have multi-cultural men and women who might become excellent missionaries if well taught and well prepared to take the gospel in their own languages to their own homelands. The strategies identified and followed by the early Christians may be exactly what we need today.

We have seen how the New Testament was written as Jewish history, a record of what God has done and showing how he wants it done. And whatever difficulties and challenges we may face today, the example we find there will surely encourage and inspire.

Looking back on our long journey through Galilee, Judea, Syria and the Mediterranean world of the first century, we see times and places very different from our own, and yet in some ways no different at all. Beliefs and cultures may change, but human nature and human frailties remain the same. And the gospel never changes. In a world still suffering violence, warfare, disease and death, the greatest and most intensely urgent need will always be for *eternal life*.

We have so often wept as Mary wept in Bethany: "Lord, if you had been here, my brother would not have died" (Jn 11:32). We long for Jesus to come. We know that when he comes everything wrong will be put right: "The dead will hear the voice of the Son of God, and *those who hear will live*" (Jn 5:25). When he comes, the kingdom of heaven will come. When he comes, the will of God will be done on earth as it is in heaven. When he comes, all the world's problems will be resolved. When he comes, the meek will inherit the earth. When he comes, the dark night of death will give way to the dawn of eternal life. In this present time, "your life is hidden with Christ in God. When Christ who is your life appears, then you also will appear with him in glory" (Col 3:3-4).

Our mission, our task, our calling is to prepare men, women and children from every tribe and tongue for that great day. We know that "Christ, having been offered once to bear the sins of many, will appear a second time, not to deal with sin but to save those who are eagerly waiting for him" (Heb 9:28). We have his promise: "Surely I am coming soon." "Amen. Come Lord Jesus" (Rev 22:20).

Additional Notes

Understanding the Methods of Jesus

The gospel of the kingdom?

When Jesus proclaimed the gospel, what exactly did he say? What was the gospel according to Jesus? And are we called to proclaim the same message?

At the very start of his ministry, we read that "he went throughout all Galilee, teaching in their synagogues and proclaiming the gospel of the kingdom and healing every disease and every affliction among the people" (Matt 4:23). Another account tells us exactly what he said: "The time is fulfilled, and the kingdom of God is *at hand*; repent and believe in the good news" (Mk 1:15).

Here we see that as Jesus started his ministry, the kingdom of God was *at hand*; it had come very near. This was wonderful news, and it required a change of behaviour and belief. It demanded personal commitment. So he would say, "Repent and believe in the good news."

Soon Jesus was fully engaged in teaching, healing and casting out demons and then he declared, "The kingdom of God has *come upon* you," and "The kingdom of God is *in the midst* of you" (Lk 11:20; 17:21). Indeed it was. When the blind could see and the deaf could hear, when the demon-possessed were set free, the guilty assured of forgiveness, the dead raised to life – when all the terrible effects of the Fall were simply vanishing away – it must have seemed like heaven on earth.

As he sent his disciples out to teach and heal, their message was "The kingdom of God *has come near* to you" (Lk 10:9) and again

"The kingdom of heaven is *at hand*" (Matt 10:7). So they would tell the people that Jesus of Nazareth is near – the Messiah has come to Israel, and with his coming the kingdom of God has come.

In our own day the good news we proclaim is the same, but our circumstances are quite different. Jesus is not physically present on earth as he was then. Now we are eagerly awaiting a Saviour from heaven (Phil 3:20). We are looking for the day when he will come in his kingdom (Matt 25:31-34; Lk 23:42).

Our message, however, is equally positive. Firstly, we describe how, when Jesus came, the kingdom of God came. It came to a small place for a short time, showing his power to meet the deepest needs of mankind. But that is not all. Soon he is coming back, and with him the kingdom of God will come again, not just to a small place for a short time but everywhere and forever. This is wonderful news, and as always, it demands a personal response of changed behaviour and belief. So we too urge our hearers, "Repent and believe the good news."

As followers of Jesus we look forward with joyful anticipation to the coming of the kingdom. Preparing for a perfect life in a perfect world, we teach and affirm the ideals of the kingdom. In our homes and families we live by the gospel culture of the kingdom. Already we see men, women and children transformed by the Holy Spirit, becoming the kind of people they will be for all eternity (2 Cor 3:18).

This is wonderful news. This is the gospel of the kingdom and we are privileged to proclaim it to the ends of the earth.

Provisions for mission?

We have seen how Jesus sent his disciples to proclaim the kingdom in the villages of Galilee and Judea, but we have not examined the instructions he gave the Twelve (Lk 9:3-5; Matt 10:5-14) and later the Seventy-two (Lk 10:1-11). Nor have we considered whether those instructions are valid for us today.

On these two short-term missions we discover several things:

1. They are sent only to the lost sheep of the house of Israel, not to the Samaritans or Gentiles or other nations beyond the borders of Israel.
2. They declare that the Messiah is present and the kingdom of heaven at hand.

3. They are sent "ahead of him", preparing the people to receive him (Lk 10:1).
4. They are given power to heal, to raise the dead, to cleanse lepers and cast out demons.
5. They must work quickly in each place and then move on to the next.
6. They will receive no payment and take nothing for their journey, "no staff, nor bag, nor bread, nor money" (Lk 9:3).
7. Their needs will be met through the hospitality of strangers, "for the labourer deserves his food" (Matt 10:10).

Jesus explained to them how it would work in practice: "Whatever town or village you enter, find out who is worthy in it and stay there until you depart. As you enter the house, greet it. And if the house is worthy, let your peace come upon it, but if it is not worthy, let your peace return to you" (Matt 10:11-13). The disciples must not go from house to house but should "remain in the same house, eating and drinking what they provide" (Lk 10:7). This was not unusual, for a Jewish rabbi would normally be supported in this way.

The strategy of arriving at a new place and looking immediately for "a person of peace" is one that some missionaries follow today. Having found such a person, they remain as guests in his house until he and all his community have heard the gospel.

But this raises a question. Were these instructions intended for the guidance of missionaries in every age, or only for the Seventy-two and the Twelve on their two short-term missions?

The answer is given at a later point in Luke's Gospel. Shortly before his arrest and death, Jesus speaks again to his disciples and asks them, "When I sent you out with no purse or bag or sandals, did you lack anything?" They replied, "Nothing." Then he said, "But now whoever has a purse should take it, and also a bag. And whoever has no sword should sell his cloak and buy one" (Lk 22:35-36).

A fundamental change of mood and method is evident here. No longer are Jesus and his disciples receiving a warm welcome wherever they go. They are beginning to face resistance and opposition. Indeed Jesus had warned the Jewish nation that "the kingdom of God will be taken away from you and given to a people producing its fruits" (Matt 21:43). The old covenant was about to give way to the new, and then missionaries of the gospel would face persecution and constant danger. They could no longer expect a welcome from the Jews, and their horizon would no longer be limited to Galilee and Judea, for soon they must go into all the world.

There is a significant difference between an itinerant Jewish disciple speaking about an important Jewish rabbi in a godly Jewish home, and an itinerant Jewish evangelist introducing an unknown Jewish saviour to an idolatrous Gentile city. The first might well expect to enjoy traditional hospitality among his own people; the second could have no such expectation among foreigners likely to view him with scorn and suspicion.

After the arrest and execution of Jesus the task would become altogether more difficult. The brief experience of the Twelve and the Seventy-two would never be repeated. Although the apostles continued to live simply in their mission after Pentecost, and they appreciated hospitality whenever it was offered, they did not insist on travelling with "no staff, nor bag, nor bread, nor money".

Nor, as we have seen, did they receive a salary or payment for their work. Why then did Jesus say, "The labourer deserves his wages" (Lk 10:7)? The word translated "wages" (*misthos*) appears many times in scripture as a reward with no thought of money (Matt 5:12, 46 etc.). When Jesus applied this proverb to the mission of the Seventy-two, the "wages" of the labourer were the food and drink provided for him in the home where he was staying. Matthew makes this clear in the parallel passage where he says, "The labourer deserves his food" (Matt 10:10).

Pioneer missionaries today will be wise to take basic supplies for their journey, and grateful too for any hospitality offered to them along the way.

Self-defence?

This raises a further question about the "sword". We have seen that shortly before his arrest Jesus told his disciples, "Whoever who has no sword should sell his cloak and buy one" (Lk 22:36).

For what purpose would a disciple of Jesus require a sword? The Greek word here translated as "sword" is *machaira*. This was a dagger or knife with many uses in fishing, agriculture, handcrafts and the care of livestock. The implement that Jesus recommends would be useful for dealing with wild animals and thorny vegetation on long difficult journeys, for gutting fish and making tents, for building shelters and gathering firewood, not for wounding or killing men.

We have no reason to suppose that Jesus intended his missionaries to proclaim the gospel with violence. That would contradict his own example and all that he had taught them about loving their enemies, turning the other cheek, doing good to everyone, and submitting patiently to the harassment of evil men (Matt 5:38-48).

When Peter reports that they have two such knives, Jesus replies, "It is enough!" In the Greek Old Testament (the Septuagint), God himself uses similar words as a rebuke to Moses, and then adds, "Do not speak to me of this matter again" (Deut 3:26). We may take this as Jesus's meaning here. When Peter attacked a man with his knife, Jesus immediately healed the injury and rebuked his foolish disciple: "Put your *machaira* back into its place. For all who take up the *machaira* will perish by the *machaira*" (Matt 26:52).

In their mission to the world the disciples suffered painfully by the sword of lawful authority and the stones of angry crowds (Acts 12:2; 7:58), but there is no sign that they ever responded with violence or gave any thought to it. As a missionary, Paul survived several riots, numerous imprisonments and "countless beatings", but he never retaliated or watched his friends fight in his defence (2 Cor 11:23). His teaching and his example were consistent: "Repay no one evil for evil, but give thought to do what is honourable in the sight of all" (Rom 12:17). And again, "Beloved, never avenge yourselves . . . To the contrary, 'if your enemy is hungry, feed him; if he is thirsty, give him something to drink; for by so doing you will make him blush with shame. Do not be overcome by evil, but overcome evil with good" (Rom 12:19-21).

A godly man might risk his life to defend his family, but none should venture to die in defence of a building. The early Christians did not worry if their houses were burned or their possessions taken. One who witnessed it reminded them, "You joyfully accepted the plundering of your property, since you knew that you yourselves had a better possession and an abiding one" (Heb 10:34b). Their treasures were all in heaven awaiting the day of full redemption.

When Christ returns, every injustice will be put right and every hour of patient long-suffering recompensed. "Then the righteous will shine like the sun in the kingdom of their Father" (Matt 13:43). It is this that makes us bold to proclaim the truth of the gospel without fear, knowing that we have little to lose in this world and everything to gain in the next – and knowing also the power of a faithful testimony to pierce the hardest heart and save even a persecuting Pharisee like Saul of Tarsus.

Understanding the Jerusalem Fellowship

All things in common?

When Luke writes about the earliest believers in Jerusalem, he makes plain his admiration for them. Many of his readers will share his admiration until they come to the place where he says, "All who believed were together and had all things in common . . . They were selling their possessions and belongings and distributing the proceeds to all, as any had need" (Acts 2:44-45) And a little later, "No one said that any of the things that belonged to him was his own, but they had everything in common" (Acts 4:32).

Some writers have dismissed this as an experiment in communism which failed and was acknowledged to be a mistake. It has been blamed indeed for the subsequent food shortage in the Jerusalem fellowship which necessitated help from elsewhere.

But Luke is not in the habit of recording bad ideas which were later abandoned. He describes effective strategies that he expects us to appreciate. He knew about the subsequent need for famine relief, but he gives no hint that this early generosity was the reason for it, or that it caused any other problems in Jerusalem. On the contrary, his conclusion is entirely positive. He says, "They shared their food with glad and generous hearts, praising God and having favour with all the people. And the Lord added to their number day by day those who were being saved" (Acts 2:46-47). These are not the words of a man who would find fault, but of one who admired what they did and saw the blessing of God upon it.

But how did it work in practice? Should we picture three thousand people all continually borrowing one another's tools, clothes, utensils, furniture and animals? Or should we imagine them all helping themselves every day from some central depot?

Firstly, we may assume that the larger part of the three thousand will have moved away from Jerusalem by this time, leaving only the long-term residents. This brings the number of people down to manageable proportions.

Secondly, we should remember that they were an intimate

community of sincere and dedicated disciples who trusted one another. They met together every day in the temple and in their homes. There had been sufficient time for them to develop close relationships and to know one another well. They could cheerfully share what they had, because they were sure their kindness would not be abused.

Thirdly, we should be aware that most people in those days possessed very little moveable property. It can be seen in our museums: a comb, a lamp, a mirror, a clay pitcher, a dice game, a cloak, a parchment, a pair of shoes, and not much more.

Fourthly, we must understand what is meant by the expression "all things in common". They would certainly not have their wives and husbands in common; nor could they easily part with the tools of their trade, or the pitcher they took to the well, or the household pots and pans, or the chickens in the yard, or the garden which grew their vegetables, or the market stall where they sold their produce.

We can reconstruct a workable scenario only by concluding that these men and women continued to use the simple items of property they possessed whilst helping one another by agreement or in time of need. A carpenter whose hammer broke might borrow his friend's for an hour while it was being repaired. A watchman whose cloak was stolen might use his neighbour's for the night until his could be replaced. Two or more families might economise by sharing certain items or by pooling their resources when visitors arrived. A number of tradesmen might share a handcart, several farmers might share a plough, and each use it in turn. All this would require a full measure of honesty, reliability and trust. When Jesus borrowed a donkey he promised to return it immediately, and its owners were happy for him to use it because they trusted him to keep his word (Mk 11:3).

But generosity among the believers went further than this. A man with two tunics or two bags of grain might easily feel led to give one to a brother who had none (Lk 3:11). In fact "there was not a needy person among them, for those who were owners of lands or houses would sell them and bring the proceeds of what was sold and lay it at the apostles' feet, and it was distributed to each as any had need" (Acts 4:34-35). This happened from time to time, perhaps frequently, but never was it compulsory. Barnabas received a special mention when he sold a field, and Ananias and Sapphira were not obliged to do the same (Acts 5:4). The proceeds were used to provide necessities for the very poorest among "those who were being saved" (Acts 2:47).

In addition to this, the believers shared food together every day, so we can be sure that anyone hungry would know where to go for supper (Acts 2:46). In these various ways the needs of all the fellowship were fully met:

1. through lending personal possessions to trusted friends;
2. through generous gifts to the poorest among the saints;
3. through simple meals shared daily in their homes.

For Luke this would be evidence not only of generosity but also of trust and honesty within the Christian community. It speaks of healthy relationships when people can move freely from house to house without fear of duplicity or theft. Having described how it worked in Jerusalem, he would expect it to continue as a normal part of church life everywhere.

Indeed it still does today. Many Christians have sold property (or avoided buying property) in order to help other believers in great need. Possessions are often lent and borrowed among trusted Christian friends. And some households welcome hungry and homeless disciples to share their supper and their roof. But this does not mean that every new convert can help himself to anything he fancies. It does not mean that valuable items will be lent to newcomers who have not yet proved trustworthy. It does not mean that converts to Christ have instant access to money.

Later in Acts we read of believers both rich and poor. We have no reason to suppose that Lydia shared her stock of purple cloth with the jailer or the slave girl or with every new convert in Philippi. And we know that the householder Philemon did not have all things in common with his slave Onesimus in Colossae. But in every age we may hope for believers with wealth to care for those who have none, and for those with moveable possessions to share their blessings with fellow-believers worthy of their trust. And it is good to hear of some whose home has become a place of comfort and refuge for believers who were hungry and homeless in a lonely world.

Lending and borrowing?

We have given thought to the lending of possessions, but what about the lending of money? On this subject Paul gives very practical advice. He says, "Owe no one anything" (Rom 13:8). These words are very emphatic, introduced by two Greek negatives: *mēdeni mēden ofeilete*, literally: To no one / nothing / owe. One translator (J B Phillips) renders it, "Keep out of debt altogether."

Experience shows the wisdom of this counsel. A debtor is always weak and vulnerable, and frequently resentful. Financial debts have destroyed many relationships and many lives (Matt 18:28). We should not get into debt ourselves; nor should we let others be in debt to us.

How then can urgent needs be met? And what did Jesus mean when he said, "Give to anyone who begs from you, and do not turn away anyone who wishes to borrow from you" (Matt 5:42)?

When a needy person comes and asks to borrow money, we should not lay on him a burden of debt but rather *give* him what we can, according to his need. Again Jesus tell us, "Do good, and lend, *expecting nothing in return*" (Lk 6:35). A loan which is not returned is certainly a gift. When Barnabas sold his field and gave away the proceeds, he did exactly this, expecting nothing in return.

We have seen that every believer must work to earn his living if he can. But our Lord has provided sufficient for all his people everywhere. Those with plenty for their comfort are privileged to care for others lacking the necessities of life. "As a matter of fairness," Paul told them, "your abundance at the present time should supply their need, so that [if circumstances change] their abundance may supply your need" (2 Cor 8:14).

There is no need for any part of Christ's body to be hungry. All will be well fed if, like the early church, we share our food with glad and generous hearts (Acts 2:46).

Understanding the Methods of Paul

The collection for the saints?

There is perhaps no subject in the Bible so misunderstood as money. In the Gospel records Jesus never asked anyone for money. Peter and John going up to the temple had no money at all (Acts 3:6). The only money Paul ever asked Christians to give, went to the relief of a suffering congregation in another country, and he arranged this collection only once.

It seems that the idea of sending this gift came not from Paul himself but from the believers in Philippi. He tells us they were "begging us earnestly for the favour of taking part in the relief of the saints" (2 Cor 8:4). The fellowship in Corinth was encouraged to follow their example, putting aside a small amount each week until he came, but he insisted that he did not want money to be collected when he himself was present (1 Cor 16:1-2). After this he did not teach the churches to continue taking a collection every week, or to request money for other purposes once that one collection had been sent.

In the New Testament, the gospel has nothing to do with money. Those who proclaimed the message and those who heard it never thought of giving or receiving money for it. Jesus said: "Freely you have received, so freely give" (Matt 10:8). It was the privilege of every Christian to pass on the good news to others without any thought of payment. The apostles who had brought the gospel to them lived by faith, supported by the work of their hands and occasional gifts from friends who valued their mission. Local evangelists and teachers who followed their example did the same. They would not think of taking collections or asking for support.

Nowhere in the New Testament are Christians taught to tithe, for they had no temple or other buildings to maintain, no priests and Levites to pay, no feasts or pilgrimages to finance, and no animals to buy for sacrificial offerings. When they met together in their homes they had no expenses beyond a loaf of bread for their common meal and something cheap to drink. In fact Christianity was the cheapest of all religions to practise. It cost nothing at all and left every believer free to be as generous as he wished to anyone in need.

Perhaps remembering the case of Judas, Paul considered a love of money to be among the most dangerous of temptations, and he was concerned for all his missionary team to set a perfect example in this. He advised Timothy, "If we have food and clothing, with these we will be content" (1 Tim 6:8). Arranging the collection for famine relief, he would not touch the money himself but asked for a reliable representative from each fellowship to deliver its own contribution to Jerusalem (1 Cor 16:3). He insisted, "We take this course so that no one should blame us" (2 Cor 8:20).

In some parts of the world today, an outsider visiting a church will be surprised and shocked at how much of the service is focused on money – several offerings and collections, honoured with great ceremony, and a sermon or two about giving and receiving money.

The leaders of the church can seem excessively interested in obtaining money. Peter insisted that a shepherd of God's flock must not be "greedy for money" (1 Pet 5:2). Paul warned that "the love of money is a root of all kinds of evil. It is through this craving that some have wandered away from the faith and pierced themselves with many pains" (1 Tim 6:10).

If church leaders do not set a good example in this, how can we expect young Christians to escape injury? There may be many outside the churches, and even some inside, who are "deprived of the truth, imagining that godliness is a means of gain" (1 Tim 6:5). Every Christian leader who follows the example of Jesus and his apostles will take care to prove this allegation false.

Various kinds of languages?

We have seen how the apostles on the Day of Pentecost preached to the crowd outside their door in the languages of Parthia, Media, Elam and Mesopotamia, Egypt, Cyrene, Rome, Crete and Arabia. This was a miracle that enabled them to communicate in real human languages.

It seems reasonable to suppose that if these were real human languages, then the same would be true of the "tongues" mentioned on two other occasions in Acts (10:46 and 19:6) and also in the fellowship at Corinth. Indeed the same Greek word glōssa (plural glōssai) is used in each case, and is later found seven times in the book of Revelation, referring to ethnic groups from all over the world, each speaking an ordinary human language.

In the fellowship at Corinth there were "gifts of healing, helping, administrating, and various kinds of languages" (1 Cor 12:28). It is often assumed that these gifts were miraculous in nature. But "helping" and "administration" would not require a miracle of any sort, and the ability to speak "various kinds of languages" would be useful but not necessarily miraculous. The fact that Paul describes the gift in this way shows that there was variety – they were indeed "various kinds of languages" such as various kinds of people would speak (1 Cor 12:10).

There is no scriptural reason to believe that these were "ecstatic utterances" or "a heavenly language", or that the speaker did not understand what he or she was saying, although experience might lead a person to this conclusion. In English translations, the use of the word "tongues" is itself misleading for it adds an element of mystery not present in the original text. We will refer simply to "languages". But what exactly does scripture tell us about these "languages"? How, for example, might we understand what happened in the house of Cornelius?

We read that the Jewish believers who had come with Peter "were amazed, because the gift of the Holy Spirit was poured out even on the Gentiles" (Acts 10:45). These Gentiles were friends and relations of Cornelius. Most would be connected with the Roman army, which at this time recruited men from all over the Empire and beyond. But why were their Jewish visitors so amazed? "For they were hearing them *speaking in languages and extolling God*" (Acts 10:46). As Peter proclaimed the gospel these Gentiles responded, each one in his own heart-language. For the first time in human history a room full of people were praising Yahweh in a whole range of Gentile languages. This was truly amazing. The gospel had moved beyond the authorized Greek and Hebrew of the synagogue into the universal linguistic world of the nations. God could now be praised by Gentiles of any race in any language. The fact that they were doing so was proof that the Holy Spirit had powerfully convinced them of the truth and added them to the church. So Peter declared, "Can anyone withhold water for baptizing these people, who have received the Holy Spirit just as we have?" (Acts 10:47).

This did not happen everywhere. When the Samaritans received the Holy Spirit we do not read that they spoke in "languages", for they would all naturally speak Aramaic (Acts 8:17). But in the cosmopolitan city of Ephesus, when Paul explained the gospel to some disciples of John the Baptist, they too were moved to express their faith in their various heart-languages, and also to prophesy (Acts 19:6). Now what was this prophesying? And how could new converts do it?

We have seen how Paul insisted on clear communication in the fellowship at Corinth (where a dozen or more languages might be represented) and how he chose to exercise his mind and prophesy rather than speak in a foreign language (1 Cor 14:19). To prophesy is to talk about God in a way that is clear and understandable to the hearers. Speaking Greek, Paul could prophesy to them; speaking a foreign language he could not. In his personal prayer and his gospel outreach he used foreign languages more than any of them, but in the congregation of believers he chose to speak clearly about God in Greek (1 Cor 14:18-19). In the light of this, we may assume that those converts in Ephesus praised God in their various heart-languages but then spoke to the assembled company in Greek "for their upbuilding and encouragement and comfort" (1 Cor 14:3).

The ability to speak "various kinds of languages" is recognised as a gift from God, and many people have this gift; it is extremely useful for missionary outreach. But to *interpret* what a foreigner says into a common language is a different gift, and fewer are able to do this with fluency and skill (1 Cor 12:10).

Paul recognizes that a person ignorant of the common language may have much to contribute to the body. In order to be understood such a person must either find an *interpreter* or else exercise his mind to learn the language of the majority (1 Cor 14:13-15). As a message by interpretation always takes twice as long, and does not easily allow for discussion and response, Paul advised that no more than two or three should speak in a foreign language lest the company become weary of listening (1 Cor 14:27).

Now if all this is correct, how can "languages" be a sign? Why is it that Paul says, "Languages are a sign not for believers but for unbelievers, while prophecy is not for unbelievers but for believers" (1 Cor 14:22)?

The simplest way to understand this is to consider the *effect* of "various kinds of languages" and of "prophecy" on those who hear them. When believers are present from many different language groups, they are living proof that the gospel has power to win the nations. Hearing them speak their various languages, outsiders will be amazed and perhaps led to enquire about the meaning of it all. In this way the languages are a sign for unbelievers, leaving them in a condition of amazement but not knowing what to believe. Prophecy, on the other hand, will be a clear communication of spiritual truth in a known language. It is "for believers", because it brings understanding and belief. For the same reason, it is "not for unbelievers", because it will not leave such people in ignorance and unbelief. By communicating clearly it leads them into assured faith.

So Paul continues, "If, therefore, the whole church comes together and all speak in languages, and outsiders or unbelievers enter, will they not say that you are all crazy?" Of course they will, for there is nothing but confusion. "But if all prophesy, and an unbeliever or outsider enters, he is convicted by all, he is called to account by all, the secrets of his heart are disclosed, and so, falling on his face, he will worship God and declare that God is really among you" (1 Cor 14:23-25). This is not merely something that took place long ago; it happens all the time. A visitor will be amazed that so many tribes and races, representing so many languages, are gathered in one place with a single purpose. But only when the visitor *understands* what is said can he become a believer and give his life to Christ. The variety of languages will impress him but clear communication will convict him. The first leads him to amazement, the second to faith.

This does not mean that every group meeting in every home must always speak a common or global language such as English, French or Arabic. A local dialect may be freely used in a fellowship that speaks that dialect. Indeed it is important for every believer to express his or her faith in the language of the heart, as they did in the house of Cornelius and in Ephesus. But when we are a mixed group gathered in one place, we should talk together about our faith and our spiritual lives in a common language understood by the majority, helping everyone to understand and participate, either directly or by interpretation, without confusion or disorder.

Itinerant evangelism?

The custom of dividing Paul's missionary career into three journeys is convenient but somewhat confusing.

It overlooks his first ten or eleven years of mission in the Middle East (Damascus, Jerusalem, Arabia, Cilicia and Syria) before Barnabas invited him to Antioch. Luke was not with him at this time and tells us little about his activities (Acts 9:19-30; Gal 1:15-24; 2 Cor 11:32-33).

It also tends to convey the idea that during his later career he was always on the move, travelling from place to place and seldom staying anywhere for long. And it implies that when he returned from a journey he remained inactive until he started another journey.

We must remember that these missions in the west were spread over a period of almost twenty years. And fifteen of those twenty years were spent in five major cities in five different provinces. These were Syrian Antioch (three visits, totalling about four years), Corinth (several visits, totalling nearly four years), Ephesus (at least three years), Caesarea (two to three years) and Rome (two to three years). More than three quarters of his missionary career after leaving Antioch was spent in these five centres. So what was he doing there?

Firstly, we have seen that in Caesarea and in Rome, Paul was under arrest. He could not travel at all. His ministry consisted of testimony to Jewish and Roman officials rather than teaching in synagogues or houses. In Antioch, he was concerned mainly to resist the influence of teachers from Jerusalem seeking to bring Gentiles under bondage to the Law. But Corinth and Ephesus were undoubtedly Paul's strategic mission centres. Each of these great commercial ports was a hub attracting people from all over the known world, and from where converts would carry the gospel to the ends of the earth. This is what made Ephesus and Corinth such significant places and caused him to settle there for extended periods.

The misconception that Paul was always travelling, and never staying anywhere for long, has had unfortunate consequences. It has led many missionaries to itinerate over wide areas, attempting to establish churches and to maintain them through brief occasional visits. After a tour like this a missionary may think he has been following Paul's method but has probably visited far more places in three weeks than Paul saw in three years.

Experience shows that brief visits rarely establish good habits in the churches. The believers may enjoy a short time of stimulus and encouragement but will then lapse back into laziness and apathy. They will appreciate their visitor while he is there but they do not expect to become like him. They would not think of doing what he does.

We have seen that Paul expected his converts not merely to understand his teaching but to follow his example. By living with them he established good habits in the Christian community. Eventually when he left them they were so well taught, and so accustomed to a healthy spiritual way of life, that their congregations continued to be centres of vigorous growth from which missionaries went out to other places. So he commended the fellowship at Thessalonica: "You became imitators of us and of the Lord . . . Not only has the word of the Lord sounded forth from you in Macedonia and Achaia, but your faith in God has become known everywhere, so that we need not say anything" (1 Thess 1:6, 8). Paul did not merely preach the gospel. Like Jesus, he made disciples.

Further Reading

Many excellent books have been written about Jesus and his apostles but very few have raised the questions that missionaries would ask of them. Many other writers have addressed current issues in cross-cultural mission although hardly any have deliberately looked for strategy in scripture. One who attempted both was Alexander Rattray Hay in South America with *The New Testament Order for Church and Missionary* (New Testament Missionary Union, Temperley, Argentina, 1947).

Another was Thomas Walker in India with his study-guide to Acts called *Missionary Ideals* (2nd edn. ed. David C C Watson, IVP, London, 1969).

Better known than either of these is Roland Allen, whose experience in China and elsewhere inspired his *Missionary Methods: St Paul's or Ours?* (Eerdmans, 1912, 1962) and *The Spontaneous Expansion of the Church* (Eerdmans, 1927, 1962).

The best evaluation of early gospel outreach is still Michael Green's classic, *Evangelism in the Early Church* (Hodder & Stoughton, London, 1970). Covering a much wider period we have W H C Frend, *The Rise of Christianity* (Augsburg Fortress, 1984).

A more recent compendium of geographical and archaeological information is provided in two massive volumes by Eckhard J Schnabel, *Early Christian Mission* (IVP Apollos, 2005). Much of this detail is repeated in his *Paul the Missionary: Realities, Strategies and Methods* (IVP Apollos, 2008).

The social context of the early Gentile churches is discussed by Wayne A Meeks, *The First Urban Christians: the social world of the Apostle Paul* (Yale University Press, 1983). Meeks suggests that

Paul's gospel appealed especially to people who were upwardly mobile in social and economic terms, and that these social risers took a leading part in the churches and missions associated with him (pp.73, 191). With particular reference to Corinth see Gerd Theissen, *The Social Setting of Pauline Christianity* (T & T Clark, Edinburgh, 1982).

Social and psychological aspects of early Christian mission are identified by sociologist Rodney Stark, *The Rise of Christianity* (HarperCollins, 1997). He depicts, for example, the terrible insecurities of life in first-century pagan cities, which made the spiritual assurance and warm compassion of a Christian fellowship particularly attractive (p.208). He observes that in general the first people to adopt cultural innovations are well above average in education and income, and suggests that this was true of Paul's initial converts in each city (p.38). A briefer sociological analysis of the early church as a movement and a community is offered by Derek Tidball, *An Introduction to the Sociology of the New Testament* (Paternoster, Exeter, 1983).

Physical and social aspects of the pagan cities at this period are well portrayed by Jerome Carcopino, *Daily Life in Ancient Rome* (Penguin, Harmondsworth, 1941).

On eyewitness accounts of Jesus's ministry, and their circulation in written form at an early date, see Alan Millard, *Reading and Writing in the Time of Jesus* (Sheffield Academic Press, 2001)

The synagogue communities of the Jewish *diaspora* are examined by Irina Levinskaya, *The Book of Acts in its Diaspora Setting* (vol.5 of series "The Book of Acts in its First Century Setting", Eerdmans / Paternoster, 1996). The author finds no substantial archaeological or historical evidence of active Jewish efforts toward the conversion of Gentiles. The God-fearers and proselytes seem to have made their own rather haphazard way into the synagogue communities.

For an account of Paul's ministry as an ambassador in chains see Brian Rapske, *The Book of Acts and Paul in Roman Custody* (vol.3 of series "The Book of Acts in its First Century Setting", Eerdmans / Paternoster, 1994). Rapske notes that "nearly 25% of Acts concerns Paul's final arrest and imprisonment", which exceeds the amount of space devoted to his journeys. Luke evidently expected his readers to be more interested in Paul the prisoner than in Paul the traveller (p.2). Rapske speaks of Paul's active "prison ministry" (p.356), noting that

"Luke closes with a picture of a prisoner whose place of confinement has become a house church" (p.313).

Data for our maps are derived from ed. Tim Dowley, *The Baker Atlas of Christian History* (Baker Book House, Grand Rapids, 1997) and from *Atlas of the Bible* (Carta, Jerusalem, n.d.).

Several other subjects mentioned in this book are worthy of more attention. On the sociology and psychology of conversion, see Lewis Rambo, *Understanding Religious Conversion* (Yale University Press, 1993).

On travel in New Testament times, see Lionel Casson, *Travel in the Ancient World* (The John Hopkins University Press, 1994).

On the kingdom of God, see Herman N Ridderbos, *The Coming of the Kingdom* (The Presbyterian and Reformed Publishing Company, 1962).

On eternal life in the new heaven and earth, see Randy Alcorn, *Heaven* (Tyndale House, 2004).

On the importance of Christian homes for mission, see Wolfgang Simson, *Houses that Change the World* (Authentic Lifestyle, reprint 2003).

On the role of evangelical mission in "cultural globalisation", see Peter L Berger, "Four Faces of Global Culture" in *The National Interest*, no. 49 (Fall 1997, pp.23-29); freely available on the internet.

Finally, for an outstanding work of fiction, bringing to life the early Christian communities, a personal favourite of mine is Patricia St John, *Twice Freed* (Christian Focus Publications, reprint 2009).

By the Same Author

This Holy Seed: Faith, Hope and Love in the Early Churches of North Africa (2nd edn., Tamarisk Books, Chester, 2010) (also available in Arabic and French).

> As an immediate sequel to the book of Acts, *This Holy Seed* charts the astonishing growth of the early churches along the Mediterranean coast of North Africa and brings to life the rich Christian heritage of this region. The narrative introduces us to some memorable characters – Tertullian, Cyprian, Augustine of Hippo, Origen, Perpetua and her friends – people whose names are now forgotten in "the land of the vanished church". How can we account for the remarkable growth of early North African Christianity, and for its equally remarkable collapse? *This Holy Seed* offers a thoroughly evangelical view of Christian history and raises important questions for the churches of our day.

The Love of God (Tamarisk, Chester, forthcoming)
> book 1: ***The Quest for the Living God***; book 2: ***The Revelation of the Living God***; book 3: ***The Character of the Living God***; book 4: ***The Plan of the Living God***

Biblical Missiology: A University Course in Cross-cultural Mission (Tamarisk, Chester, forthcoming)

(writing as Robert Bernard Dann)

Father of Faith Missions: The Life and Times of Anthony Norris Groves (Authentic, Waynesboro, 2004)
> Norris Groves was an English dentist who found promises and instructions in the New Testament that no one seemed to have noticed before. He wondered if churches and missions might

achieve more if they simply did what Jesus had told them to do. It was a theory he would put to the test. In 1829 he and his wife Mary sold their possessions, gave what they had to the poor and set off for the East, trusting simply in the care of their heavenly Father. They settled with their two small boys in a house with a courtyard in the ancient Muslim capital of Baghdad. Here they explained the gospel of Christ to anyone who would listen . . . until plague struck the city, followed by cholera, famine, floods and civil war! Here is the story of a grand experiment in authentic Christianity, and one that went on to inspire a generation of "faith missions".

> "a first rate in-depth biography . . . will stir the whole range of your emotions and thinking"
>
> (Alexander Strauch, Littleton Bible Chapel)

> "a stunning achievement. It is one of the most powerful missionary biographies that I have read"
>
> (David J MacLeod, Emmaus Bible College)

The Primitivist Ecclesiology of A N Groves (Tamarisk Books, Chester, 2006)

Norris Groves accepted the New Testament as a divinely inspired manual for church and mission. His writings and example launched a back-to-the-Bible movement that has flourished from the early nineteenth century to the present day. Groves's primitivist ecclesiology became characteristic of the open Brethren, and through Brethren influence in university Christian unions and overseas "faith missions", entered the mainstream of evangelical life in the United Kingdom and throughout the world.

The Primitivist Missiology of A N Groves (Tamarisk Books, Chester, 2006)

How can churches that are planted by missionaries become indigenous? This question has troubled mission leaders for two centuries. Varied schemes have been proposed for the transfer of authority, property and finance to suitably trained nationals but it has not been easy. Norris Groves advocated a different approach which he claimed to find in the New Testament, suggesting that churches should be indigenous from the start. With no buildings to maintain, no salaries to pay, no organisation to oversee, he encouraged his converts to meet without foreign supervision or control. His principles were adopted in India by John Arulappan and Bakht Singh, and in China by Watchman Nee, who all became leaders of flourishing indigenous movements. Like Groves, they looked directly to the New Testament as their guide to church and mission strategy.

> "a work of impressive scholarship, founded on wide reading in both primary and secondary sources . . . Dann's case is more subversive of missiological orthodoxy than he admits, but it deserves careful evaluation"   (Brian Stanley, review in *IBMR*, July 2008).

Pretty as a Moonlit Donkey: a whimsical jaunt down the proverbial byways of Moroccan folklore (Jacaranda Books, Chester, 2001)
A collection of 260 proverbs in Moroccan Arabic and southern Moroccan Berber, with English translation and commentary – humorous and perceptive, depicting many aspects of daily life and delightfully illustrated with line drawings.

Available from
www.amazon.co.uk
or
Opal Trust
1 Glenannan Park, Lockerbie DG11 2FA, Scotland,
United Kingdom
Phone / fax (UK): 01576 203670
Email:info@opaltrust.org
Web: www.opaltrust.org